THE GOVERNANCE OF BRITAIN

Also by Harold Wilson

Purpose in Politics
The Relevance of British Socialism
Purpose in Power
The Labour Government 1964–70

Harold Wilson

THE GOVERNANCE OF BRITAIN

HARPER & ROW, PUBLISHERS
NEW YORK, HAGERSTOWN,
SAN FRANCISCO, LONDON

The frontispiece photograph of Sir Harold Wilson is by Joe Bulaitis.

FIRST U.S. EDITION

ISBN: 0-06-014676-1

LIBRARY OF CONGRESS CATALOG CARD NUMBER: 76-47262

76 77 78 79 80 81 10 9 8 7 6 5 4 3 2 1

'What is a Prime Minister? That is a question which it would require a pamphlet to answer, but in a few sentences it may be possible to remove a few hallucinations. For the title expresses much to the British mind. To the ordinary apprehension it implies a dictator, the duration of whose power finds its only limit in the House of Commons. So long as he can weather that stormful and deceptive ocean he is elsewhere supreme. But the reality is very different. The Prime Minister, as he is now called, is technically and practically the Chairman of an Executive Committee of the Privy Council, or rather perhaps of Privy Councillors, the influential foreman of an executive jury. His power is mainly personal, the power of individual influence. That influence, whatever it may be, he has to exert in many directions before he can have his way. He has to deal with the Sovereign, with the Cabinet, with Parliament and with public opinion, all of them potent factors in their various kinds and degrees. To the popular eye, however, heedless of these restrictions he represents universal power; he is spoken of as if he had only to lay down his views of policy and to adhere to them. That is very far from the case.'

LORD ROSEBERY : *Sir Robert Peel*

CONTENTS

PREFACE

Professor Anthony King, in his introduction to the symposium he edited, *The British Prime Minister*, makes this comment:

> 'The Prime Minister is the most conspicuous figure in British political life; he is also, by all ordinary standards, the most powerful. The roles he plays are fascinating and complex. Yet, perhaps because scholars are over-impressed by the official reticence of Downing Street and Whitehall, the academic literature is thin. There are only three books on the office of Prime Minister, only one of which is in any sense a major study. This compares with the dozens of books on the American Presidency and, also, with the growing volume of writing on other elements in the British system . . .'

In fact, most published works are based on casual and sporadic references in political memoirs.

> 'Whatever the reason, students of the Prime Ministership have mainly to infer the view of the office held by British Prime Ministers from their casual remarks and from their actual conduct in office. It is possible that the unselfconsciousness of most Prime Ministers about the office may have concealed, not least from themselves, the full range of possibilities open to Prime Ministers.'

This work sets out to analyse the office, and to set out, with full discretion about what should not be set out, how Britain is governed. It concentrates mainly on 10 Downing Street; the office, function and powers of the prime minister as an essential part of Cabinet government within our parliamentary democracy. Certain essential elements in the governance of Britain, notably departmental administration, the role of the Civil Service and the vast and growing area of local government, are not covered. I am writing about the things I know from personal experience going back, now, more than thirty-six years.

Inevitably, the book is written from the vantage point of Downing Street, and it needs to be read with that corrective warning. But so much has been written about Downing Street by analysts writing from outside that such a corrective is needed. It is therefore a book about the governance of Britain which heavily emphasizes the prime minister's role while rejecting the philosophies of those who write of prime ministerial dictatorship. It is an analysis therefore as seen by a prime minister of the mainspring of British government, the Cabinet, Cabinet government and the Cabinet Office.

In so far as it concentrates on the prime ministerial role in Cabinet government it describes the day-to-day working of a calling that must be one of the most exciting and certainly one of the best organized – organized by history – in the democratic world: Britain's prime ministership.

When, on 16 March 1976, I told the Cabinet of my firm decision to resign after nearly eight years as prime minister, I ventured to give this advice to my then unselected and unpredictable successor:

'I want to say this to my successor, whoever he or she may be.

'This is an office to cherish: stimulating and satisfying. You will never have a dull moment; you will never get bored. But it *is* a full-time calling. These are not the easy, spacious, socially-orientated days of some of my predecessors. Apart from quite generous holidays – when, thanks to modern communications, I have never been more than moments away from Downing Street – I have had to work seven days a week, at least 12 to 14 hours a day. But the variety and interest – with, usually, at least 500 different documents or submissions to read in an average week-end after a busy week – means that you do not get bored; consequently, you do not get tired.

'Every Prime Minister has his own style. But he must know all that is going on. Even if he were tempted to be remiss in this, the wide-open nature of Prime Minister's Questions – entirely different from that of any departmental Minister – requires familiarity with, and understanding of, the problems of every Department and every part of the country.

'More than that, the price of an Administration's continuance and success is eternal vigilance – on duty or on call every minute of the day. Yet you must find time enough to stand back and think about the problems of the Administration, its purpose, its co-ordination and its longer-term strategy. Equally you have to watch for that cloud no bigger than a man's hand which may threaten not tomorrow's crisis, but perhaps next month's or next year's. In all this you have got to think and feel politically as well as in constitutional and administrative terms.

'It is not only the job here in Westminster, Whitehall and Parliament. It is the job in the country. The leader of the Party, and no less the Prime Minister, has a duty to meet the people, to address political and other meetings. For 13 years I have averaged well over 100 a year, covering nearly every constituency, some of them many times.'

The prime minister must be ever-vigilant, too, in thinking about elections – the timing of the next general election and the impact of by-elections. He must remember one of the most fundamental 'laws' of politics: elections are not in the main won by swings, nor are they capable of measurement or rationalization by 'swingometers' or similar devices. They are won and lost, in the main, by differential abstention – most often not by deliberate decisions to abstain, but just by a feeling, often as election day draws near that it is simply not worth while going down to the polling booth. This may be because of complacency – he has seen the public opinion polls and press forecasts – or because, despite his normal support for one or other party, he is disillusioned, or 'can't see any difference between the parties'. The other and newer factor is the distribution of votes normally going to one party or another which are taken by others, Liberals, Nationalists – or perhaps the National Front.

Finally, I must make clear that not a word of this book was written until 7 April 1976, two days after I left No. 10. No prime minister in the 1970s would have the time either to do that or to keep a diary.

THE GOVERNANCE OF BRITAIN

FOREWORD

Britain's Government –
Cabinet or Prime Minister?

'The Office of the Prime Minister is what its holder chooses and is able to make it.' ASQUITH[1]

This book is aimed at describing how the British system of parliamentary and Cabinet government works, and identifying the essential differences in our system and presidential systems, such as that of the United States. It is not concerned with theories.

Nevertheless, it is essential at the outset to deal with the great debate that has dominated academic discussion for many years – the question, has the system of Cabinet government described by Bagehot[2] a little over a century ago given way to a quasi-presidential prime ministerial autocracy?

Bagehot set out his then novel conclusions in the first few pages of his first chapter, 'The Cabinet'.

'The Cabinet, in a word, is a board of control chosen by the legislature, out of persons whom it trusts and knows, to rule the nation. The particular mode in which the English Ministers are selected; the fiction that they are, in any political sense, the Queen's

---

[1] H.H. Asquith, *Fifty Years of Parliament* (London 1926), II, p. 185.

[2] Walter Bagehot: *The English Constitution*, published 1867, second edition with new Introduction, 1872, which analyses the effects of Disraeli's Reform Act of 1867 and constitutional changes in France in 1868. All page references quoted are to the Fontana Edition, 1963, with an introduction by Richard Crossman, which has been widely regarded as the classical statement of the 'prime ministerial' thesis. The best commentaries on the debate are by A.H.Brown, 'Prime Ministerial Power' in *Public Law*, spring and summer editions, 1968, pp. 28–51 and 96–118, and an equally authoritative article by D.N.Chester, *Parliamentary Affairs*, Vol. XV, 1962, pp. 519–27, reviewing John Mackintosh, *The British Cabinet* (Methuen, London 1962).

servants; the rule which limits the choice of the Cabinet to the members of the legislature – are accidents unessential to its definition – historical incidents separable from its nature. Its characteristic is that it should be chosen by the legislature out of persons agreeable to and trusted by the legislature. Naturally these are principally its own members – but they need not be exclusively so. A Cabinet which includes persons not members of the legislative assembly might still perform all useful duties. Indeed the peers, who constitute a large element in modern Cabinets, are members now-a-days, only of a subordinate assembly . . .

'A Cabinet is a combining committee – a *hyphen* which joins, a *buckle* which fastens, the legislative part of the State to the executive part of the State. In its origin it belongs to the one, in its function it belongs to the other . . .

'. . . a Cabinet, though it is a committee of the legislature assembly, is a committee with a power which no assembly would – unless for historical accidents, and after happy experience – have been persuaded to entrust to any committee. It is a committee which can dissolve the assembly which appointed it; it is a committee with a suspensive veto – a committee with a power of appeal. Though appointed by one Parliament, it can appeal if it chooses to the next. Theoretically, indeed the power to dissolve Parliament is entrusted to the sovereign only, and there are vestiges of doubt whether in *all* cases a sovereign is bound to dissolve Parliament when the Cabinet asks him to do so. But neglecting such small and dubious exceptions, the Cabinet which was chosen by one House of Commons has an appeal to the next House of Commons. The chief committee of the legislature has the power of dissolving the predominant part of that legislature – that which at a crisis is the supreme legislature. The English system, therefore, is not an absorption of the executive power by the legislative power: it is a fusion of the two. Either the Cabinet legislates and acts, or else it can dissolve. It is a creature, but it has the power of destroying its creators. It is an executive which can annihilate the legislative as well as an executive which is the nominee of the legislature. It *was* made, but it *can* unmake: it was derivative in its origin, but it is destructive in its action.'[1]

It is this doctrine, indeed these quotations, that Richard Crossman specifically repudiates. Indeed, he dismisses the Bagehot thesis. The discovery of 'the efficient secret', the role of the Cabinet, as hyphen and buckle, he argues, was out of date even when *The English Constitution* was

[1] Bagehot, Introduction, op. cit., pp. 67, 68–9.

written. 'The secret which Bagehot claimed to have discovered does indeed provide the correct explanation of the relationship between the Commons and the Cabinet, as it emerged between 1832 and 1867.'

In the section of his Introduction, 'The Passing of Cabinet Government',[1] Richard Crossman attributed the change to the growth of state activity and the public services from Bagehot's time, because of 'the fantastic degree of incompetence revealed in the Crimean War'; the powers of the State and the growing efficiency of the Civil Service; the creation in World War 1 of a secretariat to keep the minutes and circulate papers; and, quoting Herbert Morrison on the 1929–31 Government, the inability of the full Cabinet to deal with economic crisis.

> 'Already, in fact, by 1931 Cabinet Government in Bagehot's sense of the word had become an anachronism. It finally disappeared under the Churchill war régime. Once Sir Winston had accepted the leadership of the Conservative Party, his ascendancy became unchallengeable. As Party leader, he controlled the Conservative machine inside and outside Parliament and could therefore dictate his terms, not merely to the House of Commons but to the Labour members of his Cabinet . . .[2]

In Richard Crossman's view there was no turning back after the war. He cites Clement Attlee and, even more surprisingly, Sir Alec Douglas-Home in support of this thesis. But he stresses particularly the further growth and power of the Civil Service, and above all its centralization, partly through the ending of the custom whereby a civil servant tended to spend his working life in a single department. He underlines, also, through the separation (by Harold Macmillan, following the Plowden Report) of the duties of the permanent secretary to the Treasury (who was also secretary of the Cabinet and head of the Civil Service) with CSD and the Cabinet secretary, both reporting to the prime minister. If Richard Crossman had foreseen when he wrote this that in 1968, following the Fulton Report on the Civil Service, the prime minister would take on the duties of the 'minister for the Civil Service' as proposed by Fulton, he would doubtless have felt his point even more fully made.

Crossman therefore concludes that the 'hyphen which joins, the buckle which fastens . . . becomes one single man' with the right to select his own Cabinet and dismiss them at will, the power to decide the Cabinet's agenda and announce the decisions reached without taking a vote, together with the control over patronage through the Chief Whip. All this, he says, had existed before 1867. In fact, as a statement of the

[1] ibid., pp. 6, 48–51.   [2] ibid., p. 49.

real position it is not true today. But his unshakeable belief in his doctrine led him, even further, to assert that 'the decline of the Cabinet has been concealed from the public eye even more successfully than its rise to power in Bagehot's era'.[1]

When he wrote in 1963, before his near-six years of Cabinet membership, the Cabinet for him had become

> '. . . the place where busy executives seek forward sanction for their actions from colleagues usually too busy – even if they do disagree – to do more than protest. Each of these executives, moreover, owes his allegiance not to the Cabinet collectively but to the Prime Minister who gave him his job, and who may well have dictated the policy he must adopt. In so far as ministers felt themselves to be agents of the Premier, the British Cabinet has now come to resemble the American Cabinet.'[2]

For me, the classical refutation of this 1963 assertion was Richard Crossman as a minister, and his unfailing, frequently argumentative, role from 1964 to 1970 in ruthlessly examining every proposal, policy or projection put before Cabinet by departmental ministers – or by the prime minister. Indeed, apart from a curious belief that prime ministerial authority was exercised by a hole-in-the-corner meeting with the secretary of the Cabinet to cook the Cabinet minutes, and falsify or qualify the meeting's conclusions,[3] he had begun to modify his views, as his magisterial Godkin lectures at Harvard in 1970[4] were to prove.

Indeed, in his concluding passage in 1963, he was already prepared to concede that the legend of autocracy and unchallengeable authority was qualified by the fact that a prime minister can be removed. But even here, he argues, he cannot be removed in real life by public *constitutional* procedure: the method, he says, must be that of '. . . undercover intrigue and sudden unpredicted coup d'état. The intra-party struggle for power that is fought in the secret committees and in the lobbies, may suddenly flare up round the Cabinet table. But if it does, the proceedings there will only be ritual, and the real fight will have finished before they begin.'[5]

Magnificent, but not real-life, as is confirmed by history before and after 1963. To be fair, however, on the most publicized, though most exaggerated, 'plot' for my own removal in 1969, Richard Crossman was

[1] Bagehot, *The English Constitution*, p. 54.
[2] ibid., p. 52.
[3] See p. 56 below.
[4] Richard Crossman, *Bagehot Revisited* (London 1972).
[5] Bagehot, op. cit., p. 54.

to be found behind my back, facing outwards, his blade directed not to me but to any possible assailant.

The debate will, no doubt, continue. Indeed, it is not new; Crossman's contribution is to have systematized a thesis that others have asserted, or in some cases hinted at,[1] and to have done so with all his formidable powers of analysis and argument.

John Morley, whose much-quoted *primus inter pares* has led to his frequent condemnation as a complacent Bagehotian, himself rightly described the prime minister as 'the Keystone of the Cabinet Arch', but went on to refer to 'powers always great and in an emergency not inferior to those of a dictator'. The key here, in my view, is the reference to an 'emergency'.

Leo Amery, too, quoted Morley's reference to power in an emergency.[2]

Even before war became total, prime ministerial involvement in a war could be almost total – this was true of the Elder Pitt, for example (never in fact prime minister or first lord), and certainly the Younger Pitt.[3]

In a world war a prime minister inevitably acts in a much more dictatorial manner. He has to, and Parliament is ready to grant him emergency powers, as long as he retains the confidence of a substantial majority, especially if he heads an inter-party coalition. Many wartime decisions involve total secrecy, and could not be discussed in full Cabinet – some of them not even in a small, compact War Cabinet. A

[1] For example, Ramsay Muir claimed that the prime minister was a 'potentate who appoints and can dismiss his colleagues. He is in fact, though not in law, the working head of the state endowed with such a plenitude of power as no other constitutional ruler in the world possesses, not even the President of the United States.' Bertrand de Jouvenel refers to 'contemporary régimes where the body politic is in fact vested in one man', making clear that in his view Britain is moving in that direction ('The Principate', *Political Quarterly* (January–March 1965), p. 21); Sir George Mallaby, a former senior Cabinet Office official: ''The deference accorded to any British Prime Minister is very striking indeed . . . Cabinet Ministers will pay special attention to his views and his leadership, with a strong inclination to sink their own opinion and defer to his.' (*From My Level: Unwritten Minutes*, (London 1965), p. 59); F.W.G.Benemy: '. . . the Prime Minister is sovereign – that is to say, he governs with an absolute authority, whereas in theory he is at bottom a Member of Parliament at the mercy of Parliament.' (*The Elected Monarch – The Development of the Powers of the Prime Minister* (London 1965), p. 245); Humphry Berkeley: 'I accept that we are now operating a presidential system; to do otherwise would be unrealistic. Let us concede the Prime Minister presidential powers and equip ourselves with safeguards.' (*The Listener*, 25 August 1966); John Mackintosh, *The British Cabinet* (London 1962), virtually *passim* asserts this thesis; indeed, in so doing anticipated Richard Crossman.

[2] In the Chichele Lectures, 1946, printed as *Thoughts on the Constitution* (1951), 2nd ed. with new introduction (Oxford 1964).

[3] See Lord Blake, *The Office of Prime Minister*, British Academy Lectures (Oxford 1975): on the Elder Pitt, p. 26; on the Younger Pitt, p. 32.

wartime premier has to spend a great deal of his time acting as a kind of super Commander-in-Chief, with the Chiefs of Staff of the Defence Services.

In World War II Winston Churchill was officially designated as minister of defence, while leaving the statutory and administrative duties to the Service ministers who were, in fact, not in the War Cabinet.

Questions of intelligence and counter-intelligence had to be on a strictly need-to-know basis; to a considerable extent the same applied to dealings with powerful allies, for example the President of the United States and, after 1941, with the Soviet leadership.[1]

I have discovered at Chequers that Winston Churchill spent a great deal more of his time directing the war from there than was known at the time, except when he had to attend Cabinet or the House. He was, in fact, there for long periods even when Parliament was sitting. He was almost invariably attended by the Chiefs of Staff, or their representatives, or field commanders summoned from abroad, and they were frequently on duty with him until hours after midnight. In the morning he usually read telegrams and despatches or dictated minutes and orders, from his bed, until near lunchtime. A high proportion of this work was in his capacity as minister of defence; much of it could not have been laid before even his small War Cabinet – there would not have been time. Only at times of full moon – 'bombers' moon' – did he leave Chequers for Dytchley.

The converse of Churchill's inevitable total absorption in the conduct of the war was his decision to leave economic and social issues almost exclusively to his principal lieutenants. Clement Attlee has outlined some of the tasks he himself took on in co-ordinating the home front.[2] Sir John Anderson, as lord president and chairman of the powerful LP Committee, had the top direction of economic policy – the Chancellor of the Exchequer, Sir Kingsley Wood, was left out of the War Cabinet. Ernest Bevin, a powerful trade union leader, whom Churchill had respected as an adversary in the 1926 General Strike, was in charge

[1] A colleague of mine in the Cabinet Office in 1940 was duty officer there when a 2 am call came in from President Roosevelt, who wanted to speak to the Prime Minister. My colleague had to decide whether to arouse Sir Edward Bridges, secretary of the Cabinet, who in turn had to decide whether to waken Winston Churchill. The latter operation successfully, if grumpily accepted, the President told the Prime Minister that he confirmed acceptance of the leasing of fifty over-age US destroyers, desperately needed for convoy duties, in return for the leasing by the United States of land for defence bases in the West Indies. But there was a condition: the Prime Minister had to give his personal undertaking that, if the Germans successfully invaded Britain, the destroyers must be ordered to proceed at once to Canada. Winston, despite his rude awakening, rose to the occasion. Yes, he said, he would certainly give that assurance, but this was a fate more likely to befall the Nazi fleet than the British. The deal went through.

[2] See p. 36 below.

of the industrial and military mobilization of Britain's manpower and womanpower, and of relations with the trade union movement – a near-dictator in his own field who realized that full participation of labour in the war effort required a social revolution in the factories, mines and workplaces. Herbert Morrison, as Home Secretary, was responsible for anti-aircraft defence and the morale of the civil population.

That is another reason for discounting Britain's wartime experience as an argument for the alleged Downing Street dictatorship. A peace-time prime minister has to be in close touch with the whole range of national and international issues and developments. In modern times a prime minister cannot become a specialist. He must fulfil, but in a far wider sense, the well-known definition of economics – economics is what interests the economist, and the economist is interested, potentially at least, in everything.

But one lesson must be drawn from war and postwar experience. After a war is over, nothing is ever the same again. There is inevitably more government involvement in our national life, whether or not the war is followed by massive unemployment, as it was after World War I and was not after World War II. Even in the feverish 'return to nor-malcy' period after 1918, particularly from 1923, this remained true.

Despite the development of the Cabinet Office between the wars, and its great strengthening after 1939, Churchill also revived, on a smaller scale, the personal prime minister's secretariat on the lines of Lloyd George's wartime 'garden suburb'[1] and it was equipped to act as his eyes and ears, and sometimes boot-toe over a wide range of subjects, including the economic direction of the war. Headed by Professor Lindemann, later Lord Cherwell, it became extremely unpopular with some departments and ministers, despite the high quality of its staff, but they could always preface a demand for information or a policy-steer by invoking the Prime Minister's name, whether or not they had previously sought his authority.

So the reference made by Morley and Amery to emergency rule, while true of wartime, is not in the least conclusive about peacetime conditions, even peacetime emergencies, economic or other. Com-mentators who have rightly quoted Neville Chamberlain's personal foreign policy before and after Munich, and Anthony Eden's pre-occupation with Egypt after the nationalization of the Suez Canal, do not in my view affect the main argument so much as draw attention to the personal characteristics of two recent prime ministers. In Chamber-lain's case there must be strong criticism of the Cabinet's collective

---

[1] On which see Mackintosh, op. cit., pp. 348–55; and S.S.Wilson, *The Cabinet Office to 1945* (London 1975), pp. 38–44.

pusillanimity – though Anthony Eden, and later Duff Cooper, resigned – and it is fair to say that Chamberlain in forming his Cabinet deliberately picked the least able and courageous among the leading Conservatives available to him. It is also clear that his partnership with Sir Horace Wilson at times amounted to a conspiracy to deceive the House of Commons, and even any members of his Cabinet showing a disposition to independence or criticism.

When Leo Amery prepared his lectures he had, of course, no knowledge of what would happen in the immediate after-war years. In fact, despite Richard Crossman's statement on Clement Attlee, already quoted, the Attlee Government was not prime ministerial. Attlee was a great prime minister, but he believed and acted in the spirit of collective Cabinet responsibility and decision. His achievement, in Cabinet terms, was to preside over an administration headed by men of the calibre of Ernest Bevin, Stafford Cripps, Herbert Morrison, Hugh Dalton and Aneurin Bevan, and to keep them together throughout the period of postwar transition. He was helped by the fact that Churchill had entrusted great responsibility to Bevin and Morrison and to a smaller extent to Stafford Cripps and Hugh Dalton, while Aneurin Bevan brought an entirely new political dimension into the Cabinet room.

But Leo Amery was right when he emphasized the essential differences between prime ministers. No two come alike, fortunately for Britain. Without going too far back into history, there was a great difference between Baldwin and Chamberlain; between Churchill and Attlee, even on problems where there is common ground, such as defence and foreign affairs; between Eden and Macmillan. Some have claimed to notice significant differences between Douglas-Home and Wilson, and even between Wilson (Mark i) and Wilson (Mark ii).

Let the debate, then, continue.

My own conclusion is that the predominantly academic verdict of overriding prime ministerial power is wrong. It ignores the system of democratic checks and balances, in Parliament, in the Cabinet, and not least in the party machine and the party in the country. The checks and balances operate not only as long-term safeguards, but also, in one way or another (often unpredictable), almost every day. Historians and academic onlookers not only have the inestimable advantage of hindsight, they span long periods at a time. History is not really like that, still less is the warp and woof of governmental decision that operate under varying but ever-present parliamentary vigilance and pressures.

Cabinet is a democracy, not an autocracy; each member of it, including the prime minister, seeks to convince his colleagues as to the course to follow. The Cabinet bears his stamp, it is true, on each and every policy issue, but it is the Cabinet not the prime minister who decides.[1]

The growth of the Cabinet committee system is one factor which would restrain the overweening desires of a would-be dictator. More and more decisions have to be taken there, or prepared there for Cabinet. Where there is general agreement on the committee, he would have to be a brave – or rash – prime minister who sought to overrule such a decision. He would not last long.

I would hazard these propositions:

1. In peacetime in this century and earlier, the prime minister in each decade has exercised, or has been able to exercise, more power than his predecessor. But this is because, over the whole period, governments have exercised more power and influence. The prime minister has shared in this increased power, and almost certainly has increased his share. In our generation this has been due less to constitutional or political change than to two facts. The first is that, partly because of the daily dramatization of politics, any crisis of whatever nature leads to a demand – genuine and popular, not merely induced by the media or the opposition of the day – that the prime minister does something. 'Action, Prime Minister.' The second is the overriding power of television and, to only a slightly smaller extent, of radio. The prime minister is not only required to make a set-piece ministerial or other broadcast on major occasions; he is constantly in the news, not least the regional news where a major part of the impact is felt.[2]

Moreover, any action of the Government is personalized. I remember, in the 1964–70 Government, seeing a local north-east Lancashire paper that had a headline attacking a planning decision in, I think, Clitheroe: the headline attributed the blame to 'Wilson'.

2. Arguments based on emergency situations such as world wars are inadmissible for peacetime conditions. The prime minister is invariably accorded emergency powers, but these are limited in duration; still more they are conditional on his maintaining parliamentary confidence, such as a coalition tends to ensure. Nevertheless, the power of government and to that extent of the prime minister never reverts to the *status quo ante bellum*.

3. The arguments in support of the prime ministerial government thesis entirely fail to allow for almost 180-degree differences in the style of individual, indeed successive, prime ministers. Constitutional rationalists fail to recognize that Cabinets, and prime ministers too, are essentially human and, being human, are essentially different.

[1] See the two quotations of Lord Rosebery in his *Sir Robert Peel* (London 1899), pp. 34–5, quoted on the title-page and at the head of chapter III. These words are still true today.
[2] Compare A. H. Brown, op. cit., p. 31.

In British politics, more than in most countries, all human life is there, varying from the occasional sub-human to the still rarer super-human, with a wide range in between. None of the prime ministers of my experience – the same goes for Cabinet ministers, and I would more guardedly make the same assertion for those about whom I have only read – has been either a puppet or a puppet-master. Harold Macmillan has been rightly praised as a successful prime minister, but this did not mean that he could impose his will. Only a madman would try; and Lord Hill has recorded of him that 'if he found himself in a minority he accepted the fact with grace and humour'.[1]

4. There has been a steady accretion to the power of the prime minister in appointing ministers, i.e. both in selecting appointees and in allocating to them their duties. But in both tasks he faces strict limitations. A modern democratic party is a broad church; its parliamentary spectrum normally covers an even wider arc than the views of the half of the country whose support it claims. So must the Cabinet. Few prime ministers, except in wartime and rarely then, could dictate to their Cabinets, except on the basis of consultation with their senior colleagues. Prime ministers who have ignored or defied that maxim, particularly if they have refused to appoint anyone who has opposed their views or in any way given offence, and have instituted 'government by crony', have invariably paid the price. Chamberlain was an obvious, but not the only, example.

The alleged freedom of a prime minister in Cabinet appointments, except perhaps on first coming into office, bears little relation to reality. There have to be consultations; cabinet re-shuffles are anything but set-piece movements on a chess board. I was fortunate in having to seek few consultations and face very few pressures. But I had to be aware of balance, not only in terms of the sometimes crudely expressed division between so-called left and so-called right, but also, in the special circumstances of a government committed to a referendum on continued membership of the E E C, to the balance between committed pro-marketeers and committed anti-marketeers. In the event, without too much calculation on my part, it transpired that I had appointed nine dedicated pro-marketeers, twelve equally dedicated anti-marketeers and one no less dedicated agnostic. The final Cabinet tally, after the re-negotiations of the terms of entry, was publicly announced to be seventeen in favour, seven against.

What I have said about the appointment of ministers applies equally to dismissal. Most prime ministers have found their freedom limited by the possible threat by a senior and politically essential minister to resign

[1] Lord Hill, *Both Sides of the Hill* (London 1964), p. 235.

if A or B were dropped. Again, I have not suffered greatly from this – apart from a little trouble in the heady post-referendum period.

5. Another defect of the prime ministerial theorem is its unrealistic assumption that everything is static. There are things he might essay in a given situation, say after a successful government election, that he would hesitate to attempt if things were going badly for him in Parliament. A bad run of by-elections or even a single bad one, or disastrous local elections, weaken his hand. Action he might want to take can be difficult on the eve of a by-election – still more a referendum – or in the run-up to a general election, the likely date of which he may see more clearly than outside commentators, or even than his colleagues.

6. If Richard Crossman is right in saying – and most historians support his thesis – that the situation Bagehot was describing was just about to end, so there is a case for saying that Richard Crossman's analysis failed to take account of the new checks and balances qualifying the power of the prime minister. These include certainly the greater power of Cabinet committees, not to mention the select committees, whose extended power is one of Richard Crossman's achievements. These checks were operating at the very time that the sheer pressure of work, and the consequent changes in government working, was rendering his sounder points out of date.

Few prime ministers this century have exercised more power, or for that matter more charisma and nonchalance, than Harold Macmillan. Even in the valley of electoral shadow, he was still able to sack a third of his Cabinet overnight – 'the wrong third', I said in subsequent elections. His period of weakness began not with the factors that had forced that decision. It followed the decision itself. He was never as strong again, though I believed at the time, and still believe, that when in October 1963 he asked the Cabinet whether they would support him in a decision to stay until after the next general election, he was already virtually assured of their support, had he not been forced to resign almost immediately afterwards because of the onset of a sudden illness.

These are my considered conclusions on the great debate on how Britain is governed, on the rationalization, mostly retrospective, of great events under successive and widely varying prime ministers.

The following pages of this book are designed to show, on the basis of one man's observations, how it all really happens. But first it is necessary to trace the evolution of the position of first minister. The historical chapter which follows lays no claim to original research or analysis: it is derivative and it possesses no authority except its faithful following of those who have blazed the historical trail. But the reader would find it difficult to understand the role of a modern prime minister without a brief account of the development of his office.

I

The Evolution of the Prime Minister

'In any sphere of action there can be no comparison between the positions of number one and numbers two, three and four.' WINSTON CHURCHILL[1]

Historians have traditionally agreed to regard Sir Robert Walpole as Britain's first prime minister.[2]

The phrase was neither new nor complimentary. It had been used in Queen Anne's reign: Godolphin and Harley were described as her 'prime ministers', a term borrowed from current French usage. It was used to denote 'court favourite', with connotations similar to 'teacher's pet'.

For centuries monarchs had had their principal advisers: in Tudor times Henry VII's Morton, Henry VIII's Wolsey and Cromwell, Elizabeth's Burghley, and in Stuart times James I's Cecil and Carr, or Charles I's Buckingham and Strafford. In many cases the monarch's favour proved unreliable, and some favourites perished ignominiously.

Against Walpole, who served the early Georges from 1721 to 1742, it was undoubtedly used as a gibe. Indeed, he denied that he was prime minister, as did George Granville (1763–5) and Lord North (1770–82) after him. The phrase 'sole minister', hated by the Parliaments of the time, and 'first minister' have tended to be used as alternatives by many commentators.[3]

---

[1] Winston Churchill, *Their Finest Hour* (London 1949), p. 14.
[2] For example, Lord Blake, *The Office of Prime Minister* (Oxford 1975), p. 6: 'I shall . . . stick to tradition and count Walpole as the first of his line.'
[3] Beatson's *Political Index* of 'Prime Ministers and Favourites from the Accession of Henry VIII to the Present Time', published in 1786, listed only one 'Sole Minister' after 1714 – Walpole. After him, though with substantial inaccuracy, Beatson chose to bracket two, three or four joint or co-equal ministers on whose advice the King relied. Blake, op. cit., p. 5.

To regard Walpole as first of his line does not mean that he was at any time head of the executive. The king was in every sense the executive, as well as the 'dignified' head of government. The departments of state, some of them extremely ancient in title and functions or non-functions, were the creatures of the throne. They were answerable to the king, though one gradual change during Walpole's period was the need to make changes in the great offices of state to meet the growing criticisms and demands of Parliament, to ensure that the king's government could be carried on.[1]

But there was more than that – Walpole's dominance over the heads of departments. Here he was helped by the fact that the Hanoverian monarchs rarely attended meetings.

Until Walpole, the first minister existed just so long as he continued to enjoy royal favour. Queen Anne's advisers had had a great struggle to keep Parliament in check, but they held office by royal favour, and as members of the royal 'cabinet' in the old sense of the word. By the time Walpole's long tenure of office ended – still longer than that of any of his forty-nine successors[2] – the test was not royal favour only, but acceptability to Parliament.

Indeed, his end came when he could no longer control Parliament. Although a first minister, right up to the widening of the franchise by the 1832 Reform Act, had vast reserves of royal patronage to ensure the return to Parliament of members acceptable to the Crown, Walpole finally fell – not through the withdrawal of royal support, but because he could no longer control Parliament.

After his resignation, royal approbation was never sufficient, if parliamentary support failed. This does not mean that Walpole's disappearance changed the whole complexion of Parliament and politics. On the contrary. Professor Plumb in his Ford Lectures makes the two salient points: 'Essential though it was to possess the confidence of the King, domination of Parliament proved more important. When at last Walpole failed to do so he went. By then, however, his system was so strong that it made little or no difference. The Whig aristocracy remained in power.'[3]

The disappearance of Walpole did not mean the resignation of the executive as a whole. There was no 'clean sweep', for the heads of

[1] Lord Blake, op cit., p. 25, has likened the relations between the head of state, prime minister and heads of departments, *mutatis mutandis*, to the constitution of the Fifth Republic in France, adopted in 1958.

[2] Forty-nine if we include the Earl of Bath, who was first minister for two days in February 1746, and Earl Waldegrave, who survived twice as long in June 1757.

[3] J.H.Plumb, *The Growth of Political Stability in England 1675–1725* (London 1967), p. 179.

departments were responsible to the king, and the king's government had to be carried on.

What went with Walpole was stability in leadership, though Pelham (1743–54) was an exception. In the next forty years there were twenty administrations – though since some first ministers served two or even three times, only fourteen individuals served as first ministers.[1]

Walpole's tenure of office was a historic turning-point, though, as Lord Blake has commented, references to him as the first 'modern prime minister' are grossly misleading. He would rightly regard Peel as the first. Peel a century after Walpole was closer to a twentieth-century prime minister than to Walpole.

Few of Walpole's twenty successors were known as 'prime minister' except colloquially. Most of them were, however, first lord of the Treasury; and again, quoting Lord Blake, 'it seems best to regard the First Lord of the Treasury as Prime Minister unless there is some palpable reason to the contrary'.[2]

Palpable reasons certainly apply in the case of William Pitt the elder (Chatham). He was never first lord. He headed two of his administrations as secretary of state for the Southern Department, and was lord privy seal in his third.

Apart from death or grave illness (the Duke of Grafton was in fact the active head of the government in the latter part of Pitt's third administration), most of the changes during this turbulent period were due to the inability of the individual first minister to retain the support of Parliament, whatever views the monarch might take. This was a proof of the change marked by Walpole.

[1] For comparison, in the forty years 1782–1822, there were seven administrations (six prime ministers); from 1822–62, sixteen (ten prime ministers); from 1862–1902 twelve (eight prime ministers); from 1902–42, fifteen (ten prime ministers); and since then ten (eight prime ministers). Some in those forty years survived for very short periods – the Earl of Bath for two days in February 1746, Earl Waldegrave for four days in June 1977: in the same month, the Duke of Devonshire got in two administrations; ten lasted for less than three years, six for less than two. Four were commoners, including Lord North, whose barony was a courtesy title.

[2] Blake, op. cit., p. 7. The prime minister has traditionally taken the title of First Lord of the Treasury. There is a widespread belief that the only exception in the last 150 years was the appointment of W.H.Smith of bookstall fame, immortalized by mutation in *HMS Pinafore* as Sir Joseph Porter, KCB. This is not so. Salisbury appointed in turn, Sir Stafford Northcote (Iddesleigh), Smith and Balfour as first lord. All of these lived in No. 10 since that dwelling is reserved for the first lord – as is shown by the plaque on the door. (Salisbury lived in his town house in Arlington Street.) He ultimately combined both posts, as all his successors have done. There is little likelihood that any future prime minister will foreswear the office of first lord of the Treasury. Since the Ministerial Salaries Act, 1937, 1 Edw. 8 and 1 Geo. 6 cap. 38, which provided for the prime minister's salary and pension, both are paid 'to the person who is prime minister and first lord of the Treasury'.

But the first minister's disappearance did not mean a mass evacuation of the departments. That did not happen until the resignation of Lord North in 1782. Rockingham's entry into office with an almost entirely new team marked a turning-point.[1] From Rockingham's administration onwards, we can speak of a new administration, a new team, known by the name of its head. The events that brought him to power marked another turning-point, Lord North's submission to the King. 'Your Majesty is well apprised that in this country the Prince on the Throne cannot with prudence, oppose the deliberate resolution of the House of Commons.'[2]

As the title 'prime minister' came more generally into use, this still carried with it no legal recognition. The first to use it in an official document was Disraeli in 1878, more than 150 years after Walpole's appointment. When the final instrument of the Congress of Berlin was agreed he signed the Treaty as 'First Lord of the Treasury and Prime Minister of Her Britannic Majesty'.[3]

After the succession of short administrations that followed Walpole, the power of the first minister was enhanced for two main reasons, war and the illness of the King. The Seven Years War called for strong ministerial leadership, and the elder Pitt provided it. The old system of departments under the king returned with the peace, the prime minister becoming more of a chairman; as Lord Blake has put it, 'a sort of liaison figure between the Crown and Commons';[4] Bagehot's hyphen, in fact, rather than his buckle. Lord North, who held this position for twelve years of national disillusionment and disaster, was the last of the old regime.

The new regime was heralded by the replacement, on the King's own decision, of the Fox–North coalition[5] by William Pitt the Younger in December 1783.

Pitt's administration lasted until March 1801, when the King broke with him over Catholic Emancipation. After the Addington interregnum ended in May 1804 Pitt retained office until his death in January 1806.

[1] North's Lord Chancellor continued in the Rockingham Cabinet.
[2] J.Fortescue (ed.), *The Correspondence of George III* (London 1938), V, p. 394, excerpt no. 3566.
[3] The office was not even recognized in the Order of Precedence at Buckingham Palace until 1904, when the prime minister was accorded precedence next after the Archbishop of York. In all previous tables he was not even referred to, although members of his administration were included, viz. secretaries of state and those whips who held household appointments. His first statutory mention is in the Chequers Estates Act, 1917, (7 & 8 Geo. 5 cap. 55).
[4] Blake, op. cit., p. 26.
[5] After a defeat in the Lords.

Pitt, both in peace and in war, provided the same dominant style of leadership as his father. In this he was assisted by the royal incapacity, and the change in the nature of the Cabinet Council.

Some of Britain's most distinguished historians have, by deep and assiduous research, uncovered and analysed the nature of the change. The consensus of those who have pronounced their conclusions is that the Cabinet Council, which under George III had developed from the meetings of officers of state and heads of departments, waned in influence and gave way to the *conciliabulum* or the so-called 'efficient Cabinet'. The prime minister was now heading a group of executive heads chosen mainly by him. The earlier body, in addition to departmental heads, had from time to time included such figures as the Archbishop of Canterbury, the lord high steward of England, the lord chief justice and the commander-in-chief. Hence Sir Lewis Namier's description of it as a 'Council of State', rather than an administration.

Pitt was dealing with the 'efficient Cabinet', as it had evolved and was continuing to evolve. They were substantially his men, his choices, and by the turn of the century the prime minister's power had extended to the dismissal of a colleague in whom he had lost confidence. It was in Addington's time that the prime minister was challenged by Lord Loughborough's insistence on retaining his membership of the 'efficient Cabinet', after he had been replaced as lord chancellor by Lord Eldon. He continued to attend Addington's Cabinet; Addington sacked him on the ground 'that the members of the Cabinet should not exceed that of persons whose responsible situation in office require their being members of it'. And the word 'responsible' by this time was related much more to responsibility to the prime minister *and Parliament* than to the king.

Earlier Pitt had taken the initiative in procuring the dismissal of a senior member of Council, and securing the King's agreement. In 1792 the Lord Chancellor made a strong attack in the Lords on Pitt's Sinking Fund. He had not protested about it in Council. In the earliest known assertion of the principle of collective Cabinet responsibility, Pitt wrote to him referring to 'the impossibility of His Majesty's service being any longer carried on to advantage while your Lordship and myself both remain in our present situation', stating that he was requesting the King to act on that recommendation. The King called for the return of the Great Seal and a new lord chancellor was appointed.

Pitt, both by his ministerial inheritance and by his dedication and singlemindedness, was less of a co-ordinator than a driving chief executive. This was so in his six years as a peacetime leader. It was intensified in war. When temporarily out of office in 1803, he told Lord Melville that it was 'an absolute necessity . . . that there should be an avowed and real Minister possessing the chief weight in the Council and the principal place in the confidence of the King'.

Pitt ensured this by unremitting hard work and by centralizing. In modern parlance, he would have been called, certainly by the standards of his times, 'a one-man band'.

After his death, there was no reversion to 'normalcy' such as had followed the elder Pitt's last administration. For one thing the war lasted for nine years after his death, with Britain facing her first blockade in the continental system and, following Tilsit, for a time standing virtually alone. Even after Waterloo the Government faced new internal and social problems, heavy unemployment, rural and urban distress, the consequences of enclosures on the land and the technological revolution in industry: for the first time a British government was facing, and felt it was facing, an unknown 'law and order' problem.

Pitt's successors, therefore, both in war and in peace, carried more power as prime minister than any of his predecessors. Addington in his interregnum, Grenville, Perceval, Liverpool – far less dominant figures than Pitt – exercised that power.

Yet they continued to rule *durante beneplacito* only as long as the king sought no change. When George III succumbed to total madness, the Prince Regent was regarded as within his constitutional rights in seeking to dismiss Spencer Perceval, and would have done so had not the assassin got in first in the House of Commons Lobby. The same Regent as king still resisted unwelcome ministerial appointments, and was successful in blocking the appointment of Canning as foreign secretary, though later he was to call him to the premiership.

The brief reign of William IV saw the fundamental changes that have led historians to describe Peel, in 1841–6, as the first modern prime minister. The general election of 1830, which had to take place on the death of George IV, altered the composition of the House of Commons and made a Whig government inevitable. From now on, the choice of the prime minister and the administration depended not on the monarch but on Parliament. The shift in power was fortified by the Reform Act of 1832. The king's patronage, exercised through the first lord of the treasury, could no longer be decisive in buying seats. The Act's final abolition of the rotten boroughs made this impossible, and with the widened franchise the money was inadequate to condition enough voters.

Moreover, despite the fact that the franchise was very much more limited than today, much more indeed than after 1867, the House of Commons could, more legitimately than ever before, claim to some

extent to represent the voice of the people – the king therefore would
have found it very much harder to resist the results of a general election.
Equally, if parliamentary opinion shifted between elections, it would
have been difficult for him to seek to maintain in office an administration that had lost the confidence of Parliament. Lord North's warning
to George III had become absolute.[1] Each of the six Parliaments elected
from 1841 to 1866 brought down at least one administration apiece, and
sometimes two. The House of Commons in being had a more decisive
voice in the survival and creation of governments than ever before or,
indeed, ever after.

The 1867 Reform Act completed the process. The franchise was
further considerably widened. The creation of much more equal electoral districts in 1885 – a demand of the Chartists – and the secret ballot
of 1872 made it still more representative of the national will, or at least
of those enjoying the franchise.

Party lines had hardened in Parliament, once the Peelites had bedded
down with the Liberals. The road was open to the creation of national
party organizations, starting with all that Schnadhorst in Chamberlain's Birmingham.[2] The prime minister – or leader of the Opposition
–secured more prestige and power as leader of his party, and as
standard-bearer in elections and between elections. Contests were beginning to be fought as much on the personality of the leader as on the
Government's or the party's policies.

Lord Shaftesbury, indeed, after the election of 1857, said, 'There
seems to be no measure, no principle, no cry, to influence men's minds
and determine elections; it is simply, "were you or were you not? Are
you, or are you not, for Palmerston?".'[3]

The classic struggle between Disraeli and Gladstone was just as personalized; their parties in all areas of the country felt almost physical
hatred for the leader of the other side, much more than in the twenty-
five years that followed.

Since the choice of the Government was clearly that of Parliament,
defeated prime ministers began the practice of resigning as soon as the
polls were declared, without presenting themselves for rejection in the
House of Commons. In 1868 Disraeli resigned before Parliament
assembled, as did Gladstone in 1874, followed by Disraeli again in 1880.
This has been the practice from that time, except when no party had a
clear majority, and the attitude of third parties had to be clarified – with
whom, if anyone, would they form a coalition? Short of a coalition, to

[1] See p. 15 above.
[2] See M. Ostrogorsky, *Democracy and the Organisation of Political Parties* (London 1902).
[3] Quoted in Blake, op. cit., p. 41.

which major party would they give non-participating support? This was the position in December 1923 and in 1929, and a similar question was raised by the result of the March 1974 general election.[1]

In the sixty years that followed the 1867 Reform Act, the position of the prime minister, his relations with his Cabinet and the relations between both and Parliament changed far less than in the previous sixty years. Survival still depended on parliamentary support. Political tidal waves were more important than constitutional ones – apart from the Irish question in the eighties, and in the years immediately before and after World War I, which was fundamentally political and religious, and the constitutional issue between the two Houses over the rejection of Lloyd George's Budget.

The Liberal Party was torn apart in Gladstone's time over Ireland, and the powerful Liberal Unionists went over to the Conservatives. Less than twenty years later, the Conservatives were rent by the Tariff Reform issue, and in 1906 suffered the biggest electoral defeat up to that point in history. By 1910 Asquith, who was committed to House of Lords reform, was dependent on the Irish vote and to a smaller extent on support from the Labour Party.

The rise of Labour created a three-party House, and minority governments in 1924 and 1929. It was not until 1945 that Labour won an overall majority, in the postwar election landslide.

Constitutional changes included the ending of sex discrimination at the ballot-box – though equal rights were held back until 1928 – and payment of Members of Parliament. Probably the most revolutionary influence on government came from outside, with the arrival of radio in the 1920s and television in the 1940s.

Apart from party splits, such as those that hit the Liberals over Unionism in the eighties and the Conservatives over Tariff Reform early in the new century, there was more stability in relations between Government and Commons. Unlike the halcyon days of parliamentary power between 1832 and 1867, there was no dismissal of an incumbent majority government by a parliamentary vote – that is to say, if one includes the extraordinary and somewhat pathetic resignation of Rosebery in 1895. Here was a prime minister of what would now be called great charisma, with a great local government reputation in the newly formed London County Council and a gift for popular mass oratory comparable only with that of Aneurin Bevan, sixty years later. Defeated on a snap vote on a Supply Day debate on the stocks of cordite in

[1] In 1929 no party had a majority in the House though Labour were the biggest single group. King George V put strong pressure on Stanley Baldwin not to resign unless and until he was defeated in Parliament, but Baldwin insisted on resigning.

government depots, he threw in his hand. It has always been understood that he found the strain of Downing Street too much for him: above all, he could not sleep. He could certainly have won a vote of confidence and survived. In any event, if things were too much for him he should have resigned and let the normal processes be followed for the choice of a successor from his own Cabinet. By surrendering the seals of office of the entire administration, he presented the Conservatives to the country as the party in government, and the Liberals as the party of abdication. Small wonder that the Conservatives were in power for ten years, and since fissiparous tendencies are harder to counter in opposition, the Liberal Party almost fatally split on the issue of the South African war. In the event it was Tariff Reform that split the Tories – in government.

In the Foreword some of the events and arguments that have fuelled the debate on 'prime ministerial government' have been assessed, together with some of the developments in the past fifty years, from Lloyd George onwards, in war and peace, which have been adduced for or against the concept. To my mind, there is more treasure to be found in examining the characters of the prime ministers of recent times, in particular their very differing styles of prime ministership: and, what is more difficult to do from any book, to get through that black door in Downing Street, and see what really happens behind it.

II

The Prime Minister
and his Cabinet

'You must have confidence in the judgment of the man in charge. If he hasn't got that confidence, he's not fit to be Prime Minister.' CLEMENT ATTLEE

There have been twenty-one changes of prime minister this century, involving fifteen men. Of these, nine have, owing to death or retirement, been the replacement of the outgoing prime minister by a colleague, who was a member of his own party; nine more have kissed hands as the result of a shift in the control of Parliament, through a general election, or a shift in parliamentary power. In addition, in 1905 Balfour resigned and let in the Liberals, who promptly called an election and gained a substantial majority.

Four changes were caused by coalition conditions – the replacement of Asquith by Lloyd George, the formation of the Ramsay MacDonald 'National' Government in 1931 with a few of his Labour colleagues and a preponderance of Conservatives, and his replacement in 1935 by his lord president, the Conservative leader, Stanley Baldwin. In 1945 the World War II coalition headed by Winston Churchill broke up, and as leader of the majority party, Winston Churchill formed a Conservative government, including a few previously non-party administrators who had been recruited during the war.

The procedures followed in a simple intra-government replacement and those adopted where a different party or coalition of parties takes over, usually after an election defeat, are different, though both involve an initiative and personal decision by the monarch.

In the relatively simple hand-over of what is in fact, though not constitutionally, a continuing government, the test, given the normal circumstances of a party majority, is whether A or B can in fact command a majority in the House of Commons. Where the party's procedure for selecting a leader is laid down and is seen to have worked, e.g. the eliminating ballot procedure used by the Parliamentary Labour Party in March–April 1976, the selection is fairly clear, though it still has to be made. The Parliamentary Party was not in fact electing a prime minister; it was electing a new party leader.

When the process is complete, the outgoing prime minister goes straight to the Palace and formally tenders his resignation; the most he needs to do is to inform the monarch, who will have been given the figures already, that the ballot has produced a given result, probably adding that in his view the newly elected leader can command a majority in Parliament. (The procedure might be somewhat different in a situation where the Government was in a minority, for example had I resigned between March and October 1974.) Contrary to widespread belief, there is no duty on the prime minister, still less any inherent right, to recommend the man to be sent for. It is the sovereign who decides whom to send for and invite to form a government.

One thing must be made clear, in view of an unfortunate incident in another of Her Majesty's dominions, Australia. In normal times – the World War II government, and two postwar governments, were obvious exceptions – there is in the British Constitution no such animal as a deputy prime minister. Even where a prime minister has formally designated a colleague as deputy prime minister, this has not created any presumption that the person nominated should be sent for on the decease or resignation of the prime minister. Had Winston Churchill ceased to be prime minister in wartime, his successor would undoubtedly have been chosen from the ranks of the Conservatives, who were by far the largest party in Parliament. Clement Attlee was deputy prime minister, as leader of the second most substantial partner in the coalition.

Herbert Morrison was officially designated by Clement Attlee as deputy prime minister.[1] But when Winston Churchill sought to have Anthony Eden recognized as deputy prime minister, George VI refused to agree, as he feared it might create a presumption about the succession (Winston Churchill was nearly seventy-seven). In 1962 Harold Macmillan refused to designate an official deputy, as he considered that there was no such recognized office under the constitution, though later in the year he announced that R. A. Butler would *act* as deputy prime minister. This announcement was not followed by any recognition in the officially promulgated list of ministers.

[1] Hugh Dalton complained in his diary of Morrison's persistent interference in the work of other ministers, saying that 'he thinks he can do this because he is Lord President of the Council, a sort of informal "Boss of the Home Front", as well as Deputy Prime Minister'. *High Tide and After* (London 1962), p. 141.

My own procedure was to rely on the order of precedence within the Cabinet, the so-called 'pecking-order', making clear that the second in the list chairs Cabinet and any Cabinet committee normally chaired by me, if I were absent, and also stands in for me in answering questions in Parliament. From 1964 to 1968 George Brown, who was elected deputy leader of the Party, held this position; after his resignation he held on to the deputy leadership outside the Government,[1] and I simply advanced Michael Stewart to second place in the list of Cabinet precedence.

The hand-over in April 1976 was the direct result of the system of election by an eliminating ballot which the Parliamentary Labour Party has always used. Since the adoption of a similar method by the Conservative Party in 1965, it is reasonable to assume that the problems of succession in any future Conservative government would be as smooth.

It was not always so. Whereas Anthony Eden followed Sir Winston Churchill in March 1955 without any opposition, this was not the case when Anthony Eden resigned through ill health in January 1957; still less was it so when Harold Macmillan resigned for the same reason in October 1963.

In 1957 there were two clear candidates, Harold Macmillan and R. A. Butler. The procedure followed is described in the respective memoirs of Lord Kilmuir and Harold Macmillan.[2] When the Cabinet met, Lord Kilmuir and the Marquess of Salisbury, above the battle as peers, went into an adjoining room and took the views of the Commons Cabinet ministers, one by one. They then consulted the chairman of the 1922 Committee of back-benchers. They concluded: 'An overwhelming majority of Cabinet ministers was in favour of Macmillan as Eden's successor, and back-bench opinion as reported to us, strongly endorsed this view.'[3]

The Queen sent for Mr Macmillan.

[1] A similar situation arose in April 1976. Edward Short, though leaving the Government, continued as deputy leader. James Callaghan, in drawing up the list of Cabinet precedence, put Michael Foot next below himself.

I was interested to note in the Labour Governments of the sixties, to a much smaller extent after 1974, how much store was set by ministers, and indeed commentators, to the 'pecking-list'; the issue quite often occupied more time in a re-shuffle than the move itself. In Attlee's Government I did not even know what my pecking-order position was. It does, however, have some prestige importance in that, in any meeting between two ministers, the junior in terms of precedence calls on the other: departmental officials tend to take it very seriously, as it affects the standing of their departments.

[2] The Earl of Kilmuir, *Memoirs: Political Adventure* (London 1961), p. 285; Harold Macmillan, *Riding the Storm* (London 1971), pp. 182–3.

[3] loc. cit. This procedure has been described, not unfairly, as 'polling the Cabinet', though little is known from published sources of the back-bench consultation. If this is so, it realized an uncharacteristic proposal of George IV, who once suggested that the Cabinet should elect his first minister.

The choice of Mr Macmillan's successor was much more sensational, not to say gory. His apparently effortless and superior conduct of government was seriously weakened by his purge of seven Cabinet ministers[1] in July 1962, following a disastrous by-election result. Following the Profumo case in the summer of 1963, there was widespread doubt about his ability to lead his party in the forthcoming general election and political commentators were virtually unanimous in prophesying his departure.

Mr Macmillan in his memoirs[2] reveals that he decided that he would either go quickly or see the party through the next election, which had to take place not later than October 1964. On the night before the crucial Cabinet he decided to face them with a decision to stay on, and it became clear that he would have strong support. So it proved; there was only one dissenter. That very night, however, he was taken seriously ill, and had to enter hospital for a prostate operation. His consequent resignation, forcing his party to select his successor, led to a public spectacle, because the crisis coincided with their annual party conference at Blackpool, in the full glare of press and television publicity, not only on the platform but in the fringe meetings, the corridors of the Imperial Hotel and outside the bedrooms of the principal candidates and kingmakers.[3]

After the narrow election defeat of the Conservative Government in October 1964, the Parliamentary Party adopted an electoral system, which when first used led to the election of Edward Heath in 1965, on Sir Alec Douglas-Home's resignation as leader of the Opposition and party leader. It was a variant of the 1965 system which was used in 1975, when Mrs Thatcher successfully challenged Mr Heath.

The procedures followed in the very different circumstances that arise from the electoral defeat of the party in power are inevitably simpler, provided that the result creates a viable situation for the majority party. The Queen, without of course receiving any advice from the outgoing prime minister, sends for the leader of the successful party. In this generation there has not been any doubt about his identity.[4]

[1] Selwyn Lloyd, Lord Mills, Harold Watkinson, John Maclay, Lord Kilmuir, David Eccles and Charles Hill. See Harold Macmillan, *At the End of the Day* (London 1973), pp. 89–96, an account that refers to only six who went, omitting Charles Hill.

[2] Macmillan, *At the End of the Day*, pp. 499–505.

[3] For informed Conservative accounts of this period see Randolph S.Churchill, *The Fight for the Tory Leadership* (London 1963), and Iain Macleod, 'The Tory Leadership' (the famous essay on the 'Magic Circle') in *The Spectator* (17 January 1964).

[4] This is to ignore, quite properly, the extraordinary attempt by Herbert Morrison, backed by Harold Laski, to dispute Clement Attlee's right to the premiership. Though Clement Attlee had become prime minister and appointed a number of senior ministers, the revolt was crushed by the summoning of all the newly elected MPs to a meeting in the

A more difficult problem is created if no party has a clear majority. King George v was faced with this situation after the general elections of December 1923 and in 1929, when no party had anything like an overall majority. In both years a minority Labour Government was formed, but only because the Liberals were willing to keep Labour in office, if only on sufferance.

The King refused to allow Stanley Baldwin to resign until he had submitted his Government's fate to Parliament in January 1924. In 1929 Baldwin pressed very strongly to resign when the election results were known, as had been the practice in cases where the Opposition gained an overall majority since the days of Disraeli and Gladstone. The King agreed.[1]

February 1974 produced an entirely new situation, in that neither of the two major parties could have reached a majority, even given the full support of the Liberals. In a House of 635, Labour had 301, the Conservative Party 296, the minor parties – Liberals, the Ulster Unionists (no longer automatically taking the Conservative whip) and the Scots and Welsh Nationalists and the Lincoln Social Democrat adding up to 37.

On the day following the polls, there was wide expectation that Edward Heath would tender the resignation of his Government, and that afternoon the Parliamentary Committee of the Labour Party – the so-called 'shadow cabinet', intimated their 'availability', even though we proved to be eighteen short of an overall majority, that is, we had thirty-four less than the combined voting power of the other parties. In the event, Mr Heath spent the weekend trying to reach an accommodation with the Liberal leader, Jeremy Thorpe, and his party, offering Liberal participation in the government. By Monday, 4 March, these negotiations had broken down, and Mr Heath tendered his resignation. When I was called to the Palace the Queen asked me if I could form an administration. Answering yes, I was authorized to form a government, and in fact submitted the names of ten of the leading members of the Cabinet for the royal approval that evening.

Over this weekend there were suggestions that, as the Conservatives had fewer seats than Labour, and were having difficulty in securing allies, the Labour leader should have been invited to try. This would

Beaver Hall, London, two days after the results were declared. The Chief Whip, William Whiteley, called on the 'Foreign Secretary' Ernest Bevin, who massively and simply proposed the confirmation of Clement Attlee as party leader. This was carried by acclamation – and a number of us among the new M Ps never really felt able to excuse Herbert Morrison's manœuvre.

[1] In 1924 the Conservatives were the biggest single party in Parliament, though Labour and the Liberals taken together outnumbered them. In 1929 Labour was the biggest single party, though still in a minority.

have been contrary to precedent. A prime minister was there – at Downing Street. If and when he resigned that would create a new situation. Alternatively, were he to face Parliament, without allies, and be defeated, he would then resign. As things were, there was no vacancy to fill.

The constitutional practice on a change of government is that the sovereign asks the party leader who has been called to the Palace whether he can form a government. There are two possible answers. One is for him to express assurance that a viable government can and will be formed. The other is a statement of willingness to hold the necessary consultations to find out *whether* a government can be formed.

In 1964, with an overall majority of four, I gave the first answer, and was in fact successful. In 1974, in a minority situation, I gave the same answer, and the minority government was formed. In 1963, on the other hand, though the Conservatives had an overall majority around ninety, Sir Alec Douglas-Home merely asked leave to go away and try, such was the disturbance in his party following the turbulent process of selecting a leader. Iain Macleod and Enoch Powell refused to serve, but Sir Alec's ability to form a government was confirmed by the decision of R. A. Butler and Reginald Maudling to join his Cabinet. R. A. Butler, in particular, received some criticism from opponents of Sir Alec's selection. In a letter to *The Times*, he explained his decision by his fear that, if Sir Alec failed to form a government, the Queen might have had no alternative but to send for Labour. I am sure that this view was ill-founded. The Conservatives still had an overall majority around ninety, and an alternative Conservative leader would almost certainly have been invited to accept the Queen's Commission.

The prime minister drives straight back to Downing Street, and after, usually, saying a few words to the onlookers and the media from the doorstep, begins the task of forming his Cabinet. If the occasion is caused by one party replacing another in forming a government, this is a most onerous task, since the administration so formed will be basically the Government for as long as the administration lasts. All re-shuffles, however far-reaching, are changes in this team. This has proved to be so even when the prime minister is succeeded by one of his colleagues.[1]

In 1964 it was a particularly difficult task. Labour had been out of office for thirteen years. In the Government I then formed, only two members of the Cabinet I formed had sat, even for a short period, in Clement Attlee's Cabinets – Patrick Gordon-Walker, who had been

---

[1] It was so in each of the three changes in the Conservative premiership between 1951 and 1964. It was so in April 1976, when four Cabinet members and five junior members, in an administration of almost one hundred, resigned or were stood down.

commonwealth secretary from March 1950 to the fall of the Government in October 1951, and James Griffiths, who had been colonial secretary for a similar period. He was brought back at the age of seventy-four because, before the election, I had announced that an incoming Labour government would include Wales's first-ever secretary of state, and none was better fitted to be, or more widely welcomed as Wales's 'charter' secretary of state. George Brown had been a 'minister of Cabinet rank, outside the Cabinet', to use a popular but totally unconstitutional concept, as had Lord Longford, who was appointed lord privy seal and leader of the House of Lords. Only James Callaghan and Michael Stewart had held office as parliamentary under-secretaries, the former as parliamentary secretary in the Ministry of Transport, and parliamentary and financial secretary to the Admiralty, and the latter in the War Office and the Ministry of Supply.

In forming the Cabinet I followed as far as possible the pattern of the parliamentary committee elected in Opposition in November 1963. It was not, in my view, in its entirety, the best shadow cabinet available, and was certainly not representative of the parliamentary party as a whole. I had not voted for all of them; even fewer had voted for me in the leadership contest. But changes became feasible over a period of time, and it was possible to create a better balance; meanwhile the Administration was made more representative of the party inside and outside Parliament than the Cabinet had been by the inclusion of Richard Crossman, Tony Greenwood, Gerald Gardiner as lord chancellor and, from the trade union movement, Frank Cousins.

In March 1974 the task was infinitely easier. We had a trained team. Thirteen of us had sat in Cabinet before. Two had sat regularly in Cabinet as chief whip, and both had been ministerial heads of a department outside the Cabinet; three others had headed departments outside the Cabinet: the Lord Chancellor had regularly attended Cabinet as attorney-general; three others had been senior ministers of state, one as chief whip in the Lords and one as under-secretary. Only Michael Foot had not been a minister, and he had been offered a senior Cabinet appointment in the sixties but declined. I was not exaggerating when I called the 1974 Cabinet the most experienced and talented Cabinet this century, transcending even the Campbell–Bannerman Administration of 1905.

There was a further advantage. The Labour Shadow Cabinet, elected just over three months before the election, was in my view virtually the best that the Parliamentary Labour Party could have chosen. It is a great advantage, on coming into office, if the Cabinet can be based in the main on an elective committee, including the leader, deputy leader and chief whip and twelve members elected by secret ballot by 280-odd MPs each with twelve votes to cast. All MPs, including some of first-class ability, who are inevitably disappointed on the formation of the Cabinet, can hardly criticize the preferment given to those so recently elected by their parliamentary colleagues.

The prime minister is uniquely free in selecting his Cabinet and other members of his ministerial team. He is not fettered, for example, in the sense that an Australian Labour prime minister is, under the unworkable system adopted there under the guise of democracy. Their 'caucus' (Parliamentary Labour Party) elects the members of the Cabinet, and the prime minister has to allocate, to a team he has not selected, the various ministerial portfolios.

Clement Attlee, in an interview, 'The Making of a Cabinet', with Francis Williams,[1] referred to a 'movement' in the Labour Party in 1931 'to set up a group that would have a say in choosing ministers'. He recorded that it fell through in 1945, 'partly because most people soon forgot about it, partly because of the time factor' – he had to go to the Allied Heads of Government Conference at Potsdam immediately after the counting of the votes.

> 'The Australian Labour Party do something of the sort, you know. Awful business. They elect a certain number of people as ministers, and then they're handed over to the Prime Minister and he's told to fit them into the jigsaw. It's quite possible that someone with particular technical qualifications may get left out because he doesn't happen to be the popular man. I don't believe in that at all. You must have confidence in the man in charge. If he hasn't got that confidence, he's not fit to be Prime Minister.'[2]

It is not a task that can be done by a group, or a selection committee. To quote Clement Attlee again,

> 'In my view, the responsibility of choosing the members of the Government must rest solely with the Prime Minister, though in practice he will consult with his colleagues. If he cannot be trusted to exercise this power in the best interests of the nation and the Party without fear, favour or affection, he is not fit to be Prime Minister.'[3]

'In practice', I did not feel it right to go into widespread consultations, either in 1964 or in 1974. In the latter year the shadow cabinet

[1] Interview included in Anthony King (ed.), *The British Prime Minister* (London 1969), p. 74.
[2] ibid.
[3] C.R.Attlee, *As It Happened* (London 1954), p. 156.

fitted into place, and almost every leading figure took up the task he had shadowed in Opposition.[1]

The March 1974 Cabinet had twenty-two members, later increased to twenty-four by the unusual inclusion of the Chief Whip (*ad hominem*, not *ex officio*) and John Silkin (minister of local government and planning). Fifteen of these were the elected Commons members of the Shadow Cabinet. The others were the Lord Chancellor (who had been shadow attorney general), the Leader of the House of Lords and Lord Privy Seal (who had been a Lords member of the Shadow Cabinet), the Secretaries of State for Industry, for Wales and for the Social Services and the Minister of Agriculture.

The need for widespread consultations varies inversely with the degree of unity the prime minister can count on. A bewildered or divided party means an unsure prime minister. Above all, it denotes cliques, factions and fights for protégés. He may not be able to count on senior minister A's continuing support if protégé B is not in a given job; senior minister C will resign if B is. It is an unhappy Cabinet with an unsure parliamentary base if the prime minister has, to any real degree, to put his Cabinet-making function in pawn, or get involved in bargaining.

The Attlee doctrine has not always been accepted in the Labour Party – certainly not on the formation of the two minority Labour administrations of the 1920s. Philip Snowden records the meeting in 1929 of what he called 'the big five' – Ramsay MacDonald, Arthur Henderson, J. R. Clynes, J. H. Thomas and himself, in MacDonald's Hampstead home immediately after the election – 'to decide portfolios'. It was all done by agreement, Snowden recording that, as George Lansbury had to be found a job, despite his 'Poplarist' reputation, it was he who suggested Lansbury for the Office of Works – to London's great benefit, as it proved. He reports, too, the argument about Margaret Bondfield. It was argued that there ought to be a woman Cabinet minister. MacDonald rejected that view but supported her on her merits. Snowden records also the violent disagreement between Thomas and Henderson about the Foreign Office, Thomas complaining that Henderson had 'tricked him'. An unhappy start to an even unhappier Cabinet, which came to the stickiest of ends.[2]

There has to be a central strategy in Cabinet formation, which must

---

[1] This was true, for example, of the incoming Leader of the House, Foreign and Commonwealth Secretary, Chancellor of the Exchequer, Home Secretary and the Secretaries of State for Scotland, Northern Ireland, Environment, Prices and Consumer Protection. Michael Foot's surprise appointment as Secretary for Employment I had long planned. Industry also followed the Shadow appointment, though Trade was separated from the ungainly Trade and Industry Leviathan we inherited.

[2] Philip Viscount Snowden, *An Autobiography* (London 1934), II, pp. 757–67.

reflect the prime minister's broader political and policy strategy. He should be prepared to listen to advice, especially that of the leader of the House and the chief whip, who are in closest touch with back-benchers, then to keep his counsel, and make his own decisions. A problem created by over-reliance on advice is that some may be based on a different strategy or approach: do not be diverted. My experience supports that of Clement Attlee when he said, 'You may talk it over with other senior ministers. As a matter of fact, my general experience was that where I accepted advice it wasn't very good. I did once or twice have people foisted on me. People don't always understand why a man who seems very clever may not turn out particularly good as a Cabinet minister.'[1]

It is usual, however, to consult with the foreign and commonwealth secretary before appointing the defence minister, and I have found it useful to discuss with the chancellor the appointments of ministers to take charge of the principal economic departments. I do not, over eight years, recall any demur over the names proposed. Apart from this, my experience of consultation is that, in ninety per cent of the cases, the senior minister concerned recommended his own PPS for promotion in his own or another department – advice I did not always follow. Colleagues also tend to offer unsolicited advice about back-benchers whom they think should be brought into the Government, almost invariably failing to suggest who should be dropped to make room for them.

The prime minister forming his Cabinet, no less in appointing ministers of state and parliamentary under-secretaries of state, has to use all the qualities he is presumed to have in order to have reached the position he holds.

First, he needs a good memory of his colleagues' specializations and past experience, or any tendencies to weakness in a crisis. Even more, he needs a good 'forgettory'. Forming a Cabinet is no time for settling old scores, or bearing grudges or associating a first-class potential minister with some groupings during some best-forgotten party argument. It is as likely to have been your fault as his, and in some past party row he had his loyalties, as you had yours. Second, the prime minister must pay full regard to preserving a real balance in the party in Parliament, and in the country. The Labour Party, and this is, I would think, equally true of the Conservative and Liberal Parties, is, as I have said, a broad church. No government should be based on a faction, still less a clique. It should embrace and reflect the whole party, though the prime minister can be forgiven if he disregards a few idiosyncratic extremists at the margins, where membership of his party seems to be asymptotic

[1] King, op. cit., pp. 73–4.

to the views of right and left groupings, owing little loyalty to the basic tenets of his party – in my own case to democratic socialism. A modern government claims, with whatever justification, to represent something like half the country: its spread of individual views may range even more widely than that. So should the government. 'What you cannot afford is a Government of cronies and like-minded people, who can be relied on for their loyalty in Cabinet, but who, for that very reason, cannot deliver a corresponding strength, whether in backbenchers or in popular support in the country.'[1]

Third, he must concentrate on the doctrine of horses for courses, not only in using the specialist knowledge of individual ministers, but also in reflecting the changing priorities of national and international relationships. A 'priority' ministry may become less important as old problems and challenges give way to new.[2] 'Horses for courses' includes the great and unteachable quality of being able to handle the House of Commons. In the first resort, as in the last, a government survives, and deserves to survive, in proportion to its success in understanding Parliament, in reflecting, and sometimes knowing when to resist, its changing moods; to its accountability to Parliament, and at times of crisis to its collective ability to lead Parliament.

Fourth, Cabinet and other ministerial appointments should reflect a real rapport with the party nationally, and above all in the country. Every member of the administration – regardless of which party is in office – must remember that he is not where he is, not even in Parliament, as a result of his own transcendent qualities: he is there because people believe in him, and work for him, not primarily as an individual but as a standard-bearer. As a member of the Cabinet, particularly, he needs them more than they need him. Whatever may have been the situation in the spacious days of the Edwardians, political inspiration comes from the country, not from the dinner tables of the élite,[3] or the

---

[1] The present writer in an address before the British Academy (25 April 1975).

[2] Shortly before he died, I invited Clement Attlee to Chequers where he had spent the happiest days of his life (having first ensured that Chequers without his wife would not be too upsetting). Following his stroke, he found speaking difficult, so I put questions to him. 'If you were in this chair,' I asked him, 'what subject would you put higher in the system of priorities than it appears to occupy today?' Immediately he answered, 'Transport.' I moved Barbara Castle there from Overseas Development within a very short period. (In a different context I asked him, parties and politics apart, whom he regarded as the best prime minister *qua* prime minister since he first took an interest in politics. He had no hesitation – 'Salisbury'.)

[3] When I was elected leader of the party in February 1963, I immediately received dining invitations from certain leading Labour MPs. In my first speech to party meeting I said that I should reject them all: instead of spending three or four hours with one or other Labour MP, the time saved would be spent in my room at the House, with the door open to any Labour member who wanted to see me.

hot-house atmosphere of London's political fringe. Members of Parliament, and ministers, may be less prone than some of the fringe to believe that as soon as you are north of Watford the Arctic Circle begins; or that when you pass Basingstoke the natives paint themselves with woad. Inspiration comes from the country. Not only party members, but wider audiences, have the right to have policies and actions explained to them: no less have they the right to be heard. There is nothing more disquieting than M Ps of any party, some ministers even, who make a profession of scorning their party conference, and refusing to attend.

That is why most prime ministers recognize the need to have a preponderance of colleagues with experience in their party machine, close knowledge of it and a real regard for it. Parliamentary democracy will be threatened, and parties atrophy, if ministerial appointments go increasingly to technicians and apparatchiks.

When choosing ministers of state and parliamentary under-secretaries, the prime minister would naturally consult – or at least inform – the Cabinet minister concerned. Clement Attlee's advice again is relevant:

> 'You must take care over junior ministers too. It's generally best to have a talk with the minister concerned in choosing an under-secretary, not just foist someone on him. But you can't necessarily accept the man a minister wants. He's the only one who doesn't know his own deficiencies. You may have picked a minister who is awfully good but, although he doesn't know it, rather weak on certain sides, so you must give him an under-secretary who fills in the gaps.'[1]

A prime minister should take as much trouble with his second team (the two levels of ministers of state) and his third, the parliamentary secretaries, as with his Cabinet. With the heavy load on a modern government they have to be in the firing line, not only for parliamentary questions, but in evidence before the new range of select committees, as well as in handling difficult deputations and meetings. More important still, they are the raw material for the future. I have always claimed, without undue exaggeration, that if the Cabinet collectively disappeared under the proverbial bus, the second team would quickly prove as good, and the third team, in time, still better.[2]

In 1964, and again in 1974, I concentrated all the available relevant

[1] C.R.Attlee, 'The Making of a Cabinet' in King, op. cit., p. 73. In forming my first administration I entirely omitted to consult Frank Cousins about the appointment of his parliamentary secretary. He was quite nice about it and accepted my nomination.

[2] For example, of the present Government (April 1976), Shirley Williams entered the Administration for the first time (as parliamentary secretary, Ministry of Labour) only in April 1966; and Eric Varley as minister of state for technology in October 1969, though he had earlier been an assistant whip.

talent in the Treasury team. Undoubtedly the 1974 team was the most highly qualified the Treasury had ever had. With the Foreign and Commonwealth Office, I virtually gave James Callaghan the team he wanted, and the same was true of the Home Office. In many departments, for example Energy and Industry, most of the incoming junior ministers were covering the same field as they had in the shadow administration.

Even after the Government is formed and functioning, it is usually not very long before changes become necessary. 'Re-shuffles', as they are usually known,[1] may become necessary through death or ill health, resignation for family reasons or disagreement with some aspect of government policy, dismissal of a minister, the desire to bring in some younger talent, the creation of a new department, changes in priorities and problems calling for a dynamic minister in the new hot seat – or simply to avoid a minister becoming stale or type-cast.

They can vary from a major series of moves affecting a number of Cabinet ministers and consequently affecting all levels of the team, to a single replacement of a departing minister, where if the post has any seniority or can widen experience, it usually pays to move a promising young minister and replace him by a back-bencher.

In the major league of re-shuffles, Harold Macmillan's night of the long knives in July 1962 undoubtedly holds the record, and no future prime minister will ever wish to be in a position where he has to challenge it.

In the 1974–6 Administration, I did not carry through any major re-dispositions apart from the two-way switch of Tony Benn and Eric Varley, in the Industry and Energy Departments: it was certainly time to consider a number from the autumn of 1975, but my decision to retire at some point from October onwards led me to postpone it so as to leave the maximum freedom of action for my successor.

In the 1964–70 Governments, and in subsequent comment, I was criticized for making too few changes. I was not enough of a 'butcher', to use Asquith's phrase. He himself was certainly not. In fact, only eight of my original 1964 Cabinet of twenty-two were still there in 1970; seven had been dropped, a similar number had resigned or had gone to other public assignments. By comparison fifteen of Edward Heath's original eighteen survived when his Administration went out of office; Iain Macleod had died, and two stood down.

It is always a good rule to create the vacancies first, and then do the more agreeable appointments with a free hand.

But it was certainly the case that I hated re-shuffles that involved

[1] More irreverently as 'shuffle-bottoms'.

dropping an old and valued colleague. Other prime ministers have told of feeling physically sick: I seemed on these occasions to be subject to psychosomatic stomach pains. Even Clement Attlee concedes that he was not immune, despite his recorded statement that he always avoided a 'cushion', a comforting explanation: 'I don't think that's playing straight with a fellow. If he doesn't measure up to the job, you should tell him.'[1]

I knew personally of a friend who, on being dropped, asked him why and was told 'You're not up to the job.' In a softer mood, his formula was, 'Well you've had a good innings. Time to go back to the pavilion and put up your bat.'

Where there is no question of a minister standing down, it is frequently wise to do a straight swap of portfolios between two ministers, or even three, enabling them to have a change of scenery. One famous case was the Roy Jenkins–James Callaghan move in November 1967: no one should be asked to hold the Treasury for much more than two years, and wisdom suggests a similar rule for the foreign and commonwealth secretary. A somewhat different example, which attracted a great deal of publicity, was the Tony Benn–Eric Varley move in June 1975, already cited.

A re-disposition affecting a substantial number of ministers at all levels is like a nightmarish multidimensional jigsaw puzzle, with an almost unlimited number of possible permutations and combinations – including the complementary qualities between the senior and junior ministers in a given department. Sometimes, after hours of juggling with the pieces, the prime minister finds that the last consequential piece will not fit, as when I was once left with a Yorkshire lady minister and a vacancy as minister of state in the Welsh Office, and had to go back to the drawing-board.

When ministers are asked to stand down, I have almost invariably found them moved more by sympathy for me than for themselves. Almost invariably, they have agreed to resign, though there was once a minister who telephoned me the following morning, after his post had been filled but not announced, to say he had thought it over and would like to stay. He went.

Suppose, one is frequently asked, a minister refuses to go. Has the prime minister the right to require his resignation, or even to recommend his deletion from the list of ministers? The answer is clear; indeed, I had to seek confirmation in a case of clear dismissal, which might have been – but in the event was not – resisted. I was told, 'A minister holds office only at the Queen's pleasure, and the Queen in such matters traditionally accepts the advice of the Prime Minister.'

[1] 'The Making of a Cabinet', in King, op. cit., p. 74.

In the nineteenth century this doctrine was in some doubt. Gladstone failed in his attempt to drop Lord Carlingford in 1884, when Harcourt said the Prime Minister 'was point-blank refused, and acquiesced'. There were, however, serious political overtones in this case as Carlingford was the only Irishman in the Cabinet.[1]

The question of the reverse process, the removal of the prime minister, has been touched upon in the Foreword. Rumours of the impending ousting of the prime minister are usually highly exaggerated. It is arguable, as a number of serious historians have commented, that had Anthony Eden not been forced to retire through illness he would have been forced out; I have expressed my doubts about similar speculation over Harold Macmillan in 1963. The removal of the leader of the party *in government* is like self-decapitation, an extremely difficult, not to say potentially dangerous, undertaking.

The prime minister, particularly if he leads from the centre or centre-left (in the Labour Party), is well fortified. He is wise, too, to ensure that there is no single crown prince. I never had less than three or four, and at one time – it happened to be crucial – six.[2]

Dalton records an attempt during the Attlee Cabinet.[3] He relates that an informal Cabinet committee on the American loan negotiations was formed of Attlee, Morrison, Dalton, Bevin and Cripps. Arising out of this, Cripps wanted Attlee to stand down and be succeeded by Bevin. Dalton wanted to be on the winning side: he would support the Cripps move if Morrison would join the band: 'that would be a decisive group'. D.J. Heasman concludes: 'Attlee survived because they were not agreed, because he knew exactly why they were not, and because he was able to act accordingly.'[4]

That is a correct assessment of Attlee. I would add, first, that, had the move become dangerous, Bevin would have interposed his *massif central* into the scales; second, that Cripps, while a great man, did not

---

[1] A.H. Brown, pp. 38–40, traces the precedents from Palmerston's dismissal over Louis Napoleon's *coup d'état* and concludes, 'If, however, a Prime Minister's constitutional right to dismiss ministers could be doubted in the late nineteenth century, it can hardly be questioned today.'

[2] In any election for my successor, no one of the candidates could in advance have had any certainty of election, and had any one been involved in plotting to create a vacancy, that would have weighed heavily against him.

[3] See Dalton, op. cit., pp. 236–47. He records (p. 242) that Cripps told him that Morrison 'fully agreed about Attlee but not about Bevin. He thought that *he* [italics Dalton's] should be Prime Minister'. Later on the page, Dalton records that Morrison said he 'wanted to be Prime Minister, not for any reason of vanity, but because he felt he could do the job better than anyone else could'. This story rings true.

[4] D.J. Heasman, 'The Prime Minister and the Cabinet', reprinted in King, op. cit., p. 64.

have an ounce of politics in his make-up;[1] and further that, knowing Dalton very well, this was one of many cases of Dalton 'meeting himself coming back'.[2]

Political assassination directed against the party leader is much easier to accomplish in Opposition, particularly if the party has been defeated in a general election and is not doing well in by-elections or local elections. All the ingredients are there – time for a change, the need for a new face, policy difficulties and confrontations – as the power, certainly in the Labour Party, swings away from the leadership and even from the parliamentary party to the party machine and conference. The highly developed stabilizers available to a prime minister no longer operate, and the unfortunate leader, who always has to be taking a long-term strategic view on how to regain office and what to do when this happens, is weakened by the need to react to day-to-day political occurrences not of his seeking. The trouble about being leader of the Opposition is that all the time you are having to say 'Yes' or 'No' to a question of the Government's devising, which is always inconveniently the wrong question to the answer on which you are working.

An observable difference between the Labour Party and the Conservative Party is that the Labour Party is always talking about getting rid of its leader and never does: the Conservative Party never talks about ridding itself of its leader and then, in a moment, in the twinkling of an eye, there is a flash of cold steel, and recrimination and denigration set in even before rigor mortis.

Even so, we no longer live in the great days of anti-leadership intrigue: the great events that ended the careers of Asquith and Lloyd George,[3] and almost destroyed Baldwin; the powers of the press proprietors, the Lords Northcliffe, Rothermere and Beaverbrook.[4] But one of Beaverbrook's laws on conspiracy still holds good in these quieter times – 'The man who wields the dagger never wears the crown.' Hence the practised performances of latter-day politicians in the game of musical daggers: never be left holding the dagger when the music stops.

Assuming that the prime minister has survived long enough, one of

[1] In 1947 Clement Attlee sent me on a visit to Cripps in hospital in Switzerland, bearing a letter about devaluation. Cripps's reaction was helpful, but one associated political proposal he set out in the letter I delivered to the Prime Minister led Attlee to say, 'Stafford is a political goose – always was.'

[2] See also Bernard Donoughue and G.W.Jones, *Herbert Morrison: Portrait of a Politician* (London 1973), pp. 413–25.

[3] See the highly readable *The Chanak Affair* by David Walder (London 1969), pp. 319–28.

[4] Compare Sir Denis Hamilton's *Haldane Memorial Lecture* at Birkbeck College (London 1976), pp. 3–4, describing Northcliffe's campaign against Haldane, including the attack in *The Times* (5 August 1914) described by Sir Denis as 'a classic example of assassination by leader-writer'.

his constitutional duties is that of recommending a dissolution of Parliament.

Much has been made of this duty, or power, particularly in the argument about 'prime ministerial government'. Lord Blake records a major change in the practice:

> 'Until the First World War no one doubted that the decision to advise the Crown to dissolve Parliament was a collective decision of the Cabinet, or at any rate of those members of it who sit in the House of Commons . . . . For reasons which are not wholly clear, the practice since 1918 has been for the decision to rest with the Prime Minister alone, taking such advice (or none) as he sees fit. The Cabinet was not consulted over the timing of the Coupon Election nor, as far as is publicly known, has it been consulted since.'[1]

He goes on to point out that Asquith emphasizes that this was 'always submitted to the Cabinet for ultimate decision', yet Balfour, writing to Bonar Law in 1918, said, 'I think that, whatever happens, the responsibility of a dissolution must rest with the Prime Minister. It always does so rest in fact; and on some previous occasions the Prime Minister of the day has not even gone through the form of consulting his colleagues.'[2]

I do not believe that there is any profound constitutional issue here. Nor have I ever heard much discussion about the practice followed by previous prime ministers. The evidence is scrappy and indeterminate, partly because of the informal nature of Cabinet proceedings in matters with a marked political content. Clement Attlee is recorded as having 'consulted a few senior colleagues but clearly made up his mind about the dissolutions which terminated his two administrations'.[3] This is not my recollection in respect of 1950. In my view most prime ministers would be likely to indicate the decision that was hardening in their minds, but be ready – although not for long – to listen to a contrary view. Certainly he would almost certainly consult senior colleagues, perhaps the chief whip and leader of the House, to see what MPs were thinking. In other cases he would consult those closest to him, the chancellor if there might be any question of economic repercussions, or the foreign secretary. He would be likely, also, to get the views, in strict confidence, of the head of his party machine.

[1] Blake, op. cit., p. 58. Lord Blake points out that when Disraeli consulted Cabinet in 1880 about dissolution, only the Commons members spoke up. He was not clear whether this was the practice, but the decision was regarded as that of the Cabinet. Professor Plumb reminds me that in the 18th century Walpole's rare dissolutions were on his recommendation, not the Cabinet's.

[2] ibid. (quoting from the Balfour papers).

[3] John P.Mackintosh, *The British Cabinet* (London 1962), p. 24; John P.Mackintosh, 'The Position of the Prime Minister' in King, op. cit., takes the same view (p. 23).

There seems to be little doubt from leaks at the time that Mr Maudling, as chancellor, opposed the postponement of the 1964 election from the spring to October, and failed to secure support. In 1951 I was told that the Chancellor, Hugh Gaitskell, wanted an immediate election, and that Herbert Morrison, on returning to London from Ottawa, was horrified at the Prime Minister's decision to support the Chancellor. In the event, the economic situation, and especially the soaring commodity prices, greatly improved immediately after the election: a contest in the spring of 1952 might have produced a very different result. The Prime Minister was understood to be as just worried about a forth-coming by-election, Droylsden, the loss of which would have reduced the overall majority to four: Clement Attlee always took the conventional view that anything much less than ten was not viable.

There is, then, no obligation on the prime minister to consult. But in my view he would be foolish not to discuss his ideas with leading colleagues, better still with the Cabinet, if he could trust their discretion.

In 1966 I was in favour of a March election many weeks before any discussion with my colleagues. Our majority – four in October 1964 – had fallen to two when we lost Leyton, the seat where a vacancy had been created to enable Patrick Gordon-Walker, the foreign secretary, to return to the House. In January 1965 we held a by-election in a reasonably safe seat, following the death of the member, but I was becoming increasingly interested in going to the country to seek a working majority as early as possible.

My reasons for this, the problem of overcoming an almost universal belief that an election was improbable and untimely, and the precise events leading up to the announcement, on 28 February, that Parliament would be dissolved and an election would take place on 31 March, are set out in *The Labour Government, 1964–70*.[1] I had made up my mind with no consultation whatsoever, though after doing so consulted the Deputy Leader, and found that he was of the same mind.

In 1970 I consulted fully. We had bad county council results in April, including Lancashire though with a favourable swing in Greater London, but our standing seemed to improve between then and the borough and district council elections in early May. I was attracted by the idea of calling the election for 11 June, and most were in favour of a June election. I wanted more than that – unanimity. An election mood grew in the country, and by this time the press were chiding me for dithering and not seizing what they regarded as a favourable opportunity. The borough elections reversed the verdict of the April county voting, and

[1] H.Wilson, *The Labour Government, 1964–70: A Personal Record* (London 1971), pp. 199–201.

the election was duly called, thirty days before the chosen date, 18 June. Had the idea of a three-week election period, which Edward Heath initiated in February 1974 and I followed in October of that year, occurred to me we could in fact have awaited the borough election results, and avoided the disasters of the fourth week of the campaign.[1]

In 1974, when we were working with an all-party majority against us of thirty-four, the only argument was whether to go to the country in June or wait until October. There were strong arguments both ways, though I firmly favoured October. There was vitally important legislation to get on to the Statute Book, including the repeal of the Conservatives' Industrial Relations Act and the enactment of other labour legislation to which we were committed. It would have been extremely messy, and of dubious constitutional propriety, to have failed to carry into law the Finance Bill which embodies the Budget proposals. The country, in my view, was hardly in a mood for a second general election in three or four months; we might have been greeted with a big yawn, and a low turn-out. Against this, we might have to face humiliating parliamentary defeats in the close season when regional holidays precluded an election.[2] In favour of October, although there was much essential legislation promised in the Queen's Speech that simply could not be prepared in time for introduction into Parliament before an October election, the extra time would enable us at least to make clear our detailed legislative intentions by publishing White Papers, as we had done in the months immediately preceding the 1966 general election. In the February election we had suffered a heavy loss of votes by the characterization of our proposal for the public ownership of development land as involving a takeover of privately owned houses and gardens. By deciding on an October election, we were able to issue a White Paper showing in detail what the legislation would do, and categorically denying election scare stories. Again, we were able to prepare and announce our detailed proposals for North Sea oil – the legislation took another year. And it was vital to end doubt and the possibility of scaremongering by publishing our White Paper, *The Regeneration of British Industry*, setting out exactly what the promised National Enterprise Board and the planning agreements system would do and what they would not do. I was driving my colleagues on White Papers all that summer, even to the point of taking over the drafting of key ones.

Once we had decided in favour of October, I was studying with great care the incidence of local holidays, as well as the date of Yom

[1] H. Wilson, op. cit., pp. 778–81, 786–90.
[2] This in fact happened on major legislation but we were able to turn this to our advantage in the election.

Kippur, on which a number of friends obligingly but unnecessarily hastened to enlighten me.

The close period proper begins early in July, with the Glasgow and other Scottish holidays. A prime minister must, and if he is a northerner usually does, understand the complex of Wakes Weeks and Feast Weeks,[1] to say nothing of Longwood Thump and the late long weekend holidays in the textile area and elsewhere, including Glasgow's October break. (For any future successor not fully informed on these arcane matters, I would advise him or her to get in touch with the Blackpool Borough Entertainments Office.)

I had told my colleagues I was studying these matters for any 'social options' I might wish to take up in the autumn. I received a charming note from Barbara Castle:

'Prime Minister:

'Please bear in mind in deciding your "social" options, that Blackburn has an *autumn* town holiday, as well as a July one.

'It is from September 13th–September 18th.

'So, no "social options" before September 26th, please.

Barbara.'[2]

As a footnote to the discussion of dissolution, it would be well to deal with a widely canvassed legend that has started a new academic hare, namely the power of the prime minister to bring his colleagues to heel by the unilateral threat of a dissolution.

A prime minister who decided to act in such a way would be certifiable. In order to punish his critics in the Cabinet or parliamentary party, he threatens them, it is suggested, with the loss of their seats: but if such a threat became a reality the first result could well be his departure from Downing Street. As Mr G.W.Jones rightly points out, '. . . since he wants to win, he is hardly likely to enter an election campaign wielding the weapons of dissolution against his own party, for the Opposition will make much capital out of the splits within his party'.[3]

Nor is it realistic to say that the prime minister would not need to act, he need only threaten. Since deterrents must be credible, the threat would be unavailing. The only consequence would be the image of a rattled prime minister and a split party.

One final issue involved in the constitutional relations between the prime minister and the Cabinet – the voluntary resignation of the prime minister.

[1] The National Union of Mineworkers appeared to have forgotten Barnsley Feast when they were planning their referendum on pay for August 1975.

[2] In suggesting 26 September she herself forgot Yom Kippur.

[3] G.W.Jones, 'The Prime Minister's Power', in King, op. cit., pp. 177–8.

D.J.Heasman criticizes Harold Macmillan for

'. . . disrespect for the royal prerogative: namely, the way in which Mr. Macmillan, by announcing his intention to resign, instead of actually resigning, contrived to retain control of "the customary processes of consultation" which led to the evolution of his successor. When he finally did resign, the Queen acted with unprecedented haste – presumably on Mr. Macmillan's advice, even though this was no longer binding – in sending for Lord Home.'[1]

Certainly, as the authorities quoted in the reference to the Conservative leadership crisis of 1963 made clear, Mr Macmillan seemed markedly allergic to the idea of being succeeded by Mr Butler, and took some part in ensuring that he was not. But in defence of his announcement of his intended resignation it must be said that he was ill; the Queen's Government had to be carried on, and an immediate resignation would have forced an extremely hasty decision. Certainly the Queen cannot be criticized. The machinery of the Party, such as it then was, had ground itself out to the end.

In any case the fact that the Conservative Party have now adopted an elective process instead of relying on a leader's emergence means that it is not only defensible but right for a prime minister to announce, not his immediate resignation, but his intention to resign. In March 1976 I acted as Mr Macmillan had done, at the same time asking the back-bench authorities of the Parliamentary Labour Party to speed up the electoral process as far as possible, compatible with the need for proper deliberation and consultation. Clearly no disrespect was involved. Had I forced a decision on the succession within hours in order to maintain continuity of government, not only Labour MPs but the country would have the right to complain that so important a decision had been taken with frivolous haste.

[1] Heasman, op. cit., p. 49.

III

The Cabinet at Work

'A First Minister has only the influence with the Cabinet which is given him by his personal argument, his personal qualities, and his personal weight. All his colleagues he must convince, some he may have to humour, some even to cajole; a harassing, laborious and ungracious task. Nor is it only his colleagues that he has to deal with; he has to masticate their pledges, given before they joined him, he has to blend their public utterances, to fuse as well as may be all this into the policy of the Government: for these variations records must be reconciled, or glossed or obliterated. A machinery liable to so many grains of sand requires obviously all the skill and vigilance of the best conceivable engineer. And yet without the external support of his Cabinet he is disarmed.'

LORD ROSEBERY[1]

The prime minister, when appointing the Administration, sees each individual Cabinet or junior minister, and on receiving his acceptance of office immediately sends a written submission to the Queen recommending her approval of the appointment. When this is secured the prime minister tells the new minister to report for duty at his department or other office, and the way is prepared for him by a telephone call from No. 10 Private Office to the permanent under-secretary concerned. On arrival he is welcomed, briefed and handed a mass of documentation for reading himself in.

The Civil Service is extremely agile and politically, almost cynically, dispassionate in reading the electoral portents. Not only does the Cabinet Office, during this election period, prepare two alternative Queen's speeches reflecting the respective parties' election manifestos; each department of state is preparing the necessary policy guidance on the main issues affecting its departmental work. For example, the two principal parties will have campaigned on two alternative, perhaps diametrically opposed, policies on North Sea oil. One would be the policy of the incumbent Administration, which would have been worked out before the election as a continuing process, amended perhaps by any tactical change announced by the Government in the course of the election. The other would be the department's first attempt to translate manifesto and campaign commitments into a practical policy, including the outlines of the legislation required.

[1] Lord Rosebery, *Sir Robert Peel* (London 1899), pp. 34–5.

In cases of extreme urgency, proposals for immediate action will have been worked out, ready for submission to the minister and to Cabinet. For example, the incoming Government in March 1974 was committed to ending the previous Government's confrontation with the National Union of Mineworkers. Michael Foot, on his appointment on the evening of Monday, 4 March 1974, found on his desk the relevant proposals for departmental action and for submission to Cabinet. Cabinet was able to take the necessary decisions on the Tuesday afternoon, and renewed negotiations between the Coal Board and the mineworkers began and were successfully completed on the Wednesday. (The state of emergency, the compulsory three-day week and other concomitants of the confrontation were formally ended on the Thursday.)[1]

Meanwhile, in the Department of the Environment, the incoming secretary of state found that work had gone ahead on another campaign commitment, the rent-freeze, involving the cancellation of the increased rent notices due to take effect on 1 April, which had gone out from local authorities during the election campaign. By Friday, 8 March, he was able to announce that they had been abrogated. In the Foreign Office similar work had been done on the promised ban on arms shipments to South Africa.

On the first two days of a new administration, Cabinet ministers kiss hands on appointment, and any who are not already privy councillors take the oath, or are sworn by affirmation on their appointment.

The prime minister, on being commissioned to form a government, is announced as having 'kissed hands'. He does not in fact do so, but is simply authorized to form an administration. The following day, he attends a Privy Council where the secretaries of state kiss hands and receive their seals of office – those not already privy councillors being sworn of the Privy Council. The prime minister is the first to kiss hands, as first lord of the Treasury.[2] (He does not in fact kiss hands, having done so the previous day as prime minister – or rather, having been deemed to have done so.)

Junior ministers (including ministers of state) – other than those whips who hold Household appointments – do not attend on the Queen, nor do they, or the whips, kiss hands. Any senior ministers of state who subsequently become privy councillors in New Year or Birthday Honours Lists, or for operational reasons,[3] have of course to go to the Palace to be sworn.

[1] See Harold Wilson, *The Labour Government, 1964–70: a Personal Record* (London 1971), p. 640.

[2] All prime ministers have been first lord since Salisbury in the 1880s: see p. 14 above.

[3] In 1974, Stanley Orme, Minister of State, was so sworn, because of the need for him to receive particularly sensitive information. I was announcing in Parliament the

Every member of the Cabinet, every junior minister, on appointment receives a document, hallowed over the years, and amended and updated regularly, which sets out the conduct required of ministers, from broad and clearly defined rules setting out the requirements of collective ministerial responsibility to mundane matters relating to travel, the use of service aircraft and the duties of and limitations relating to parliamentary private secretaries. It is one of the prime minister's responsibilities to ensure compliance with these rules.

It became my duty in subsequent months to draw to the attention of certain ministers the overriding requirements of this code of conduct, particularly in relationship to their membership of the National Executive Committee of the Labour Party and its sub-committees. I circulated to all ministers a copy of the instruction I had laid before Cabinet in the difficult circumstances of April 1969 and, with Cabinet approval, made public at that time. This appears in the Appendix, Note I.

As soon as may be after the Cabinet is formed – without necessarily waiting for the junior appointments – the first meeting is called. In March 1974 this took place, as recorded above, less than twenty-four hours after I had become prime minister. But, apart from the urgency of ending confrontation, two urgent problems pressed upon us, one normal to every incoming administration, the other of seasonal urgency. The normal priority is the approval of the Queen's Speech; the seasonally urgent priority was the Budget.

The civil service machine, as always, had a draft Queen's Speech ready, setting out the main lines of government policy, and also informing Parliament of the legislation we intended to introduce in the coming session. In the special circumstances of March 1974 there were complications here: we had to prepare a Queen's Speech for a session of normal length, but as a minority government we could not be sure how long the new session, indeed the new Parliament, would last. I decided that we would base the legislative programme on a normal session, while clearly reserving the right to seek a dissolution earlier. The Lord President, or Leader of the House, had an unenviable task in preparing his legislation programme – and ministers and parliamentary draftsmen a still tougher task in preparing bills for introduction before Easter. These, we decided, should include that providing for increased social benefits, and the new price control legislation, which Shirley

discovery of documents envisaging an IRA offensive and virtual 'scorched earth' policy. The Secretary of State for Northern Ireland could not leave Belfast, and I had to make the announcement because Stan Orme could not receive the briefing necessary to deal with supplementary questions, as he was not a privy councillor.

Williams carried through all its legislative stages before the Easter adjournment on 11 April.

Cabinet meets normally on Thursday mornings, usually at 10.0 or 10.30 (a long agenda might dictate a 9.30 start) and it lasts until around 1.0 pm. It is not good to go on much later than that. If business is relatively light, it can meet as late as 11.0 or 11.30, and this enables the prime minister to hold one, or perhaps two, Cabinet committees before-hand, e.g. on economic affairs, Northern Ireland, defence or foreign policy questions, or some *ad hoc* issue requiring collective consideration, not necessarily by the full Cabinet.

When business is heavy, a supplementary Cabinet can be put in on Tuesday mornings, and meetings on Mondays, Wednesdays and Fridays are not unknown when urgent problems have to be dealt with, or when the prime minister (and often the foreign and commonwealth secretary with him) have to be abroad, e.g. for a Common Market summit meeting (the European Council) or for a head of government visit to a foreign capital.

I always made it a point of honour, so far as possible, to complete the business on the day for which it was tabled. This was not always possible; rarely it spread over into another session. Occasionally, it was necessary to adjourn in order to get additional information, or to consult perhaps with industry or some overseas government, or our NATO or EEC partners or the Commission – or again, if a *prima facie* attractive alternative solution to some difficult problem was proposed, requiring further examination, by a Cabinet committee or Cabinet itself. But in the sixties, still more the seventies, far fewer Cabinet decisions were deferred for further consideration than in, for example, the time of the Attlee Cabinet, particularly after 1947, when deep rifts developed between leading members of the Cabinet.

Cabinet procedure is reasonably and helpfully stereotyped: Cabinet discussion is not.

Every Cabinet minister has his own regular seat. The secretary of the Cabinet sits on the prime minister's right; the most senior ministers on his left or across the table. Thus, in 1974–6, the Lord President (Leader of the House and Deputy Leader of the Party) sat on my left, and across the table were the Foreign and Commonwealth Secretary, the Home Secretary and Lord Chancellor. Others were seated, in some relation to Cabinet precedence, further from the centre – the seating being decided by the prime minister before the Cabinet first meets.[1]

[1] At one time there were problems connected with lady members. Until the early seventies, the chairs at the Cabinet table were of somewhat rough design with splintery legs. On a number of occasions the even tenor of Cabinet discussion was interrupted by

It should be made clear for the benefit of cartoonists, not to mention those responsible for television reconstructions of Cabinet meetings (e.g. Granada on Chrysler), that the prime minister does not sit at the end of the table, or with his back to the window. His seat is in the middle, in front of the Walpole portrait, facing out to Horse Guards. The table is neither oblong nor oval; it is in fact rather coffin-shaped, this design having been introduced, I understand, by Harold Macmillan, so that by leaning forward – or rocking backwards – the prime minister can see ministers far to his right or left (in geographical, not political, terms) and satisfy himself that they are paying attention to the business.

At the regular Thursday meeting two items, 'Parliamentary Business' and 'Foreign and Commonwealth Affairs', head the agenda.

On 'Parliamentary Business' the leader of the House outlines the course of debates for the following week, together with the proposed ministerial speakers, so that the programme can be confirmed in time for him to announce it that afternoon in reply to the leader of the Opposition's routine question about the business of the House for the week ahead. The chief whip then indicates the kind of whip he will issue for each day – one-line, two-line or three. Should ministers for any reason ask for a switch of business from one day to another, or a postponement to the following week, the chief whip rushes out to confer with the opposition chief whip, who is usually helpful.

On 'Foreign and Commonwealth Affairs', the secretary of state opens up informally, usually without circulating documents on the issues with which he is immediately concerned – it may be Cyprus, Rhodesia, Chile, the Icelandic negotiations, Anglo–US or Anglo–Soviet questions, or issues connected with forthcoming meetings of NATO or EEC ministers. More often than not he is not seeking agreement to particular lines of policy – on a major issue he would circulate a paper for decision later on the agenda – he is more concerned to keep Cabinet informed on a developing situation, which might have to come up for a formal decision at a subsequent Cabinet. Alternatively he may be reporting to Cabinet, for information or endorsement, a decision or provisional decision taken by the relative Cabinet committee, which

Barbara Castle, who complained that her hose had been laddered. Following one occasion when she threatened to sue me for the damage involved, I gave instruction for the legs of the chair to be encased in cretonne covering, *à la* Victoria. I have reason to think that when the Heath Administration took over, the chair was allocated to Mrs Thatcher. By munificence of that Administration not only was the table replaced – or re-covered, orange in place of brown – but the chair legs were rendered smooth and inoffensive to lady members. In two years after March 1974, I never had a complaint from either Barbara Castle or Shirley Williams.

will have met under his own or the prime minister's chairmanship.

Mr Heath has recently made it clear[1] that under his Administration there were two further regular items on the agenda, Europe (during the E E C negotiations) and Northern Ireland, once direct rule was introduced. In 1974–6 these two subjects, in so far as they could not be adequately dealt with in the appropriate Cabinet committees, would appear on the Cabinet agenda not as routine items, but whenever necessary as separate items.

The agenda for Cabinet and for all Cabinet committees chaired by the prime minister is approved by the prime minister in consultation with the secretary of the Cabinet. (The forward programme of Cabinet and its committees – irrespective of who chairs them – is masterminded by an informal meeting of the prime minister, lord president, chancellor, foreign and commonwealth secretary, chief whip and Cabinet secretary each Friday morning, when the issues coming up for decision are surveyed for a period of roughly a fortnight ahead.)

It has been suggested that the prime minister is in unique control of the agenda.

'Meetings of the Cabinet are held twice a week [sic] during the Parliamentary session but the Prime Minister arranges the order of business and can keep any item off the agenda indefinitely. It is regarded as quite improper for a minister to raise any matter which has not previously been accepted for the agenda by the Prime Minister.'[2]

In theory of course, he is in charge as chairman, but this is not how things are done.

In any case, ministers are free to raise matters under 'Parliamentary Affairs' or 'Foreign and Commonwealth Affairs'. If a minister (or ministers) is worried about an issue that is disturbing M Ps he can raise it under the former item, or if he is concerned over some development

---

[1] *The Listener* (22 April 1976), recording a radio discussion by Mr Heath and Lord Trend, with Robert Mackenzie.

[2] John P. Mackintosh 'The Position of the Prime Minister', in *The British Prime Minister*, ed. Anthony King (London 1969), pp. 20–1. He also mentions the frequently quoted case of Neville Chamberlain's attempt to raise House of Lords reform after the forward agenda had been settled, an attempt frustrated by Stanley Baldwin's walking out of the room – thus ending the Cabinet meeting. Too much can be made of an action taken, probably in a moment of irritation. Any prime minister I have known would presumably have suggested how the proposal might be considered, either at a subsequent Cabinet or in a committee of the Cabinet. Nor should much be made of another case cited in the same context, a Hore-Belisha initiative in the Chamberlain Cabinet.

in, e.g., Eastern Europe, or Rhodesia, he can ask about it. The appropriate minister would then explain how things stood, or he or the prime minister could say that this was coming up the following week in Cabinet, or was being currently considered by the relevant committee. There is no rigidity of style in Cabinet: the best style is the one that gets the boat along fast and in the right direction.

The successful working of Cabinet government depends, first, on documentation. From my earliest days in the Cabinet secretariat thirty-six years ago, through the Attlee Administration and in two periods as prime minister, I have seen successive improvements in the quality and method of documentation, improvements brought about under successive governments, wartime coalition, Labour and Conservative.

The requirement is that, except in an emergency, documents relating to the main items on the agenda must be circulated a clear two days in advance, so that ministers can study them, form views on them, and be briefed both on the implications for their own departments and more generally. Only the prime minister can relax this requirement, and the minister concerned has to produce a cast-iron case to justify waiving the rule.

It has been a standing Cabinet rule for a generation – my recollection is that it was begun by Clement Attlee – that ministers submitting proposals, whether for legislative or for executive action, must state what they would cost, the estimate to be confirmed by the Treasury. If the department and the Treasury cannot agree on the cost, both estimates must be quoted.

In the 1960s I gave instructions that documents must also include an initial estimate of total requirements for additional staff, agreed with the Treasury – later the Civil Service Department. In 1975, following a helpful proposal from a Conservative Member of Parliament, I announced that I had directed Cabinet ministers to include estimates of local government staff requirements and costs for any new proposals.

Attendance at Cabinet is normally strictly confined to Cabinet ministers, though the attorney-general is called in for individual items where his advice is needed. Exceptionally the senior minister of state, Foreign and Commonwealth Office is called in for the 'Foreign Affairs' item on the Thursday agenda, and for any substantive Foreign Office subject due to come up later in the morning, if the secretary of state is abroad. Rarely, for example if another minister is ill or abroad, his deputy is called if there is a clear departmental interest in a subject under discussion. In all cases where non-Cabinet ministers are invited, they wait in the ante-room until their item is reached, and leave when it is concluded. It has become the practice that, where major decisions on public expenditure are involved, and during the annual review of public expenditure,[1] the chief secretary to the Treasury, who has been responsible for all the in-fighting with the departments, usually attends and sits alongside the chancellor.

The normal procedure is for the prime minister to ask the minister tabling a paper to speak to it, and to be immediately followed by any other minister who has himself submitted a paper disagreeing with, qualifying or supplementing the first.

The prime minister may then wish to indicate how the discussion should be handled and decisions taken. He may, for example, say that the question raises, say, three issues, and it might be helpful to discuss each separately, without prejudice to the decisions to be taken at the end. Or interim decisions on each of the three may be taken, and the viability of the package as a whole considered at the end, when it will be necessary to deal also with a fourth question, handling and presentation. Alternatively, particularly on a major or new issue, he might suggest that Cabinet begins with a 'second reading' debate, which enables members to make their set-piece contributions, which must be short, possibly raising fundamental and long-term issues. This averts the need for wide-ranging oratory when the meeting comes to decide detailed practical questions requiring a clear decision. Again, at the first meeting on a major issue – e.g. devolution, the EEC negotiations in 1967 and 1974–5, the EEC referendum, House of Lords reform or pay policy – a wide-ranging second reading debate is virtually mandatory, and saves much time in the end. Even with such cases, a great deal of preparatory work will have been done in clearing the ground and identifying points for decision at high level Cabinet committee meetings, usually with the prime minister in the chair.

It would be usual for the prime minister to open such a discussion. On other issues, where papers had been submitted by departmental ministers, he would be unlikely to speak first, but would be ready to steer and guide the discussion to the point of taking the required decision. Very occasionally he opens the discussion, usually on a procedural point. For example, he may feel it right to remind the Cabinet that they have not met to review a broad policy decision – that has been taken – but are concerned with this or that point of implementation. Alternatively, he will point out that they are not this morning taking the major decision on subject X – that will be the subject of a further meeting, separately documented – but that an interim decision on a narrower aspect must be taken now. Or if he feels, from the papers submitted

---

[1] See pp. 68–72 below.

and his knowledge of the strength of different ministers' feelings, that there is a danger of perhaps unnecessary polarization, he may suggest at the outset that there is a possible third course which might be more productive, and on which agreement might be possible.

The prime minister must be ever-alert to issues which raise fundamental, doctrinal or almost theological passions on the part of one or more ministers, and do all he can to avert an unnecessary clash without sacrificing principle, and without fudging an issue on which a clear decision has to be reached, binding the Cabinet. Not only at that point, but by possible frequent single-sentence interventions, he has to concentrate on face-saving and binding up wounds, intervening also to soften asperities and curb the invocation of personalities. Above all, the prime minister must be ever-watchful of the political implications and dangers of a given course of action, particularly when a departmental minister might be tempted to under-emphasize them, because of his immersion in administrative technicalities or his proneness to accord too much weight to outside pressure-groups on his department. It is a constant vigil, requiring full concentration not only in Cabinet itself, but in days and nights of studying Cabinet papers, departmental minutes addressed to himself and to other relevant ministers, seeking clearance of a particular proposal.

To judge from comments by both historians and writers on current affairs, many of those concerned would, I think, be surprised at the relative informality of Cabinet proceedings. As a novice Cabinet minister I was myself surprised, even with Clement Attlee in the chair, running the Cabinet like a nineteenth-century dominie. Every prime minister has a different style, in Cabinet and outside, but the aim should be informality combined with total orderliness. A touch of humour to calm things down, or to stop excessive length and preoccupation with technicalities, is not out of order. The purpose is to get the business through, with full consideration, and to reach a clear decision, with nothing fluffed or obscure – and, so far as possible, an agreed decision, with the maximum emollient to wounded pride. Above all, the prime minister must keep his head, when all (or some) about him are losing theirs. In this respect as in others, Clement Attlee was a prince among prime ministers. Professor Mackintosh has commented:

'At Cabinet, Mr. Attlee's great objective was to stop talk. There is evidence that two ministers rightly talked themselves out of the Cabinet. Discussion was limited by the Premier's habit of putting his questions in the negative. A non-Cabinet Minister with an item on the agenda would be called in at the appropriate point, simply bursting to make a speech. Mr. Attlee would begin: "Mr. X, your memo says all that could be said – I don't suppose you have anything to add to it?" It was hard to say anything but "No". Then, "Does any member of the Cabinet oppose this?" Someone would indicate a desire to contribute, and say "An interesting case occurred in 1929 which was very similar to this, and I remember then that we . . ." "Do you oppose this?" "Er . . . No." "Very good that is settled" . . .'[1]

I can confirm that Professor Mackintosh's description of an Attlee Cabinet is entirely accurate, and would add only that he was savagely cruel in rebuking, in a very few words, any minister who didn't know the subject adequately, had not been briefed, hadn't read the paper, particularly if it was his own. The Prime Minister spared no one, except Ernest Bevin, and reserved his most cutting quips for his most powerful colleagues. He himself, in an interview with Francis Williams, summarized his style:

'A Prime Minister has to know when to ask for an opinion. He can't always stop some ministers offering theirs, you always have some people who'll talk on everything. But he can make sure to extract the opinion of those he wants when he needs them. The job of the Prime Minister is to get the general feeling – collect the voices. And then, when everything reasonable has been said, to get on with the job and say, "Well, I think the decision of the Cabinet is this, that or the other. Any objections?" Usually there aren't.'[2]

Clement Attlee was almost certainly the coolest prime minister this century.[3] I only once saw him ruffled: he was rushing along the corridor

[1] Mackintosh, op. cit., p. 29. The quotation is from Francis Williams, *A Prime Minister Remembers* (London 1961), p. 81.

[2] Reproduced in King, op. cit., p. 71. Referring to Winston Churchill, Clement Attlee cites an occasion when Churchill as leader of the Opposition complained in Parliament that a particular issue had been brought up several times in the wartime Cabinet. Attlee replied: 'I must remind the Right Honourable Gentleman that a monologue is not a decision.'

[3] In early 1951, an extremely serious two-day debate was taking place in the House on international affairs. On the afternoon of the second day, the ticker-tape carried a story that President Truman had said that General MacArthur, supreme commander in Korea, had the authority to use the nuclear weapon there, without reference to the President. There was uproar in the House. Clement Attlee was to wind up. Early in the evening he called a Cabinet in his room at the House. He referred calmly to the report, and said he had concluded he must fly to Washington – then anything but a routine operation – and see the President. He would have preferred Ernest Bevin to go, but his health precluded flying, and a ship would take too long. He would try to contact the President, hoping not very confidently to get his agreement in time for an announcement in the Prime Minister's winding-up speech at 9.30. Telephone communication was difficult and not as secret as it is now. At 7.0 pm I was at the Cabinet table having dinner when the Prime

to the House (we then sat in the Lords at the other end of the building) for a statement on Hugh Dalton's resignation after the Budget incident.

It should be a matter of pride, so far as possible, to get the business through, without deferring it to another meeting. To defer a decision simply to cloak a disagreement is a defeat, above all for the prime minister. Even when there is a case for deferment, for example to consult an overseas government, a heavy cost may be involved. I have recorded the sad story of the case of the Kenya Asians, where a decision was deferred for Malcolm Macdonald to see President Kenyatta, and in the interim Richard Crossman, as lord president, in his constant educative mission described the possible alternative courses to the parliamentary press lobby, who were less interested in erudition for its own sake than in securing an authoritative story of a split Cabinet.[1]

Postponed decisions happened in the sixties, as I have recorded, over certain issues of defence policy, principally the cancellation of certain aircraft, such as TSR-2 in 1965 and F-111 in 1968. But it happened far less frequently in our five years and eight months of government (1964–70) than in the three years eight months I was a member of Clement Attlee's Cabinet, under the clearest and most concise of prime ministers. From 1948 onwards, as a number of autobiographies have since revealed, it was a seriously divided Cabinet, divided more on personalities than on doctrinal issues of Left versus Right, at least until 1950–1. In 1974–6 deferment because of an inability to agree was almost unknown.[2]

Cabinet has sometimes to take decisions, not just recorded in the conclusions, but to be announced in Parliament as an oral statement, written answer or as a White or Green Paper. On lesser issues, the draft can be cleared by inter-departmental circulation and comment, or at most by consideration by a Cabinet committee. In major cases Cabinet itself has to consider a draft. It is an old canon of Cabinet lore that 'Cabinets can't draft'. They can go, however, and frequently must go, through a prepared draft, amending it where necessary.

With Command Papers, White or Green, I made a rule in the sixties

Minister came down and sat next to me. As his other neighbour was a minister of Cabinet rank not in the Cabinet, I could not comment on events which we were pledged to keep secret. Equally, I felt he would be too preoccupied for small talk. Suddenly he turned to me and said, 'Just been reading Guedalla. Tell me, which of the popular historians do you prefer – Guedalla or Arthur Bryant?' I answered, 'Arthur Bryant'. 'So do I', he said and for half an hour we discussed their books. At 9.0 pm the President's agreement came through, and Attlee's speech steadied the entire parliamentary situation.

[1] Wilson, op. cit., pp. 504–5.

[2] Even in the much-publicized Chrysler case, deferment was in every case for the purpose of examining alternative proposals, e.g. the Coventry-to-Linwood move, or new proposals to the main Chrysler Board, from the time they dropped their insistence on getting out within weeks, and their refusal to undertake to share future losses.

– whether following precedent or not I do not know – that every such state document should be gone through by Cabinet, paragraph by paragraph. In 1974–6 I started off with this procedure, but the process of Cabinet Office clearance with departments had so improved that this was rarely necessary, and at most the Cabinet were taken through the document page by page. Any minister is free to raise any question of drafting – policy having always been cleared at previous substantive meetings of Cabinet or the appropriate Cabinet committee.

The formal taking of a decision by Cabinet depends on the form of words used by the prime minister in summing-up, subject to their agreement by Cabinet with such drafting amendments as might be proposed.

Winston Churchill, though a great and heroic war leader and an unrivalled master of the English language, has no claims to crispness and conciseness in reaching a decision and embodying it in a summing-up, certainly on non-military issues, which tended to bore him.

In my address to the British Academy, I described my own experience.

'In 1940, on a famous occasion, I recorded the Cabinet minutes, at the age of 24. Sir Edward Bridges, Secretary of the Cabinet, came into my room – a gross breach of protocol: he should have sent for me – and said "I want you to write the Cabinet Minutes. I can't make head or tail of the discussion." I stuttered that I had not been there and did not know what they had said. He said if I had been, I would not have been any better informed than he was. I tried vainly to excuse myself, and he thrust his notes across the table and asked me to read them. I was still no better informed. In the event he ordered me to produce the minutes in one hour, saying "This is your subject. You know what they ought to have decided, presumably. Write the Minutes on those lines, and no one will ever question it." He was right. They didn't. That could not have happened under Attlee, whose summing-up was superb, crisp, clear – and let no one try to go against it.'

I also told them of a story I had heard at second hand from a minister who had just come from Cabinet, in the closing stages of the war. There were six or seven subjects on the agenda. The earlier ones were on straight war issues, relations with allies and similar topics. A 1.0 pm Winston Churchill closed his Cabinet folder and lit another cigar. Sir Edward Bridges drew his attention to the fact that there was still one remaining item.

It was town and country planning. The determination of those days that we should not go back to the 1930s had inspired Beveridge, the Cabinet White Paper on full employment, and also the three classic reports on town and country planning by Uthwatt, Barlow and Scott. Winston had created a minister of town and country planning, Mr W. S. Morrison (later Lord Dunrossil). Starting the postwar housing programme after six years in which hardly a house had been built depended on decisions about planning, betterment and compensation.

W. S. Morrison had assessed these reports and was presenting his conclusions. Winston was not amused. 'Ah, yes,' said he. 'All this stuff about planning and compensation and betterment. Broad vistas and all that. But give to me the eighteenth-century alley, where foot-pads lurk, and the harlot plies her trade, and none of this new fangled planning doctrine.'

If Morrison had been wise he would have said that he fully agreed with the Prime Minister; that he assumed the Prime Minister was approving his paper, that he assumed the Cabinet agreed, and that in all his planning he would take care to make full provision for narrower vistas and alleys for appropriate activities such as those mentioned. Winston would have said, 'Quite right, my boy, you go ahead.' Instead, Morrison stammered out, 'I take it, then, Prime Minister, you want me to take it back and think again.' Winston replied, 'Quite right, my boy.'

Morrison went back without any guidance about redrafting and did not emerge before Cabinet for some months – a vital loss of time before Britain's postwar housing programme could effectively begin.[1]

Cabinet colleagues of Winston Churchill have commented on his discursive style in Cabinet – not only in summing-up. Lord Woolton in his memoirs, referring to the 1951–5 Administration, says:

'. . . in his earlier days in office he had never hesitated to mix freely with the people, [and] to the intense irritation of his Government officials, and in these last years of his ministerial life he distilled all this experience at Cabinet meetings for the benefit of his colleagues. It was not always for their pleasure, because not infrequently the entire time of the meeting had gone before he arrived at the first item on the agenda; he had no hesitation in keeping other ministers waiting in the corridor for an hour or more after the time when they had been called to attend the Cabinet meeting, whilst he talked to us

---

[1] It is fair to add that, after the delivery of this address before the Academy, a historian at the Cabinet Office examined the Cabinet files of the time and threw some doubts on certain details of the story I had been told. Possible Cabinet meetings had been identified, but there were discrepancies with the original story. Perhaps the fitting comment, as with other Churchill stories, is that it is the legend that counts. From other sources I have received confirmation about the 'eighteenth-century alley' and all that occurred therein; the doubts surround the occasion and the general Cabinet ambience.

about the things that he thought important for the country, but about which the Cabinet Secretariat had been given no notice and about which, of course, there were no papers.'[1]

Summing-up is vital: it is the fine art of Cabinet government. The great improvement over the past thirty years is due not only to the style of Clement Attlee: the consistent improvement in the service provided by the Cabinet Secretariat is itself a guarantee of clarity.

Ex-prime ministers have confirmed – as I can – that in reaching a decision Cabinet does not vote, except to save time, on minor procedural matters.[2] On many issues, discussion is confined to one or two, or very few ministers; and, perhaps after suggesting a formula which appears to command assent, the prime minister asks 'Cabinet agree?' – technically a voice vote, sometimes just a murmur. On a major issue it is important not only to give the main protagonists their heads, but to ensure that everyone expresses an opinion, by going round the table to collect the voices. The prime minister usually keeps a tally of those for and against, after which he records his assessment of the predominant view – or occasionally puts forward a suggestion of his own which all, or nearly all, can support. Sometimes on a minor issue where all the arguments are known – perhaps they have been discussed at an earlier Cabinet – and no arguments are likely to make converts, it saves time to go quickly round the table and take the sense of Cabinet.

In the very major issue of the recommendations the Cabinet was to make to Parliament and the country about continued membership of the EEC, following the re-negotiations, the numbers for and against were reported to the press. This was inevitable, because of the unusual decision to permit an 'agreement to differ'. The House of Commons was informed of the guidelines to be followed, and Parliament and the country were entitled to know which ministers had been granted a dispensation from the normal obligations demanded by collective Cabinet responsibility.[3] Cabinet leaks, for example those at the time of the aircraft purchasing decisions in January 1968, sometimes purport to give the numbers on each side, as recorded by an unauthorized keeper of the tally. There have been one or two recent attempts to challenge the

[1] Lord Woolton, *The Memoirs of the Rt. Hon. Earl of Woolton* (London 1959), pp. 376–7.
[2] Clement Attlee, 'The Making of a Cabinet' in King, op. cit.: 'You don't take a vote. No, never. You might take it on something like whether you meet at 6.30 or 7.30, I suppose, but not on anything major.' Edward Heath, in *The Listener* (22 April 1976), p. 501: 'As a Cabinet, when I was Prime Minister, we never voted.' He went on to say that, during his attendance at Cabinet, as chief whip in 1955–9 and as a member of Cabinet in 1959–63, he could not recall a vote, those years spanning the premiership of Anthony Eden, Harold Macmillan and Sir Alec Douglas-Home.
[3] See pp. 72–6 below, and Appendix Note III at the end of the book.

Prime Minister's weighing of the Cabinet voices, by those who claimed to have counted them – a practice that I very severely discouraged.

The clarity of the summing-up, and the Cabinet's decision, is, of course, essential to the recording of the Conclusions. (The word 'Conclusions', in place of 'Minutes', was adopted in August 1919.)[1]

Because of recent comments by Richard Crossman and others, it must be made clear that the writing of the Conclusions is the unique responsibility of the secretary of the Cabinet, aided by members of his staff who have been present at the meeting, making notes, but not – this is important – a shorthand word by word record of the discussion. He may also retain the prime minister's own notes or draft of his summing-up, which the Cabinet will have heard verbatim and agreed in terms. The Conclusions are circulated very promptly after Cabinet, and up to that time no minister, certainly not the prime minister, sees them, asks to see them or conditions them in any way.

A few days before Richard Crossman went to America to deliver his Godkin Lectures at Harvard on 'Bagehot Revisited', he thought I ought to look at them. His main thesis, in support of his doctrine of 'prime ministerial government', was that Cabinet was controlled by a conspiracy between the prime minister and the secretary of the Cabinet, who sat down the day after the meeting virtually to cook the Cabinet Conclusions.[2] He was incredulous when I told him that, not only had I never seen them before circulation, but that it was only very rarely that I would read them after they were circulated – only then for purposes of refreshing my memory, if the subject came up again. He duly rewrote the lectures, though I doubt if I fully convinced him. Perhaps, recalling the view he took of most senior civil servants, he was content to believe – wrongly – that the Cabinet secretary was capable of doing the necessary cooking without my help. The Cabinet minutes are immaculately conceived.

This doctrine is, of course, pure fantasy. It is the rarest occurrence for any of those who do pore over the Conclusions, officials as well as ministers, to query their accuracy or fairness.

There can be occasions, now very rare, when the Cabinet meets without officials – perhaps two or three in 1964–70, mainly about election timing, once on an apparently serious breach of collective responsi-

---

[1] See the history and developing practice on Minutes and Conclusions, together with references to the earlier practice of the prime minister's letter to the sovereign after each Cabinet, in Public Record Office, *The Cabinet Office to 1945* (London 1975), paras 209–13, 411–13, 907–8 and 916.

[2] The prime minister did, indeed, approve the Conclusions in draft, until May 1917. After that the Cabinet secretary wrote them, referring to the prime minister only when in doubt about what had been decided.

bility; and only once, I recall, in 1974–6, again on election timing. It is appropriate on such occasions for the prime minister to write or dictate a short, usually uninformative, note for the Cabinet records.

Cabinet Conclusions in the present form are a twentieth-century development.[1] At first, when they replaced the older minutes, they were more bold, setting out the decisions with only a brief record of the arguments deployed for and against a particular proposition. By World War II they were again a fairly full record of the points made by individual ministers, and these were very carefully perused by the ministers concerned.

A point to note is that the record summarizing the statement by the minister or ministers tabling papers includes a short summary of the paper itself, as though it had been orally stated. This is done even when the minister introduces his paper very briefly, without going over the ground: it has the advantage that the Conclusions stand on their own, and are intelligible without having to refer back to the paper submitted. This practice goes back well before the war; on 23 March 1931 Lord Hankey wrote: 'In the Cabinet minutes I have for many years made a practice of providing a very brief summary of the main points in the report . . . Whenever it is possible I consider it important that the minute should be intelligible in itself without turning up other papers.'

Significant changes – and improvements – have been made over the years. Under the Attlee Cabinet there was much fuller attribution of points made by individual ministers at all stages of the discussion: for example, 'The Minister of Health expressed the view that . . .' and then followed a brief summary, while the next paragraph attributed some totally opposed thesis to the Minister of Fuel and Power. This led to correspondence, after each meeting, as ministers complained that they had not been correctly reported. The re-draft volunteered by the minister was invariably at least three times as long. Successive prime ministers tightened up the individual attributions, confining them in the main to those speaking to circulated documents, apart from the

---

[1] The confusion that could result in the days before minutes were recorded is shown by a letter written in 1882 by Lord Hartington's private secretary to one of the Prime Minister's secretaries:

My dear Eddy,
   Harcourt and Chamberlain have both been here this morning and at my chief about yesterday's Cabinet proceedings. They cannot agree about what occurred. There *must* have been some decision as Bright's resignation shows. My chief has told me to ask you what the devil was decided for he be damned if he knows. Will you ask Mr G. in more conventional and less pungent terms.

Yours ever

prime minister, whose summing-up was strictly recorded. The points made were de-personalized, e.g.:

'In discussion, it was urged that the moon was made of green cheese and that in view of the attitude of New Zealand it was important to ensure that . . . Moreover, at the European Council in Dublin in March 1975 the Commission had reserved their position, pointing out that the definition of "green" varied from country to country.

On the other hand, the view was expressed that the moon when at the full had only a limited cheese content, and . . . Attention was drawn to the draft ruling of the European Commission in relation to the regime in force in respect of dairy products, and the views of the Irish Government on the definition of "green".

Summing up, the PRIME MINISTER said . . .

The Cabinet endorsed the PRIME MINISTER's summing-up, and invited the Minister of Agriculture to make a statement accordingly in the forthcoming debate.'[1]

The minutes are succinct with a strong emphasis on brevity. This owes much to Winston Churchill, who minuted Sir Edward Bridges on 25 June 1940: 'Far more brevity should be practised in the Cabinet reports, and in principle conclusions are all that is necessary to report.' Specific instructions were given to Cabinet secretaries in 1944 which are still, *ipsissimis verbis*, in force today.

Ministers still tried from time to time to have a clear attribution inserted, and of course it was traditional for any minister who disagreed deeply with the decision to ask for his dissent to be recorded. The Public Record Office's *The Cabinet Office to 1945* sets out a number of prewar instances, including a facsimile of a Cabinet minute – 'Record of Dissent from Cabinet Conclusions', dated 25 July 1922, as drafted by Sir Maurice Hankey and amended in manuscript by Austen Chamberlain.

In 1964 I decided to end the practice, and as the new ministers were almost all without Cabinet experience, it was a good time for reform. When, quite soon, a minister asked for his 'dissent to be included in the Minutes', I refused to agree, and suggested he should send me an official minute, recording his views. My reasoning was that, since such statements of dissent were required mainly for future memoirs or histories, his purpose could be achieved by minuting me, no doubt keeping a copy.

---

[1] It should be made clear, to avert allegations of improper disclosure, that these prototype 'Conclusions' and the purported discussion underlying them are entirely fictitious.

This was accepted happily for a time, until a minister contumaciously asked what would happen to such a minute. I told him that it would be 'registered', and that satisfied him, and one or two others who later asked the same question – until one of the keen 1974 Cabinet entry asked me what happened when the minute was 'registered'. He for his part was happy when I told him that it would be 'entered in a register', as in fact are all minutes on all subjects.

An exception to the established Cabinet routine is the Budget Cabinet, usually now held the day before Budget Day. No papers are circulated. After the prime minister has opened the proceedings with a blistering invocation of secrecy, with dark hints about leak tribunals and what happened to J. H. Thomas, the chancellor is invited to make an oral presentation of his Budget proposals. This he does from many pages of notes, usually in his own handwriting, and for something like an hour gives the arguments he will be deploying the following day, outlining his strategy, listing the options he had considered, and setting out his decisions, answering questions and then listening to his colleagues' comments. Only the prime minister will know what the proposals are, though decisions affecting other departments (e.g. Transport on vehicle licensing; Industry on automobile taxation; Trade on shipping, etc.) will have been discussed on a 'need-to-know', basis with the secretary of state concerned and his officials.

The Public Record Office history of the Cabinet Office sets out the practice, and the traditional form of minuting:

> 'The Chancellor of the Exchequer communicated to the Cabinet particulars of the proposals in the forthcoming Budget
>
> In accordance with precedent, details are not recorded in the Cabinet conclusions.'[1]

This formula is still used today. The Cabinet Office history on the basis of the pre-1945 practice regards it as axiomatic that 'there was insufficient time to make changes in his plans.' In fact, Hugh Gaitskell was forced by Cabinet objection to drop a proposal for a differential fuel tax.

When the Cabinet Conclusions are circulated, reference to a particularly sensitive matter can be confined to a statement that the discussion is recorded in 'the standard file of Cabinet Conclusions'. When the Cabinet Conclusion has been promulgated, it is binding on the whole Government, including all departments. I remember an exchange during the Attlee Government. Following the circulation of a Cabinet

[1] Public Record Office, op. cit., p. 9, para. 215.

decision, a subordinate department – I think the Ministry of Works –
sent a minute to the Prime Minister, which began 'with reference to the
suggestion of the Cabinet that . . .' then proceeding to suggest that the
Ministry did not agree with it and did not propose to comply. The
Prime Minister responded with a characteristically short reply: 'The
Cabinet does not make suggestions. It takes decisions.' I was much
gratified to receive a similar minute soon after the 1964 Government
was formed, and took great pleasure in a reply that used Clement
Attlee's exact formula.

Another special type of Cabinet is the all-day meeting which some
prime ministers, by no means all, like to hold from time to time at
Chequers.

There is a theory about surroundings conditioning action. It certainly
seems to hold good in relation to decision-making. Downing Street is
the place for decision *par excellence*. Ministers go there to take decisions,
and know that these must be taken before Cabinet breaks up. Its fur-
nishing, décor and facilities – particularly since it was 're-furbished' by
Edward Heath – create the right atmosphere for decision.

The prime minister's room at the House of Commons is inimical to
clear discussion and crisp decision. It has its uses for the prime minister,
for example going over parliamentary questions and anticipating possible supplementaries ready for 3.15 pm on Tuesdays and Thursdays;
and also for working on boxes until late at night on a three-line whip,
particularly if the timing of divisions is unpredictable (for example, on
the report stage of a Bill or consideration of amendments made in the
Lords). It is totally integrated with No. 10 for communications and
office facilities, with staff in attendance.

But it is too small to accommodate the whole Cabinet, or even a
fairly large sub-committee. Worse, the frequent interruptions for divisions make continual discussion and decision very difficult. The division
bell goes, and all who are not paired (and by definition no one should
be) troop off into the division lobby. Any number of them may be
intercepted, by back-benchers with an urgent point to make, by their
shadow opposite number or their PPS. The return is ragged and
business is held up.

Chequers, on the other hand, is the ideal place for contemplative
discussion, particularly on long-term strategic questions, where ministers for a whole day, with a break for a buffet lunch and a stroll round
the rose-garden, can discuss major problems in depth and at a greater
length than is possible in a normal Cabinet meeting. In the 1960s I used
it for our first discussions on our contemplated application for membership of the European Economic Community and, after we had held

a series of Downing Street meetings on individual issues, for the meeting where we came up to – but did not ratify – the decision to apply for entry. In 1974–6 I used it for wide-ranging meetings on devolution, on industrial strategy – the National Enterprise Board and Planning Agreements – and on the first approach to the long process of working out our Public Expenditure Survey decisions for the five years to 1979–80. This meeting or 'PES C' was concerned not with detailed allocations of expenditure, as finally announced in February 1976, but with basic priorities, on which our discussion conditioned many months of work on the individual departmental estimates. An exception to the 'contemplative' role of a Chequers meeting was a further discussion on devolution, which was, unusually, concerned with decisions. There were some seventy or eighty points, some of detail, some of great principle, which had not been resolved in the appropriate Cabinet committee and its sub-committees and working parties; as was another meeting on individual policy. In addition, Chequers is used for smaller meetings, sub-committees or informal groups, for example on the future of Northern Ireland.

Sometimes a full discussion, for example on entry into the EEC in October 1967, leads to a clear attitude. Even so, no formal decision was taken: that was to come up at a formal Cabinet two days later. I told Cabinet that I would, in the light of the discussion, make a formal proposal to Cabinet and ask for a decision. No one after our discussion was in any doubt what it would be.

A Chequers meeting is informality at its best, and it usually inculcates informality and comradeship in the follow-up meetings in the Cabinet room. (See Note II in the Appendix, which includes an interesting quotation from Lord Lee of Fareham's original settlement of Chequers on the nation 'for the rest and recreation of her Prime Ministers for ever'.)

Two questions require decisions by the prime minister that bear on the informality of Cabinet proceedings: the manner of address, and smoking.

In 1964, with an almost totally inexperienced Cabinet and a filial desire to base my Cabinet style on that of Clement Attlee, as far as in me lay, I adopted his method of address; all Cabinet ministers were to refer to one another by their official title – chancellor, foreign secretary, chancellor of the Duchy and so on. One minister attempted to introduce Christian names, and tried it on until he was stopped. At our first meeting in March 1974, I ruled that ministers were free to use either Christian names or official titles. They became, in fact, interchangeable.

Newspaper reports suggest that my successor has reverted to the more formal system. In April 1976, a press report that I am unable to check suggested that the Heath Administration was still more formal, in that all ministers had to address the Prime Minister as '*Mr* Prime Minister', commenting that after a particularly long and critical Cabinet meeting Anthony Barber, the chancellor, rose to make a statement in Parliament and addressed Mr Speaker as 'Mr Prime Minister'.

Smoking is a difficult question. The Attlee Cabinet certainly became more quarrelsome after the Prime Minister, in 1947, forbade smoking in Cabinet until 1.0 pm as a gesture recognizing the severe dollar crisis and the emergency budget increase of a shilling on twenty cigarettes. It was more probably the strain created by the crisis that caused the dissension rather than the more austere régime. I have set out the arguments in explaining the decision I took in October 1964 to allow smoking. As with party conferences, fewer ministers keep stepping out ostensibly to telephone their departments if smoking is allowed, and there is less disposition to bring the meeting to an end prematurely, with decisions deferred to a later time.[1]

Edward Heath, it is understood, banned all smoking, and on my entering No. 10 on 4 March 1974 the staff had difficulty in finding an ashtray for me. At our first Cabinet the next day, I simply announced 'Smoking is not compulsory', and lit up.

So far the discussion has been in terms of the Cabinet itself. No modern Cabinet could function for a month without the extensive infrastructure of Cabinet committees. Most ministers, including the prime minister, spend more time in such committees each week than in Cabinet.

Cabinet committees are not new. There was a Crimean Committee in the Aberdeen Government in 1855, and a Cabinet committee to draft the abortive Reform Bill of 1854. Lloyd George made great use of them in World War I. There was later a corresponding cutting back of the Cabinet committee system. (Sir Warren Fisher, permanent secretary to the Treasury, strenuously tried to merge the Cabinet Office in the Treasury; it continued as an independent organization, though severely reduced, particularly from 1923.)

The committee system and the Cabinet Office were both greatly strengthened in World War II. These changes are recorded by the Public Records Office in *The Cabinet Office to 1945*, which sets out the principal committees serviced by the Cabinet Office between December 1916 and May 1945, as well as the number of committees and committee meetings.[2]

---

[1] For a serious discussion of this controversial item, see Wilson, op. cit., pp. 17–18.
[2] Public Record Office, op. cit., paras. 108, 222–35, 525–32 and 973–4. The Cabinet

The contrast between the period after World War I, particularly after 1923, and the years after 1945 owes something to the degree of state intervention in World War II, something also to a public determination not to suffer the earlier scandals of demoralization and the mass unemployment of the early twenties, but more to the difference between the 'Back to Normalcy' ideologues who swept into power in the Khaki Election, and Clement Attlee – together with Ernest Bevin, who had master-minded the successful and smooth 1945–6 demobilization, with a minimum of transitional unemployment.

The success of wartime Cabinet committees was another important fact. Sir John Anderson's successful chairmanship of the Lord President's Committee – later chaired by Clement Attlee – directing economic affairs, and that of other Cabinet committees by Herbert Morrison and Lord Woolton, helped to create an administrative revolution.

Sir John Anderson, while still a member of the wartime government, wrote an internal report recommending the retention of the Cabinet Office and, by implication, the system of Cabinet committees after the war.[1]

Clement Attlee retained the system. As he recorded in his memoirs, 'I had a good deal of responsibility for arranging committees during the war-time Government and the experience so gained stood me in good stead when making arrangements for Government machinery in the Labour Administration.'[2] He experimented in particular with a number of strategic economic committees, mainly chaired by Herbert Morrison and Sir Stafford Cripps, until the 1947 crisis led the Prime Minister to chair a still more high-powered one. As an economic minister I was on a number of these, and since the Board of Trade was regarded as neutral and uncommitted in the struggle to the death between the Ministries of Agriculture and Food, I had to spend what seemed years as one of the 'independent' members of such exciting committees as White Fish, and Farm Gate Prices, both of which had to settle the precise boundary where Agriculture handed over its produce and Food took over. Eventually, under Winston Churchill, the two departments merged in November 1954 and, inevitably, it became a virtual takeover by Agriculture. (In 1974, as a believer in creative tension between contesting departments based on interest, I gave the consumer

Office staff fell from 162 in 1919 to 120 in early 1923, being cut in that year to 39. It rose again to about 200 by 1939 and 600 by 1945. See also Thomas Jones (secretary of the Cabinet under Lloyd George and his successor up to 1930), *Whitehall Diary* (Oxford 1969), *passim.*

[1] Cited in Peter Hennessy's portrait of the Cabinet Office, 'A Magnificent Piece of Powerful Bureaucratic Machinery', *The Times* (8 March 1976).

[2] Attlee, op. cit., p. 154.

a champion once more by appointing Shirley Williams as secretary of state for prices and consumer protection.)

During the thirteen years of unbroken Conservative rule from 1951 to 1964, the committee system, so far from being weakened, was strengthened and developed. The Conservatives of those days had a number of experienced administrators well qualified to take the lead, such as Lord Woolton (in the early years), Harold Macmillan, R.A. Butler, Derick Amory and Iain Macleod. Harold Macmillan's highly revealing autobiography, based on a very full diary, shows his faith in the system, which equally benefited from the growing strength and quality of the Cabinet Office. The process had begun when Sir Edward Bridges relinquished the secretaryship of the Cabinet, which was taken by Sir Norman Brook. It was Harold Macmillan, towards the end of his premiership, who completed the process of separation by creating the modern system by ending the unitary control, where the permanent secretary of the Treasury, aided by deputies, was at one and the same time the head of the Treasury as the principal economic department, and head of the Civil Service. Harold Macmillan, following the Plowden Report, created three virtually equal-ranking officers at senior permanent secretary level, separating the secretary of the Cabinet, while the Treasury and Civil Service functions were directed by two co-equal joint permanent secretaries. The operation was completed by me in 1968, following the report of the Fulton Committee on the Civil Service.[1] I set up the Civil Service Department, with the prime minister as minister for the Civil Service, assisted by the lord privy seal and leader in the Lords, and now by a minister of state as well, and with the joint permanent secretary to the Treasury for the Civil Service in a separate command as permanent secretary to the Civil Service Department and head of the Civil Service.

The undoubted success of the Macmillan reform owes a great deal to Lord Plowden and the then Prime Minister, but no less to the fact that the civil servants who have been appointed include some of the best – indeed, the best – I have known in thirty-six years of close and intimate knowledge of the machine and its leading[2] personalities.

We have seen that the development of Cabinet committees has been used by adherents of the Crossman school to suggest that the power of the prime minister is enhanced thereby. This is a facile view: what it

[1] *Hansard* (26 June 1968), cols. 454–9. The relevant order was laid on 16 October, and the changes took effect on 1 November 1968.

[2] Even during the thirteen years of unbroken opposition, I had the good fortune to be chairman of the House of Commons Public Accounts Committee, whose witnesses, for half a year at a time, are the departmental accounting officers, in almost all cases permanent secretaries.

does is to make the whole government more effective, and to shield Cabinet from over-absorption in detail. Business coming before Cabinet is reduced to the extent that it puts its work, so to speak, into commission, by committees with power to act. The principal checks on over-delegation, or lack of co-ordination with other sectors of the government, are, first, the right of any minister to ask for the matter to go to Cabinet on appeal, or at least be reported there; second, the ability of the prime minister to direct that such and such an issue shall go straight to Cabinet, or a committee decision be reported to the senior body, for confirmation or second thoughts – a power very rarely used in my recent experience; and, third, where the membership of an established committee seems inappropriate for a particular reference, a decision to make it more representative, *or* to create a special *ad hoc* committee to deal with this particular issue, a so-called MISC (jargon for 'miscellaneous'). The Government does not publish the names or number of Cabinet committees, but there are currently about 25. *The Times* profile of the Cabinet Office also records some 118 official sub-committees.

But it is fanciful to suggest that by these means the prime minister's power is enhanced at the expense of that of the Cabinet. For one thing, it would be extremely difficult for even a megalomaniac prime minister (who would not last long) to plan to set aside an agreed, or substantially agreed, decision of a powerful committee consisting of seven or eight of his Cabinet colleagues. His role is to see that the committee system, as an indispensable part of the Cabinet machine, works satisfactorily – by delegating enough to the committee and giving them authority, but also by being sufficiently politically and administratively sensitive to know when to respond to an appeal by a dissatisfied minority, or to spot the case that ought to go straight to Cabinet. But when this is what he decides he must make this clear in advance, not weaken counsel and the standing of his ministerial colleagues by invoking Cabinet to reverse a decision they have taken.

Another positive duty he has is to ensure that the principal Cabinet committees, including *ad hoc* groups set up for a specific problem, are not packed with adherents of a particular departmental or political viewpoint. It is for him to ensure that a Cabinet committee is the Cabinet *in parvo*, a microcosm of the Cabinet itself.

On the question of 'appeals' to Cabinet, a tendency developed in the 1960s for a defeated minister almost automatically to seek for a re-run at Cabinet, even if he was in a minority of one. This threatened to congest the work of Cabinet, and to weaken the authority of the committees and their chairmen. I had to direct – and make public – that no appeal to Cabinet could hope to succeed unless it had the backing of the chairman of the committee. Under any government, committee chairmen are experienced ministers who have enough *nous* to know when, for administrative or political reasons, the matter should be taken higher, irrespective of their own views on the decision reached.

A better judgment than that of the confrontation school is that of Lord Blake: '. . . It is by no means clear that this procedure, [i.e. the greater use of Cabinet committees] makes the Prime Minister a more dominant force. It could be equally well argued that it strengthens – by making more efficient – the Cabinet itself.'[1]

When the prime minister, through Cabinet or a senior Cabinet committee, moves in and takes a subject over, it can well be for the purpose not of weakening Cabinet control, but of strengthening it against action by an individual department which is striking a discordant note against the orchestrated harmony which it is the purpose of Cabinet government to aim at, and the duty of the prime minister to ensure.

To take an example, which, unless millions of copies of national newspapers are regarded as secret documents, is public property. There were the anxieties in the summer of 1974 that work on the manifesto commitments on the National Enterprise Board and Planning Agreements was, in the first place, going too slowly for announcement by the Government before the planned October election, and, secondly, that there seemed to be some departure from the precise manifesto language, in favour of an earlier National Executive Committee document, which had not been adopted as an election programme, and which had in fact not been approved by the Labour Party Conference in 1973.[2] I had insisted that, since legislation could not possibly be introduced before the October election – and 'industrial regeneration' was bound to be a central issue on the hustings – there must be a government White Paper setting out the policy, and saying precisely not only what we were going to do, but what we were not going to do. As the draft was unsatisfactory, I put it into commission – to a Cabinet committee representative of all shades of opinion – with myself in the chair. The White Paper was produced on time, and was the basis for the legislation introduced after the general election, enacted in the 1974–5 parliamentary session, receiving the Royal Assent on 12 November 1975.

An act of prime ministerial authority? Or the assertion of Cabinet supremacy? It has a potential for unending academic argument: but this was an assertion by Cabinet, on prime ministerial initiative, of its collective authority. It also illustrated the duty of the prime minister

[1] Lord Blake, *The Office of Prime Minister* (Oxford 1975), p. 53.
[2] See p. 158 below.

to enforce a time-table as well as his duty arising out of his position as political, as well as administrative, head of government.[1]

For the reasons I have given, the use of the Cabinet committee system, serviced by the Cabinet Office on behalf of the Cabinet as a whole, has increased, is increasing, and ought not to be diminished – give or take the removal from the list of Cabinet committees of one or two which have served their purpose, and rarely if ever now meet. If the system had not existed, it would have had to be invented. The enormous increase in the work load on ministers, senior officials and the machine itself following the oil crisis and the problems of world inflation, world depression and world payments imbalance, if it could be statistically measured, must be, I would estimate, between thirty and fifty per cent. This, together with the volume of legislative and other action required of a reforming government elected on a specific manifesto, means collective delegation from the Cabinet to bodies deriving their authority from the Cabinet and answering to it.

This is not to say that there are no problems. The sheer weight of business in the departments and at inter-departmental level means that at important committees junior ministers have sometimes to stand in, lacking the authority of their secretaries of state. It is more difficult for the chairman, however experienced, to collect a sense of the meeting; and decisions by voting or counting of heads are utterly wrong in such meetings. One cannot equate the voice of the foreign secretary or chancellor with that of the most recently recruited parliamentary under-secretary.

Another problem arises when the issue under discussion involves public expenditure. At any Cabinet committee there is a danger that the chief secretary, or other Treasury representative, is in a minority of one. (Strangely, while spending ministers in Cabinet hardly ever form a bloc against the chancellor, in Cabinet committees there is a tendency to do so.) In recent months decisions have had to be taken to obviate this danger. The public expenditure decisions announced to Parliament in Cmnd 6396 are overriding by Cabinet directive. The contingency fund for the current year is not up for grabs at a committee: all claims on it must be tabulated, assembled, assessed and brought to Cabinet for decision.

I have referred to junior ministers. On occasion, following Clement Attlee's example, I have found it useful on an important but not crucial issue to set up committees consisting entirely of junior ministers. One such was responsible for the reorganization and strengthening of the Government's statistical service. I set up a committee under the chairmanship first of Peter Shore, later of Edmund Dell, which also included

[1] See chapter IV, below.

the principal heads of statistical departments, though I chaired the first
meeting to show that I meant business and received regular reports
from the Chairman (and from the head of the Government's statistical
service, Sir Claus Moser) on the progress recorded.[1] This, incident-
ally, was a mixed committee, including junior ministers and officials
(mainly from the Central Statistical Office and departmental statistical branches). Mixed committees are a practice I would normally
deprecate.

Looking back, I regret that I did not set up more committees of
junior ministers; no less that I did not follow Clement Attlee's precedent
of calling groups of young ministers at all levels to meet under his chairmanship to discuss fresh ideas for the future. The work some of us –
particularly Fred Lee – did in 1950–1 opened up a great deal of new
thinking. Lee's work foreshadowed new thinking on industrial democracy; my own contribution prepared for thinking that paved the
way after many years for the philosophy that produced the Industrial
Reorganisation Corporation (IRC) and the NEB.

I have briefly referred, for example in the Chequers context, to the
annual problem of deciding the public expenditure limits for the five-
year period ahead.

The Labour Government in 1969 introduced the concept of a five-
year rolling programme. After full consideration by the Cabinet, under
Treasury leadership, the Government each winter published a White
Paper[2] setting out for the financial year (1 April to 30 March) immediately ahead the Government's firm decisions on expenditure limits,
department by department and item by item: these are later set out in
the published estimates for the coming financial year. The Estimates
Volume for 1975–6 encompasses some 880 pages, weighs 2¾ lb, lists the
detailed figures by departmental heads setting out in the fullest detail
the provision for each activity of government. Supplementary Note I V
in the Appendix sets out a facsimile of typical pages, and also a representative table from the forward expenditure programme referred to
in Cmnd 6393.[3]

For the second financial year, 1977–8 in the White Paper referred to,
the proposed expenditure limits are pretty firmly decided, though subject to final decisions before the following White Paper is tabled. For

[1] The results, including continuing reforms under the succeeding administration, were
set out in my Presidential Address to the Royal Statistical Society, on 15 November 1972,
reprinted in the *Journal of the Royal Statistical Society*, Section A (1973), Part I, pp. 1–16.

[2] For example, Cmnd 6393, published on 9 February 1976, which has 149 pages of
detailed forward expenditure programmes.

[3] H.C. paper 210.

the third, fourth and fifth years the figures are increasingly less firm, since it is not always possible to forecast particular contingencies, or to forecast such heavy expenditure items as unemployment benefit or the scale of expenditure on nationalized industries.[1]

Nevertheless, the forward programme is of fundamental importance, because of the nature of the central problem of controlling expenditure, a fact that so many political and press comments fail to appreciate – particularly those demanding drastic and immediate cuts in state spending in the current year, or the financial year that is about to begin.

Expenditure decisions cannot be programmed in this manner. To attempt to do so would mean, for example, that local authority houses would be left half-built; schools, hospitals and old people's homes would be abandoned without a roof over them; the construction of motorways and other work would be left unfinished, with unsightly semi-finished roads petering out in a field somewhere or other; naval vessels and air-craft would be left half-constructed; pay decisions announced for the armed forces and social commitments relating, for example, to retire-ment pensions and supplementary benefits would be dishonoured. The practical way in 1976 of restraining public expenditure on, say, motor-ways, schools or hospitals, is not to stop work on a construction project in 1976, but to desist from starting on an intended motorway scheduled to begin in 1977 or 1978.

Some social expenditure is determined by demographic factors totally outside the control of any government. The proportion of the population represented by the elderly directly conditions expenditure on pensions, and – in the absence of new and harsh decisions about care of the elderly – the provision for old people's homes and other forms of assistance.

The preparation of the Public Expenditure White Paper begins in the spring of the year preceding the beginning of the first of the five financial years covered in the annual statement. Estimates of the amounts required are worked through in the spending departments, in conjunction with the Treasury, the latter usually reserving their position both on the figures and on their right to propose minor or major changes in policy commitments, so as to secure a reduction.

In the heated debates in Parliament and the country in 1975–6 on public expenditure, with the Opposition demanding sweeping cuts in

---

[1] On 17 December 1973, Mr (now Lord) Barber, then chancellor of the exchequer, announced a programme of expenditure reductions for the financial year beginning on 1 April 1974. A central element was Exchequer provision for the deficits of publicly owned industries. In December last year the House was told that the deficit in the nationalized industries would be about £500mn. That turned out not to be the case. By the beginning of March when we took office – only ten weeks later – it was not around £500mn; it was around £1,400mn – *Hansard* (24 July 1974), col. 1632.

the total, and the Government challenging the Opposition to say which spending programmes they would cut and by how much, I quoted the words of Disraeli in 1862: 'Mere abstract and declaratory opinions in favour of reduction and retrenchment are of no use whatsoever. I have so often maintained it in this House that I am almost ashamed to repeat it, but unfortunately it is not a principle which has yet sufficiently entered into public opinion – expenditure depends on policy.'[1]

As I have suggested, the practice now being developed involves a general discussion on priorities such as the Chequers talks I have described, followed by detailed scrutiny of expenditure proposals prior to collective consideration and decision.

Expenditure control is becoming more sophisticated and detailed but it can never become an expert science. By its very nature it is political and involves clear and unequivocal decisions, measured in precise expenditure estimates, the Cabinet itself deciding the figures for each programme and major sub-heads within programmes.

There can be differing views on how collective Cabinet examination of spending programmes can best be organized. On first becoming prime minister in 1964, and recalling the experience of the Attlee Cabinet, I feared an unacceptable ganging-up by the ministers heading spending departments against the Treasury. 'If you'll back me on housing – or social services – or education, I'll back you on defence.' As I have suggested, whatever may be the case in Cabinet committees, for example consideration of drawings on the contingency fund, this has not happened in Cabinet,[2] and in committee it has been stopped.

One experiment tried in the sixties was to set up a group of non-spending ministers (or ministers with small budgets), such as the lord president, lord privy seal, lord chancellor, foreign secretary and the chancellor of the duchy, to sit in judgement, with Treasury help, on the claims of the major spending departments, and to report their suggested priorities, allocations and cuts in departmental programmes. It was my impression that this worked fairly well, but chancellors have on the whole preferred to do it by direct in-fighting followed by clear submission to Cabinet, strongly sustained there with the support they can usually get from the prime minister.

---

[1] Labour Party, *Annual Conference Report, 1975*, p. 185. See also D.H.Macgregor, *Public Aspects of Finance* (Oxford 1939) for an account of classical economic discussion on this issue, and in particular the Disraeli–Gladstone dialogue, pp. 21–4 and 45–50.

[2] It clearly did happen in the Macmillan Government, when the entire Cabinet rejected the Chancellor's demand for a further cut in expenditure, leading to the resignation not only of the Chancellor but of the entire Treasury team, an event described by Macmillan as 'a little local difficulty', as he coolly and characteristically set off on a six-week tour of the Commonwealth.

Nevertheless, I think there is a case for considering its re-introduction. The chancellor must seek allies. Provided that, I repeat *provided that*, the Cabinet adheres to recent practice in setting an overall total that must not be exceeded for any given year, there is no danger of softness setting in: the committee of non-spending ministers has to recommend priorities and allocations within that total. The independent judgement of non-spenders provides the chancellor with a built-in alliance, and other ministers uncommitted as between, say, education and health are likely to be influenced by that judgement.

Established procedure would begin with the spring and summer Chequers-type general discussions, followed by bilaterals, then an action meeting, which lays down the total spending limit, which must be absolute, followed by specific Treasury proposals for each thesis of expenditure. These can be flat figures, in which a given percentage reduction is applied to the main spending programmes to bring them down to the agreed limit, or a selective series cutting bids by different percentages reflecting differential priorities, or a combination of the two.

The most difficult problem a Cabinet has to face is when it has, for whatever reason, perhaps foreign confidence, perhaps budgetary considerations, to make reductions in the announced programme for the year immediately ahead, as happened in Anthony Barber's announcement in December 1973, of cuts for the fiscal year 1974–5, or the review of the 1977–8 programme in July 1976. For the reasons I have given these are much more difficult – especially when unemployment is already high.

I should add that a great deal of thought has been given in recent months to improving expenditure procedures and making the approach more sophisticated: I shall be surprised if processes already set in hand do not lead to further reform in the next year or two. But the problems will remain, and they are indescribably painful for the whole Cabinet, not excepting the chancellor.

One of Aneurin Bevan's phrases has passed into the folklore of the democratic socialist movement, indeed more widely: 'The language of priorities is the religion of socialism.' This is right, but it is a religion that needs a further secular process before it becomes a rule of life. In government there are no absolute priorities – if there were, and, say, the health service were given an *absolute* priority over education or housing, then any conceivable improvement in health would take priority not only over improvements in the other areas of government, but over existing services and expenditure. Any democratic movement, of any party, has its priorities which it asserts as part of its philosophy: when the leaders of that movement become the leaders of a government they are faced with the harsh reality of translating those priorities into allocations.

This is what government is about. The classic proof occurred just after the fall of France in 1940. Winston Churchill issued a 'priority directive' governing, in particular, the use of raw materials for specific war and civil requirements. At the top of the list coast defence, the naval construction programme and the production of fighters for the Battle of Britain, all jostled for top place, because priorities involve an *ordinal* list. In the event, the naval programme was given '1AA' (the top) priority. Aluminium was for a time the material in shortest supply. The Admiralty invoked their priorities. *Any* Admiralty use took priority over the most important requirement of a non-Admiralty programme. Aluminium was therefore specified by their lordships for lavatory pans on naval vessels. 1AA priority meant that the specification had to be met even if Lord Beaverbrook (minister for Aircraft Production) had to go short for his Spitfire programme. In no time at all, priorities gave way to allocations – the allocations being in specific quantities reflecting the priorities laid down, but on the basis that no priority can be absolute and pre-emptive, that no one could apply an 'absolute priority' slip on any of his programmes, regardless of whether they were essential or not.

The lesson learnt in 1940 applies equally in peacetime as in war to public expenditure, which is basically the allocation of the taxpayer's money, on the basis of priorities.

No treatment of Cabinet government can be complete without dealing with a subject which, for a number of reasons, became a matter of public debate in recent months – the question of collective Cabinet responsibility.

The collective responsibility of the Cabinet for every decision was firmly laid down long before the Cabinet, with its responsibility to Parliament, developed in its present form. In chapter I above I described how the younger Pitt in 1792 dismissed his Lord Chancellor for publicly dissociating himself from Pitt's creation of the Sinking Fund, 'the earliest known assertion of the principle of collective Cabinet responsibility'.[1]

From that time the doctrine has never been seriously challenged. Lord Salisbury in 1878 set it out in what has been regarded as the classic formulation:

'Now my Lords, am I not defending a great Constitutional principle, when I say that, for all that passes in a Cabinet, each Member of it

[1] Chapter I, p. 16 above.

who does not resign is absolutely and irretrievably responsible, and that he has no right afterwards to say that he agreed in one case to a compromise, while in another he was persuaded by one of his Colleagues . . . It is, I maintain, only on the principle that absolute responsibility is undertaken by every Member of a Cabinet, who, after a decision is arrived at, remains a member of it, that the joint responsibility of Ministers to Parliament can be upheld, and one of the most essential conditions of Parliamentary responsibility established.'[1]

Another classical Salisburyism is reproduced in the *Report of the Committee of Privy Councillors on Ministerial Memoirs*, presided over by Lord Radcliffe (Cmnd 6386 of January 1976, paragraph 32) under the heading 'Principles':

'Originating in a spontaneous gathering of friends, legally unrecognised [the Cabinet] system had inherited a tradition of freedom and informality which was in its eyes indispensable to its efficiency. A Cabinet discussion was not the occasion for the deliverance of considered judgements but an opportunity for the pursuit of practical conclusions. It could only be completely effective for this purpose if the flood of suggestions which accompanied it obtained the freedom and fulness which belong to private conversations – members must feel themselves untrammelled by any consideration of consistency with the past or self-justifications in the future . . . . The first rule of Cabinet conduct, he used to declare, was that no member should ever "Hansardise" another – even compare his present contribution to the common fund of counsel with a previously expressed opinion.'[2]

A more cynical and oft-quoted statement was that of Lord Melbourne, as his colleagues were leaving the room after reaching a conclusion on the Corn Laws in 1841: 'By the bye, there is one thing we haven't agreed upon, which is, what we are to say. Is it to make our corn dearer or cheaper, or to make the price steady? I don't care which; but we had better all be in the same story.'[3]

Professor Ivor Jennings, in his authoritative *Cabinet Government*, favours Joseph Chamberlain's definition:

'Absolute frankness in our private relations and full discussion of all matters of common interest . . . the decision freely arrived at should

[1] *Hansard* (8 April 1878), cols 833–4.
[2] Lady Gwendolen Cecil, *Life of Robert Salisbury* (London 1921–32), quoted in the Radcliffe Report, op. cit., p. 13.
[3] Spencer Walpole, *Life of Lord John Russell* (London 1889), I, p. 369.

be loyally supported and considered as the decision of the whole of the Government. Of course there may be occasions in which the difference is of so vital a character that it is impossible for the minority . . . to continue their support, and in this case the Ministry breaks up or the minority member or members resigns.'[1]

There has been some difference on whether the doctrine is binding on all ministers or only on those who participated in the decision. Gladstone, when prime minister, took a limited view: 'The rule I have stated as to the obligations of Cabinet Ministers has for its correlation the supposition that they have been parties to the discussion of the subject in the Cabinet.'[2] This would not be accepted today. The modern doctrine is undoubtedly as formulated by Lord Simon, as lord chancellor, in a memorandum to a War Cabinet Committee on the machinery of Government:

> 'A husband is responsible for his wife's debts even though he does not know where she goes shopping or how big a bill she is running up. He trusts her, unless indeed he finds it necessary to give notice that she is not his agent. The same thing happens in a Cabinet. Ministers who are not in the inner circle trust the Ministers who are. Perhaps it leads to greater clearness, not to speak of ordinary Ministers as being "responsible" but to describe them as being "answerable" for what the Government does. But the Government is one, and since the whole Government may be held answerable for some act of a single department, there is nothing surprising in the proposition that Ministers must stand together, even if an individual Minister did not know and might not have approved the policy adopted by the War Cabinet.'

The principle must be strongly upheld that the doctrine of collective governmental responsibility is totally binding on a minister, whatever he is doing or in whatever capacity he may be acting. A minister is a minister, and there can be no derogation from his obligation always to act in that capacity. This applies in particular to his membership of party bodies; for example, in the case of the Labour Party, the National Executive Committee.

In 1974-5 there were strains arising from certain aspects of foreign policy, including Chile and South Africa – and to some extent on EEC including the establishment of a Transport House Committee to monitor the Government's actions in the re-negotiations about the terms of

---

[1] Ivor Jennings, *Cabinet Government*, 3rd ed. (Cambridge 1935), p. 277.
[2] Quoted in D.J.Heasman, 'The Prime Minister and the Cabinet' in King, op. cit., p. 63.

entry. Letters I sent and published to certain ministers on this question also appear in the Appendix.[1] In 1976 I had to direct that no minister who was chairman of a sub-committee of the National Executive Committee should undertake press briefing on behalf of the sub-committee, despite a National Executive decision that he was free to do so, if it meant announcing NEC policies that were opposed to, inconsistent with, or even different from the policy of the Government, or in any way blurred the clarity of government policy.

Under the constitution of the Labour Party the Executive has a duty to work out policy for submission to the Annual Conference. Inevitably, an Executive elected by Conference includes a substantial number – frequently amounting to a majority on particular issues in 1974–6 – who were concerned to prepare policy statements on almost every subject under the sun, home and abroad, inconsistent with, sometimes sharply critical of, government policies. This was liable to cause confusion in certain quarters, including national and international financial markets, where there are many who are singularly uninformed, not to say naive, about our political institutions, and on where power really lies. Quite often, therefore, I had to make this point clear, by answers to questions in Parliament or published replies to anxious letters from City-based financial institutions such as the British Insurance Association or the merchant banking community, on more than one occasion drafting the letter, to which I was at pains to reply myself.

There were times when I wondered whether a rule would have to be made precluding ministers from being members of the NEC. I was very loath to take such a decision, as the presence of ministers, however unenviable their position, would help inculcate realism in the Executive and prevent the two bodies growing far apart. Richard Crossman did in fact decide not to stand for re-election in 1967, but I was, throughout my premiership, anxious that ministers should stand and seek election, in addition to the leader and deputy leader of the party who are *ex officio* Executive members.

There was great interest in constitutional circles in my announcement on 23 January 1975 that collective responsibility would be relaxed for the period of the referendum campaign on membership of EEC – the famous 'agreement to differ'. I said:

'The circumstances of this referendum are unique, and the issue to be decided is one on which strong views have long been held which cross party lines. The Cabinet has, therefore, decided that, if when the time comes there are members of the Government, including

[1] See Appendix Note I.

members of the Cabinet, who do not feel able to accept and support
the Government recommendation, whatever it may be, they will,
once the recommendation has been announced, be free to support
and speak in favour of a different conclusion in the referendum
campaign [HON. MEMBERS: "Oh!"]'[1]

In the subsequent questioning there were many members of the
House, including Edward Heath, then leader of the Opposition, who
queried the right of a minority to differ from the majority decision of
Cabinet; some feared, or affected to fear, that a precedent might be
created. To all of them I stressed the 'unique' character of this referendum.

There was something of a precedent, though not an exact parallel,
in the public agreement to differ of the 'National' Government in 1932
on import duties. The events of 1932 are set out in the Appendix Note
III.

In the run-up to the referendum campaign I repeatedly claimed not
only that there would be a complete return to full collective responsibility
as soon as the votes had been counted, but that the party and the
Government would thereafter be stronger, not weaker, more united, not
divided, as a consequence of the agreement to differ. So it proved, and it
was decisive in securing an overwhelming majority in the referendum,
which ended once and for all the previous doubts about the support of
the British people for membership of the European Community.

[1] *Hansard* (23 January 1975), col. 1746.

IV

No. 10 and the Cabinet Office

'In recent years . . . it has become clear that the structure of inter-departmental committees, each concerned with a separate area of policy, needs to be reinforced by a clear and comprehensive definition of government strategy which can be systematically developed to take account of changing circumstances and can provide a framework within which the Government's policies as a whole may be more effectively formulated.' EDWARD HEATH[1]

No. 10 is best regarded as a small village. During Sir Alec Douglas-Home's premiership, I described it as a monastery and declared my intention of changing it into a power-house. Whether I succeeded or not, or whether it was the right objective, historians may debate. The function of No. 10 – and clearly of the Cabinet Office – is to make Cabinet government work.

No. 10 reflects the style of the prime minister of the day. The prime ministerial style of Clement Attlee was markedly different from that of Winston Churchill,[2] and that of Anthony Eden differed from both of

[1] *The Reorganization of Central Government* (Cmnd. 4506), presented by the Prime Minister to Parliament, October 1970, para. 45.

[2] Sir David Hunt, as Foreign Office Secretary at No. 10, overlapped the Attlee Government and the early period of Winston Churchill's last administration. His comparison of the two premiers is perceptive: 'While Attlee had a great power of decision, Winston Churchill, on subjects in which he took little interest, affected horror when his advisers pressed for a decision; they were confusing him with a dictator, and he said, '"This is a democratic government. These matters must be decided by the Cabinet as a whole; I cannot possibly settle them on my own authority."' Hunt regarded this as sometimes being a way of deferring a decision: he goes on to comment: 'Many people have expressed surprise to me when I have mentioned this as a point of contrast between Attlee and Churchill. It goes completely contrary to the popular idea of both these men. Attlee is usually thought of as good-natured, a compromise, but not a strong character and it is always supposed that Churchill was one of those determined men who made up their minds in a flash. To assert that the opposite was true might make it seem that I was disparaging Churchill.' He goes on to develop the point, concluding that Churchill 'was a very great man, and, for all my affection for Attlee, a greater man in world history than his predecessor'. His further analysis throws an interesting and intimate light on both premiers. *On The Spot: An Ambassador Remembers* (London 1975), p. 53.

them. Harold Macmillan gave the public impression of being something
of a dilettante, fainéant and disdainful – and enjoying it immensely.
Nothing could be further from the truth. Reviewing the sixth and final
volume of his memoirs, I said:

> 'I am simply moved to confirm the provisional judgment inspired
> by an earlier volume I reviewed in *The Times*. Those of us were
> wrong who regarded him as a "Premier Ministre Fainéant".
>
> 'He was utterly hard-working, even discounting the long hours he
> must have spent recording the events of each day for posterity, and
> the time he spent on detailed and perceptive letters to Buckingham
> Palace.
>
> 'As I wrote two years ago, Mr. Macmillan's role as a poseur was
> itself a pose.'[1]

There was a general impression that my No. 10 style was somewhat
different from that of Sir Alec. In a radio interview in 1964[2] I said that,
if elected, I intended to run No. 10 not only as chairman, but as a full-
time managing director or chief executive, for my incoming team would
have almost no Cabinet or administrative experience.

The style even of the same prime minister can itself change over time,
as requirements change. Reference has been made to change of style of
Labour premiership between the sixties and 1974–6. On the final meeting of the Shadow Cabinet on 4 March 1974, as we were waiting for
news that the Heath Administration was finally going, I said that I
would run the new government very differently from that of the sixties.
James Callaghan exchanged a knowing and disbelieving wink with
Denis Healey. Within a fortnight they both agreed that the style was
entirely different. At the first meeting of the Parliamentary Labour
Party, I told them that, whereas in the sixties I had played in every
position on the field – goalkeeper, midfield, taking penalties and corners
and bringing on the lemons – I was going to be an old-fashioned deep-
lying centre half, lying well back, feeding the ball to those whose job it
was to score goals, and moving upfield only for rare 'set-piece'
occasions. A few weeks later, commenting on the metaphor, the *Liverpool
Daily Post* said that the analogy was rather that of the manager, sitting
on the bench and encouraging his team. This was flattering, as Liverpool
is Shankly country, but pursuing the theme I reminded colleagues that
managers frequently sit on the substitutes' bench, pulling players off the
field and replacing them at short notice.

[1] *The Times* (27 September 1973).
[2] Harold Wilson, 'Whitehall and Beyond' (London 1964), pp. 11–28; reprinted in
Anthony King (ed.), *The British Prime Minister* (London 1969), pp. 80–92.

In the two administrations, March–October 1974 and October 1974–April 1976, No. 10 and the Cabinet Office were working with me to strengthen the power and effectiveness of Cabinet government, taking advantage of the successive improvements in the servicing of the Cabinet as a decision-making body, which had been introduced over the previous six or seven years.

No. 10 is not only a village; it is a small village. In his authoritative review of No. 10 Private Office, G. W. Jones records the numbers of private secretaries proper in No. 10.[1] In 1870 there were three, and the number remained constant until the 1920s; today there are five, apart from the appointments secretary. In 1951 there were 52 clerks, typists, messengers and cleaners in No. 10; by 1964 there were 59 and in 1974 98. The figures for private secretaries are, as Mr Jones points out, not strictly comparable. Nineteenth-century private secretaries had to do a great deal of copying, and until modern times the No. 10 Private Office was responsible for relations with the press. The creation of a separate press office, and in particular the establishment of typing pools, electronic communications and copying machines, has made the figures something less than perfectly comparable.

The Lloyd George Administration provided a unique aberration, the 'Garden Suburb' private Cabinet Office and a Lloyd George oriented private office. His successor, Bonar Law, was served by unpaid, privately recruited informal advisers, together with one Treasury appointment.

It was Ramsay MacDonald who changed the system, against the strong criticism of his party colleagues. He ended the system in which the principal private secretary, and others, were changed when the party complexion of the Government changed. 'None of the private secretaries who served Liberal Prime Ministers from 1868 to 1921 ever served a Conservative Prime Minister, and none of the private secretaries who served Conservative Prime Ministers from 1868 to 1905 ever served a Liberal Prime Minister.'[2] Ramsay MacDonald took over his predecessor's secretaries. 'The Civil Service took over the private office.'[3]

Since then each incoming prime minister following a change of government has retained his predecessor's principal private secretary,

[1] G. W. Jones (ed.), *From Policy to Administration: Essays in Honour of William A. Robson* (London 1976), pp. 13–38. For the history of the office see pp. 14 *et seq*. Prime ministers have had private secretaries since the Duke of Newcastle (1757–62), though paid from public funds only since 1806; the secondment of a 'Treasury clerk' dates from the early nineteenth century.

[2] ibid., p. 30.

[3] ibid., p. 31.

with one exception: Edward Heath in 1970 got rid of a civil servant I had appointed a few weeks earlier – a career civil servant who had in fact been private secretary to Lord Hailsham during the Macmillan Administration. I followed a different course. I kept on Sir Alec Douglas-Home's private secretary for nearly two years, and in 1974–5 retained Edward Heath's post-election appointee for more than a year – though he was due for a change and in fact, after nearly five years of No. 10 service, he was almost the longest-serving principal private secretary since the war.

After Robert Vansittart (later Lord Vansittart) was appointed to the Private Office in 1937, no appointment except from the Civil Service (usually from the Treasury) was made to Private Office, with one exception. Harold Macmillan appointed John Wyndham (whom he later created Lord Egremont) not as a political or private adviser, but in Private Office. As a wealthy man, he was unpaid – in fact a dollar-a-year man. Pay is not the test: here was a political appointment brought into Private Office itself. All other prime ministers, including Edward Heath and myself, have kept the administrative Private Office and the Political Office apart (though people associated with Mr Heath were included in the Central Policy Review Staff, as mine were not).

As G. W. Jones, who in the essay quoted really has got the feel of what No. 10 is about, has commented, 'The Prime Minister is the one minister who stands on the peaks of both politics and administration . . . at the top politics and administration could not be kept distinct . . . at the top politics and administration are inextricably entangled.'[1]

Hence the tendency in recent years to create a political office to advise the prime minister and to provide a means of contact with the party machine, which it would be unprocedural, if not improper, to attempt through the Civil Service machine. To this I will return.

No. 10 is a deceptive building. From Downing Street it appears a tiny house, but in fact it is two houses linked by a passage, the larger one being built to face Horse Guards.[2]

It has, in fact, over 160 rooms, mainly offices, together with the Cabinet room, reception and dining rooms, and a small flat on the second floor. To the north it links directly with the Cabinet Office; to the south there is a through passage to No. 11 and No. 12. No. 11 is the chancellor's official residence, No. 12 the office of the chief whip (his main office is at the House of Commons). Hugh Dalton used to tell me, when he was chancellor and I was a young minister, that you could

[1] Jones, op. cit., pp. 14, 35, 36.
[2] For a description of the house and its history, see R. J. Minney, *No. 10 Downing Street* (London 1963).

always measure the situation within the Cabinet by the door covering the passage between No. 10 and No. 11. If it was locked, as it had been for long periods, that augured an unhappy ministry. It was a free-way through all the years I was at No. 10; and it was used for two-way traffic.

The present No. 10 is a new building. In the fifties its foundations began to shift, and an expensive and protracted rebuilding took place, during which time the then prime minister, Harold Macmillan, lived in Admiralty House, and made it the seat of government for meetings of the Cabinet and Cabinet committees. He always made clear that he preferred it to No. 10. In fact he returned to the by-then rebuilt building only in October 1963 and within days left it for hospital, where his resignation took effect.

Clem Attlee used to work from his seat at the Cabinet table, and received his official visitors in the Cabinet room. In 1964 I followed his example, despite the handy little study on the first floor. Three years later I took over the study and worked from there, except for formal committees, deputations and overseas visitors, as did Edward Heath, who greatly extended and refurnished it. It was there I went on the evening of 4 March 1974, to set about forming the Cabinet.

Others have written about the facilities for work there – and at Chequers. The secretarial services are of the highest standard, provided by the so-called 'garden room girls' (their offices are on the sub-ground floor, level with the garden). The communications are superb. No. 10 has the best telephone switchboard in London.[1] Communications between Chequers and Downing Street are total, and secure, in contrast to the facilities in Neville Chamberlain's time, when he used to be alerted after each of Hitler's acts of weekend aggression on an ancient upright telephone, with a rotary handle, in what used to be the butler's pantry. Chequers is linked with the Downing Street communications system with secure access to hot lines, etc., to Washington (and, a reflection of recent troubles, to the secretary of state's office in Belfast).

The service the prime minister gets would soon persuade any incoming premier who had delusions about setting up the often-advocated 'Prime Minister's Department', and I was not one of these, to think

---

[1] During the world financial crisis that followed rumours created by the German Finance Minister's careless reference to parities (see H.Wilson, *The Labour Government 1964–70* (London 1971) pp. 506–10), all the activity centred on Washington; No. 10 was the operational headquarters in London. About 11 pm a senior Treasury official asked for a call to be put through to the Economics Minister at the British Embassy in Washington, which is on the 'Hobart' exchange. He gave the number 'Hobart etc' and fifteen seconds later was put through to a bewildered Tasmanian doctor who was just finishing his breakfast.

again. Everything he could expect to create is there already to hand in the Cabinet Office. Should he pursue these illusions his first visit to Washington should put paid to them. The president – who is of course head of state as well as head of government, as a result of the decision of the founding fathers two hundred years ago[1] – can hardly move for staff. (In President Lyndon Johnson's time, I was told his staff was 2500: I understand it increased still further under President Nixon.) He is pressed on all sides for signatures, approvals, ratifications – I have seen presidents badgered to sign them in the lift, an action that must be a more or less automatic reflex. Contrast with that a *total* staff in No. 10, including private secretaries, garden room girls, the Honours and Church sections, telephone and communications operators, messengers and cleaners, of less than one hundred.

G. W. Jones, whose study, as I have said, is the best one so far written on the history and organization of Private Office, summarizes the case against a Prime Minister's Department in these words:

> 'The present system of small groups of civil service, political and personal advisers is flexible and easily adaptable to the changing requirements of a Prime Minister. If he had his own department, formal and structured, his personal power and influence might well be reduced. A department might, especially if large, develop a view and momentum of its own and even begin itself to rule. To control it the Prime Minister might have to acquire another set of private secretaries and political aides.
>
> 'The political executive of Britain is not one man but a collective entity, the Cabinet. The plural nature of the executive means that its chairman, the Prime Minister, has no real need of a department of his own to control the work of government as a whole. The reason is that British government is more cohesive, less fragmental, than a system with a single executive. The Cabinet is a force for unity. It is supported by the Cabinet Office, which is the guardian and sustainer of the collective nature of British government.'[2]

To cite the American analogy in favour of such a department is totally to misconceive our respective constitutional institutions and two hundred years of history.[3] The president is the chief executive. His cabinet is not a cabinet as we understand it: it is his instrument, as his departmental secretaries are his instruments. They act in his name. In

---

[1] See p. 171 below.
[2] Jones, op. cit., p. 37.
[3] See chapter X below on the contrast between the constitutions of the two democracies.

fact, they bear the same relationship to him that eighteenth-century functionaries bore to George III, whom the founders of the American republic thought they were supplanting, not following.

Now I turn to the pattern of a prime minister's day, with two qualifications. No two days are the same; no day ends as it began; the tidy list of six to twelve fixed engagements is not only increased; it may – and probably will – be broken into by a sudden crisis, minor or major. This could be international, parliamentary, administrative, financial or political in a party sense – not to mention a departmental problem which, on the initiative of the minister concerned, or one called in by the prime minister, becomes No. 10 business.

In 1964–70 I lived in No. 10. In 1974 I decided that I did not want to live over the shop again, and I slept each night in my home in Lord North Street, five minutes' walk from the House of Commons. Most days, after reading the morning press – two or three are delivered overnight to the prime minister's home – I would be at my desk in Downing Street at 9.30 am. Unless there was a ministerial committee due to meet under my chairmanship at that hour, I would have a quick check with Private Office to learn of any overnight developments or crises – for example a meeting of the Security Council of the UN – I had not been apprised of through a late-night or early-morning telephone call or overnight overseas telegram, and would make dispositions for the work of the day.

On Thursdays, and sometimes Tuesdays – other days more rarely – there is a Cabinet, usually lasting the greater part of the morning. On other days there will be Cabinet committees to chair, usually two, sometimes three. There may be speeches to prepare, an ambassador or high commissioner to call or a visiting president or prime minister or colleagues to see, a meeting with the appointments secretary about a vacant bishopric, deanery or lord lieutenancy. The leader of the House or chief whip might call to discuss overnight parliamentary developments or parliamentary prospects for the day or longer ahead. Boxes would normally have been done the previous night, however late that might be, as would parliamentary Questions on Monday and Wednesday nights.

Late morning – after 1.0 pm if Cabinet or a Cabinet committee had run late – I would meet with my Political Office for up-to-date political issues, arrangements for political meetings in the country or messages from party headquarters. At 1.45 or later I would have a quick lunch at the House, almost always at the table where the whips and senior ministers foregather. Depending on which back-benchers were there, informal government business would continue throughout lunch and over coffee.[1] I might ask two or three back-benchers or junior ministers from other tables to join us for coffee. After that I would usually go to the tea-room for informal chats with back-benchers or ministers, and then to the afternoon's work. In all, I probably spent more time in the members' dining room and the tea-room than any of my postwar predecessors.

On Question days I would return to my room at the House to prepare for the 3.15 pm ordeal. Usually, after that, I would return to No. 10 for a routine similar to that of the morning.

In the 1960s I extended the time for meeting back-benchers. On Tuesdays, Wednesdays and Thursdays I was available in my room, on an open-door basis, for any members or groups of members who wanted to see me. In 1974 I tried to revive this practice. It was less successful, partly because of the immensely increased work load at No. 10, which meant that I had to be back at the ranch. Another problem was that through the open door came more clearly defined groups, not only those from the Tribune or the Manifesto caucuses, but regional groups and groups concerned with individual industries, not to mention the highly articulate group concerned with members' pay, allowances and pensions.

The pattern of the day's activities could be rudely disturbed not only by a sudden crisis (including, twice in 1974–6, a hijacking), but also by overseas visits or by state visits or head of government visits from foreign or Commonwealth countries. Such visits virtually took over the day. A state visit by a president or monarch involves joining the receiving line at Victoria Station or Windsor, attending the formal royal banquet at the Palace, Windsor or perhaps Holyrood, giving a formal lunch at No. 10, sometimes a dinner at Guildhall, and almost invariably attending a return dinner given by the visiting head of state. In addition, where the head of state is also head of government, e.g. many of the African and Latin American presidencies, the prime minister is engaged in very full talks on all aspects of bilateral and international questions.

Though the hospitality is more restricted, a prime ministerial visit usually involves a full day's talks, perhaps more, and this means several hours of reading the very full and invaluable briefing on anything Whitehall wants raised, anything we expect the visitor to raise, and what to say, and what not to say, when he raises something we hope he will not raise ('defensive brief'). For really key discussions – also before international conferences, e.g. with Commonwealth heads of government, European Council (EEC Summit), NATO heads of government, Helsinki – full briefing meetings are held, of ministerial colleagues

---

[1] In Clement Attlee's day there was a large Cabinet table, by convention used only by Cabinet ministers and those who were then described as 'ministers of Cabinet rank'.

and Foreign Office and other departmental officials. The briefing for conferences also inevitably includes 'bilateral briefs' for discussions which we or the other country want to seek, or which happen socially.

Very many overseas colleagues have briefing systems similar to ours, especially in Commonwealth countries.[1]

The best impression of the pattern of the prime minister's day or week is to analyse his diary for a given period. An analysis of these for the last three months of 1975, 1 October to 31 December, covering a period that began in the middle of the party conference and ended during a brief holiday in the South-West, leads to the following tabulation:

Audiences of the Queen	8
Cabinet meetings	11
Cabinet committees	24
Other ministerial meetings	43
State visits	1
Other head of government visits	5
Other foreign VIP visits (deputy prime minister, finance, foreign ministers etc.)	8
Visits abroad	2
Visits to Northern Ireland	1
Meetings with industry, prominent industrialists etc.	28
Official meetings	27
Ministerial speeches	17
Political speeches	9
Visits within Britain	13
Official lunches and dinners	20
Political meetings – no speech	11
TV or radio broadcasts	8 (excluding party conference)

Christmas apart, I was not able to record a single private or social engagement.

Apart from pre-arranged ministerial meetings with documents circulated and written and sometimes oral briefing, each day sees a number of often unprogrammed meetings with ministers. Most days the prime minister will see the foreign and commonwealth secretary, and the chancellor. Each Friday, as already stated, I would have the informal scheduled meeting, to which reference has been made, with the leader

[1] See the account of the late Lester Pearson's amusing handling of a 'defensive brief' in Wilson, *The Labour Government 1964-70*, p. 503.

of the House, foreign and commonwealth secretary, chancellor and the chief whip, mainly to survey the progress of administrative business over the following two weeks, arrangements for Cabinet and Cabinet committee meetings. This meeting gave the opportunity for reports on the parliamentary situation and forward programme. It was not, in any sense, an 'inner Cabinet'; no policy decisions were taken, it was concerned purely with business. Usually the foreign and commonwealth secretary would stay on for a discussion of problems arising in his rather extensive diocese or to discuss diplomatic appointments; when more urgent problems arose, an *ad hoc* meeting was arranged, or if we were both in the House he would come round to my room. Similar arrangements applied with the chancellor. The lord president could even more easily drop round from the Cabinet Office whenever necessary on any parliamentary matter, including the progress of the legislative programme or the preparation of the programme for the succeeding session, as well as anything within a subject specifically remitted to him, such as arrangements for the EEC referendum and the enabling legislation, and devolution. Other ministers usually called by appointment, or one or two would stop to raise some matter after Cabinet or a Cabinet committee. Still more frequent – several each day – were meetings with the staff of Private Office and with the secretary of the Cabinet.

Formal deputations would come from the principal national organizations: the Confederation of British Industry, the Trades Union Congress, the National Farmers Union and many others. The Labour Government took office in March 1974 during a period of great anxiety in the medical profession and occupations ancillary to medicine, about salaries following stage III of the 1972–4 pay policy and associated problems of status – these anxieties increased in the next two months; accordingly on 20 May I met a deputation consisting of the Royal Colleges of Midwives and Nursing, the Association of Nurse Administrators, the National Union of Public Employees (NUPE), the Confederation of Health Service Employees, the Health Visitors Association, the National and Local Government Officers Association (NALGO), and the Managerial, Administrative, Technical and Supervisory Association (ASTMS).

When fresh concern arose about government legislation and action in connection with pay-beds and private practice, in October and December 1975, I received two deputations of the principal professional bodies, including the Royal Colleges; the British Medical Association; the Central Committee for Hospital Medical Services; the Hospital Consultants and Specialists Association; the Junior Doctors and the

British Dental Association. In all these meetings the prime minister is, of course, flanked by the ministers principally concerned.

In the week that ended with the announcement of the Government's counter-inflation policy on 11 July 1975, I called in the TUC, the CBI and the chairmen of thirty-one publicly owned industries and services. Other ministers saw the representatives of all the relevant organizations such as the local authorities and the farmers.

Sometimes the prime minister takes the initiative to invite representatives of an important profession, or group of people, to come for an informal evening meeting or dinner. In the sixties, for example, I had two such gatherings with representatives of the Church of England; and early in 1974 with representatives of the 'Charities', a convenient but inadequate description of a voluntary association of six bodies concerned with problems of poverty and deprivation, some on the domestic front (such as Help the Aged and Save the Children Fund), others with overseas countries such as War on Want and Oxfam. Their joint memorandum, based on the assertion that poverty was one single problem, home or overseas, and their determination to act on the principle of all for each and each for all, was carefully studied by departments and centrally, and response was further discussed over a working dinner at No. 10.

Working dinners at No. 10 are of course nothing new, though the phrase came into use after 1964. (This is a phrase not to be confused with 'working funerals', invented by Robert Carvel, political editor of the *Evening Standard*, after the attendance by the world's leaders at the Requiem Mass for Dr Adenauer in 1967, and much used after the memorial service for Mr Harold Holt, the Australian prime minister who was drowned, in the same year: it is now in general journalistic – if not diplomatic – use.)

Recent working dinners at No. 10 have assembled, on separate occasions, groups of leading industrialists, merchant bankers and other City leaders, and representatives of the film industry; in addition, there was a small lunch to discuss the NEB and another to consider the provision of public (or private) funds for technological innovation in industry. After March 1974, a series of 'City' dinners was arranged, alternately in No. 10 and the Governor's flat in the Bank of England, with the City representatives, including some of the younger generation, chosen by the Governor. Unfortunately, the sheer pressure of work with the economic crisis and other problems made it harder to set aside an evening in advance to follow up these extremely valuable occasions. The same demands, together with the need to settle the forward public expenditure programme in May–December 1975, led to repeated

postponement of the follow-up (proposed for Chequers) of the work
we were doing on the 'Charities' front.

Different entirely from these occasions was the use of No. 10 on behalf
of charitable organizations, which, in common with my predecessors, I
arranged very sparingly. I recall only four in nearly eight years: one
for the United Nations Association – U Thant had arranged to fly over,
but was prevented at the last minute and sent his deputy; another for
the Roundhouse ('Centre 42') in Camden Town, with whose establishment I had been much involved before becoming prime minister;
another for the Children's Theatre. In 1974–6 there was one only, for
the Attlee Memorial Foundation, to raise money for the work done for
very young deprived children in the East End, under the dedicated
direction of John Profumo.

All this and speeches too. In three months from mid-September to
mid-December 1975, I had forty-four speeches to prepare and deliver,
eighteen of them major ones, involving a great deal of research, briefing
and preparation. This excludes some seven or eight speeches each
evening during Party Conference, on the nightly tours of dinners
or receptions given by regional parties, associated organizations and
trade unions. The heaviest concentration was the forty days between
3 November (at the opening of the Forties Field) and 12 December when
there were fifteen speeches, nearly all of them major, including the Lord
Mayor's Guildhall Banquet, the main speech in the debate on the opening of the new session of Parliament and, within twenty-four hours, the
Local Government Conference at Eastbourne, the London Mayors'
Association dinner, two political speeches on the same day in Carlisle
and Newcastle, the first Blackett Memorial Lecture, the annual conference of the National Council of Social Services and my Guildhall
speech on receiving the Freedom of the City of London. The only way
I could keep going was to dictate the first draft of the speech on the
Saturday and Sunday mornings at Chequers eight to ten days ahead of
its delivery, leave it for checking and revising in Downing Street, and
approve the final draft with whatever alterations I wanted the weekend,
or night, before delivery.

I have always liked to prepare my own speeches. The transatlantic
custom of using speech-writers, recently imported into Britain for the
use of certain eminent politicians and others, is only to be deplored. If
you are to speak to the House of Commons, a party conference, the
CBI or the TUC, an important national conference or to anyone who
has issued an invitation that you have accepted, they do not want to
know whether you can read – that is assumed – they want to know what
you have to say in your own words, even if it rates only B-plus, B-minus

or lower. For that reason, for thirty years I have prepared my own speeches, sometimes writing them by hand (taking up to twenty hours), sometimes dictating; most recently preparing a full set of notes, then dictating.

No. 10 has every facility for assisting the preparation of speeches. A draft can be prepared based on a departmental brief or a set departmental speech, some of which are very good, some of which need to be redrafted in more comprehensible language, or simply to 'make it sound like me'.

I never used any drafting, or speech contributions, until the 1974 elections, when I was faced with two or three or even five and six a day, plus a hand-out for each day's press conference. New material, especially for the press conference, and basic strategic speeches I dictated. Towards the end of each election when it was a question of hammering home the salient points and issues, I weakened into having these assembled from my earlier efforts and given more direct appeal and emphasis.

At No. 10 I reverted to dictating (very occasionally writing) my speeches, both political and official. On specialized subjects, e.g. those on the National Council of Social Services and the Local Government Conference at Eastbourne, I began with a departmental brief, and suggested draft passages. Then my own draft would be dictated, followed by the processing by those concerned at No. 10, as described above. Copies were sent to the departments concerned and in all cases to the Treasury, even if it was not in the lead in the speech – or Foreign and Commonwealth Office if it had international implications – and comments, including re-drafts of any sensitive passage, required by a given time-table. I would then go through the draft, approving or rejecting the suggestions. (A note to public speakers, in all walks of life: do not let them retype with their amendments, and force you to collate their re-draft with yours: insist on having your own speech, with their suggested amendments written in. Theirs may be improvements, but don't risk any fast ones.)[1] Only one or two of the series of speeches in October–December 1975 started with a draft by others: one of those was the speech to US correspondents about American supplies of money and munitions to sustain the terrorist campaign in Northern Ireland, drafted in the No. 10 Press Office.

Political speeches, for example for party conferences, regional conferences, party and other meetings, are done by the prime minister with

[1] One day I hope to write a piece, not necessarily too serious, on the preparation of speeches: as one who for thirty years never quite knew how to begin, and who only at the end of that period began to get some glimmering about the right approach to it; it may be that others may be helped to a quicker perception.

the help of his Political Office. It would be contrary to established practice to ask civil servants, whether at No. 10 or in the departments, to prepare drafts. But increasingly, and in my view rightly, it has become normal for his draft to be circulated to the relevant departments for comment and suggestion. For through every hour of his life, the prime minister is acting as administrative head and political head of No. 10 and of the entire government machine. Every word he uses can, and should, be taken, unless he is a schizophrenic, as the official word of the head of government by everyone who studies his words at home or abroad. If it is true – or should be – that in all he does he himself never neglects the political implications of his actions, it is equally true that every word he utters in his political capacity is carefully construed by industrial, labour and financial circles at home as an act of government, and equally by the chancelleries of the wider world. Moreover, some speeches by their nature cannot be a-political even though specifically directed towards a governmental objective. No speech I made in 1974–6 had, or was designed to have, a more governmental impact than one to the annual conference of the National Union of Mineworkers at Scarborough on 7 July 1975, just four days before the announcement in Parliament of the counter-inflation policy for 1975–6. Every word I wrote, and rewrote, and the final passage that I added was based on my long association with the N U M (and their predecessor organization, the Miners Federation of Great Britain, at national and area level), and was clearly political.[1] Many observers have said that at a time when the votes seemed to be going in a way that would have made an agreed national policy an impossibility, it was a turning-point in the battle against inflation.

Standing on 'the peaks of both politics and administration', as G. W. Jones has said,[2] any modern prime minister, unless he seeks to be a political eunuch, gives primary attention, by whatever means seem appropriate, to his political advice within No. 10: this is over and above anything he receives from his own party organization, and his parliamentary party. He must also ensure a continuing relationship with the party machine at party headquarters, and with the members of his party in the House of Commons.

[1] 'It is now *Labour's* Prime Minister, your Prime Minister, at a critical hour in the nation's history, enjoining this community, once again, to assert loyalty *for* the nation. It is not so much a question of whether that loyalty, that response, will be forthcoming in sufficient measure to save this Labour Government. The issue now is not whether this or any other democratic socialist government can survive and lead this nation to full employment and a greater measure of social justice. It is whether any government *so* constituted, *so* dedicated to the principles of consent and consensus within our democracy, can lead this nation.'

[2] Jones, op. cit., p. 14.

All prime ministers do it, though it is a law of nature that Conservative prime ministers do not receive, or suffer, press comment on it, while Labour prime ministers can count on almost daily animadversing on the subject, even though they are adopting the practice of Conservative predecessors; and as for those they appoint to the Political Office, God help them.

I have recorded that Harold Macmillan was the first for twenty years to insert a political appointee into Private Office,[1] in the same role as the other private secretaries, all of whom, like their predecessors for a generation past, were civil servants. This was not criticized by the press of the time; it was excused by the fact that, being a dollar-a-year man, he was not in receipt of public funds. Nor have the staff of successive prime ministerial political offices, but they have not gone into Private Office proper. Both Edward Heath and I, in the sixties and early seventies introduced outside economists who had worked with us in opposition; they were employed in the Cabinet Office. The system of political advisers – the Policy Unit – has now supplanted that practice. In fact, no member of my Political Office ever had access to classified documents. That was not the case with the appointees of Harold Macmillan or Edward Heath. Yet unremitting press comments, including unwarrantable invasions of personal and family privacy, have been addressed, uniquely, to my appointees.

The Policy Unit – and the corresponding appointments by departmental ministers – was the right solution, following the recommendations of the Fulton Report; it was based on the recruitment in specific fields of government of persons qualified and recognized in their particular disciplines, but with political affinities to the party of government — most of them were experts who advised the incoming government when the party was in opposition. But this is no substitute for the Political Office. Their roles are entirely different. First, the prime minister has a constituency. He must have the means of maintaining personal contact, not only with every constituent who approaches him by letter or at 'surgeries' (advice sessions), but with his agent, his local authorities, whatever their political control, and local officials, as well as local industrial, social and charitable organizations.

Second, he needs a continuing, almost daily, relationship with the back-bench members of his parliamentary party – and with them one must include junior ministers, who in administrative terms have only limited access to the prime minister, since in governmental matters they normally act through their ministerial chief. But in their political

[1] Lord Wyndham.

capacity they have much to contribute, and the prime minister cannot afford – nor would he wish – to discount that contribution.

Third, he needs to maintain an intimate and continuing relationship with his party – the general secretary, other officials, his colleagues on the governing body of the party, and regional and constituency officials all over the country. This includes a great deal of consultation in the months preceding the annual Party Conference.

Fourth, there is his contact with supporters of his party all over the country, elected representatives, particularly local councillors, officers of constituency and local parties and local branches of trade unions affiliated locally and approaching him in that context. His post-box will include hundreds of letters a week from self-identifying officials or members of local organizations of his party.

Fifth, there are individuals, many of them held in great esteem in almost every walk of life – for example the arts and entertainment – who are passionately loyal to the prime minister and his party and whose ideas and experience should be welcomed and used.

Mr G. W. Jones, in his perceptive understanding of the prime minister's dual political and administrative role – and an average prime minister's inability ever entirely to separate them – includes in his monograph on the No. 10 secretariat an interesting section headed 'The Search for Political Assistants'.[1]

After reviewing the Lloyd George 'Garden Suburb' and the political reactions of Stanley Baldwin and Ramsay MacDonald, he records Neville Chamberlain's reliance on Horace Wilson (as political a civil servant as one will find) and Mr Churchill's political – or at least personal – team.[2] He records the limited but clearly political advisers appointed by Clement Attlee, and Harold Macmillan's Wyndham appointment. While the Churchill and Macmillan appointees inevitably had the same access to secret and top-secret documents as any civil servant appointee, which my own small separate political secretariat did not have, more thousands of acres of Swedish and British Columbian forests have been devastated to provide the newsprint for comment on my political secretariat, and everything that could be dug up about their social engagements, than was deployed on all the appointments made by every Establishment prime minister, back to the Duke of Newcastle, not excluding the Rockingham Whigs.

What I had was loyalty, the political advice that every prime minister

[1] Jones, op. cit., pp. 34–6.
[2] Winston Churchill had been obsecrated in the 1930s, notably by the second-rate team of Neville Chamberlain, broadly corresponding to the then Conservative Establishment; his own No. 10 team comprised a number of those who had been loyal to him in the dark years, personal, but no less political.

needs to counter civil service and departmental ministers' pressure, advice inspired by the closest contact with party feeling, from Transport House level right through the party in the country – with continuing Parliamentary Labour Party contact throughout. The political secretariat, in particular, maintained close relations with the press department of Transport House, made the more effective by personal relations over many years. The prime minister's speeches on party occasions are not issued to the press through the Government Information Service or No. 10 Press Office, though these have access to the material should they receive inquiries from the overseas press. This is essential, for the prime minister, being a composite being, political and administrative, cannot utter a word that is not that of the head of the British Government. For that reason they see, comment on and suggest revisions on speeches on party occasions, which are issued to the press by the Labour Party Press Department.

The Press Office is a relatively new creation in No. 10. The Private Office of bygone years was responsible for press relations, and those prime ministers who made quasi-personal appointments sometimes did so in order to ensure that press relations were covered by one of the private secretaries able to represent the political and above all personal views of the prime minister.[1] They had full access to classified documents. The first recorded as having specific press responsibilities was Sir William Sutherland, in the Lloyd George Administration. George Steward was seconded from the Foreign Office News Department in 1931, as the first press officer serving No. 10 and the Treasury, working from the area of the present Press Office. In 1937 he was appointed chief press liaison officer, HM Government, still working from No. 10. James Margash refers to his appointment in an article reviewing, on his retirement, forty-eight years in journalism: 'Prime Ministers and I', *Sunday Times* (9 May 1976). He comments that this and similar appointments made it more difficult for an enterprising journalist to get stories – for example, on asking Steward about Neville Chamberlain's Deeside fishing plans, he was told to await the official announcement.

No. 10 is not part of the Cabinet Office. Departmentally, it is under the Civil Service Department, and all the staff are on the establishment of CSD for 'pay and rations', as well as being directly concerned with all those duties of the prime minister that relate to his position as minister for the Civil Service, including civil service and many other public appointments. But by far the highest proportion of the work of No. 10 is done in the most intimate connection with the Cabinet Office.

[1] Jones, op. cit., p. 15.

The Cabinet Office is next door to No. 10, and though its main entrance is in Whitehall, the two offices are linked by a corridor and a flight of steps. The secretary of the Cabinet walks through many times a day, not only for Cabinet and other set meetings, but for talks with the prime minister or with Private Office.

The Times 'Profile', headed 'A magnificent piece of powerful bureaucratic machinery'[1], includes a photograph of Sir John Hunt, secretary of the Cabinet and head of Office, with the caption 'A sentinel guarding the corridor linking the Cabinet Office and Number 10 Downing Street'. The comment is as justified as the high praise in the same article describing it as 'the magnificent Rolls-Royce that is the Cabinet Office machinery'.

The history of the Cabinet Office has been summarized in the previous chapter; its progressive development, and rapidly increasing efficiency, particularly in the sixties and seventies has been noted.[2] When it was formed it brought, in the words of Sir George Mallaby, a degree of 'indispensable articulation' to the machinery of government.

The secretary of the Cabinet, once appointed, is permanent until his retirement. He is selected from the very best in the Civil Service. His deputy secretaries, under-, and assistant secretaries and others are usually there on a roughly two-year secondment from their departments. This is deliberate Cabinet Office practice, to avoid any tendency to create a 'Cabinet Office view', still less a 'Cabinet Office policy'. The purpose of the Cabinet Office is to make Cabinet government work, not to be an *imperium in imperio*. It services the Cabinet, discusses the forward programme of the Cabinet with the prime minister, including, where appropriate, the consideration in the first instance of specific issues and papers in the relevant Cabinet committee – or a Chequers 'contemplative' meeting. In addition to the Friday morning meetings covering the succeeding fortnight, other time-tables are worked out for a month or more ahead, and sometimes speeded up. In major questions like public expenditure or the time-table for E E C negotiations and the referendum, the planning is for six or nine months ahead.

With a sudden crisis, or a specially urgent and important issue such as the negotiation of the counter-inflation policy in June–July 1975, the most detailed programme is set out. The key date was the Mineworkers' Conference at Scarborough, with my speech on Monday 7 July (see p. 90 above). This included a key meeting of the special sub-committee of ministers immediately before that weekend; considera-

---

[1] *The Times* (8 March 1976).
[2] See also J. R. Starr, 'The English Cabinet Secretariat', *American Political Science Review* (May 1928) and H. Craik, 'The Cabinet Secretariat', *Nineteenth Century* (June 1922).

tion by the TUC Economic Committee on the Monday morning: preparation of an outline of the draft White Paper by officials and consideration of it by the relevant ministers, later by me on returning from the NUM; further meetings on the Tuesday between ministers and the TUC and of ministers that evening on my return from Edinburgh;[1] the meeting of the General Council of the TUC on the Wednesday morning and the special meeting of the National Economic Development Council (Neddy) in the afternoon, followed by ministerial consideration of the draft White Paper; the full Cabinet meeting on the Thursday to approve it, followed by further consultations my colleagues and I had with the TUC, CBI and the thirty-one chairmen of publicly owned industries and services. Late on Thursday evening I had to dictate the draft of my statement to Parliament for the following morning at 11.0 when the White Paper was laid before Parliament: after well over an hour's questioning by MPs a mass, open, on-the-record press conference followed and radio and television broadcasts.

The Cabinet Office also regularly reviews Cabinet procedures, such as a Chequers suggestion that the whole of the Government's social services expenditure should be looked at from time to time, rather in the manner of a defence review, to assess the balance of the various programmes and identify priorities.

Reforms introduced by Edward Heath have contributed greatly to its effectiveness. In addition to establishing the Central Policy Review Staff (the Think Tank), a project that was being worked up before Labour left office in 1970, and showing inspiration in the appointment of its first head, he initiated the practice of the Cabinet Office Units, which has been developed since.[2] When the Conservative Government's negotiations for entry into EEC began, the Prime Minister decided to centralize their planning and conduct in the Cabinet Office by setting up a 'Europe Unit' under a 'second permanent secretary', with the relevant departments interlocking through a network of interdepartmental ministerial and official committees. This decision was not only right administratively; it showed great wisdom in political terms. A number of departments, such as Agriculture, Energy, Trade and Industry (as it then was), Employment, Health and Social Services, while

---

[1] My time-table was complicated by the state visit of the King of Norway, who arrived in Edinburgh on the Tuesday morning. I had hoped to fly on from Scarborough to Edinburgh but had to return for key meetings on the Monday night: I flew to Edinburgh early on the Tuesday, and after the morning's ceremonies had an audience of the Queen at Holyrood and a meeting in Edinburgh, before my return to London.

[2] Not to be confused with the No. 10 Policy Unit, which consists of outside advisers on temporary secondment to Government (see below); the Cabinet Office Unit consists of regular civil servants, mostly seconded from their own departments.

committed by Cabinet decision and (usually) departmental conviction to seek success in the negotiations, might well have suspicions about Foreign Office leadership, as the FO was believed to desire entry, on international grounds, almost at any cost, while there were important economic interests to be preserved which were of high priority in the minds of the ministers and departments concerned. Moreover, Edward Heath had appointed a non-departmental minister, Geoffrey Rippon (as chancellor of the Duchy of Lancaster), to carry the main weight of the negotiations, and he needed central co-ordination of the briefing material covering all relevant departments.

The Labour Government, for the 're-negotiation' of the terms of entry, continued with this machinery, including the Cabinet Office Unit. In 1974, a further unit was added, again under a second permanent secretary, to co-ordinate the work on the vast implications of the manifesto commitment on devolution. Edward Short, lord president and leader of the House, was put in ministerial charge, with a minister of state to assist him. With the government changes in April 1976, James Callaghan appointed Michael Foot as lord president, with the continued responsibility for devolution.

The prime minister's responsibility for relations with the Cabinet Office is well described by G. W. Jones.[1] 'As chairman of the Cabinet the Prime Minister is particularly close to the Cabinet Office; he is in a sense the director of its work, but it is not his department since it serves the whole Cabinet.' This is true. The secretary of the Cabinet is, in a sense, the 'prime minister's permanent secretary', to use a phrase of the present Secretary's predecessor on handing me my first brief in 1964; but his loyalty is, no less, to Cabinet and the doctrine of Cabinet government. Were any prime minister – and in my view this is inconceivable – to seek to change the conventions and challenge the concept of Cabinet government in a major sense, as Richard Crossman believed, as a step to some form of unconstitutional personal rule, he would find not only his Cabinet, but the whole of Whitehall against him, and rightly.

Within that clear setting, the secretary of the Cabinet, as already made clear, does brief the prime minister for meetings of Cabinet and Cabinet committees, and in recent years his staff has provided a similar service for the lord president, who has no department in the real sense.[2]

---

[1] Jones, op. cit., p. 36.

[2] This goes some way to redress the fundamental weakness of a non-departmental minister's position. I remember in 1946 Aneurin Bevan prophesying to me that Herbert Morrison's power and influence would decline because he had no department behind him.

He advises also on the practices and conventions about the conduct of ministers in relation to collective Cabinet responsibility, as well as on other matters affecting collective responsibility and loyalty, such as the issues raised therefore by the Crossman memoirs, and the consideration of these issues by the Radcliffe Committee of Privy Councillors.[1]

The establishment of the Central Policy Review Staff, on which planning had been continuing for some time before the 1970 election, was announced by Edward Heath in a White Paper, *The Reorganization of Central Government*,[2] laid before Parliament in October 1970. The need for it was explained by the fact that existing inter-departmental committees, concerned with specific areas of policy, needed to be reinforced by a clear definition of government policy as a whole, a framework within which government policies could be more effectively formulated.

'For lack of such a clear definition of strategic purpose and under the pressures of the day to day problems immediately before them, governments are always at some risk of losing sight of the need to consider the totality of their current policies in relation to their longer-term objectives; and they may pay too little attention to the difficult, but critical, task of evaluating as objectively as possible the alternative policy option and priorities open to them.'[3]

Stating their intention to proceed gradually to what they had in mind, they proposed '. . . to begin by establishing a small multi-disciplinary central policy review staff in the Cabinet Office'. Edward Heath made a first-class appointment in Lord Rothschild, and the quality of the top appointment was reflected in those lower down. Before long the four-word title was upgraded by the use of capital letters; in common use they have almost invariably been known as the 'Think Tank'. They have remained small, with a total staff of about sixteen, consisting of both Civil Service 'fliers' and recruits from business and the universities, on the basis mainly of short-term appointments. They are adequately provided with money to commission research by outside consultants and expert bodies. Experience with two successive governments of different parties suggests that they have come to stay, an integral part of the decision-making centre of government.

Their work closely follows the White Paper remit: they stand aside

---

The reference earlier (p. 22) to the successful attack by other ministers to prevent him from becoming an economic supremo has a bearing on this. Hugh Dalton, on returning to office in June 1948 as chancellor of the Duchy of Lancaster, expressed similar anxieties to me, when he asked me to release a Board of Trade under-secretary to run his mini-office.

[1] See pp. 72–6 above.

[2] E. Heath, *The Reorganization of Central Government*, Cmnd 4506 (London 1970).

[3] ibid., paras 45–6.

from day-to-day in-fighting and departmental issues – though their head was involved in the Chrysler crisis – and their reports are utterly fearless, related to strategy and singularly unworried about upsetting Establishment views or producing conclusions extremely unpopular with those who commission them.

In addition to their main reports, some of which are very long-term in concept, and often long-time in production, they are involved in the work of many inter-departmental committees, especially those operating at top level. On short-term problems and those requiring rapid decision, they have acquired the facility of putting the central issues with greater brevity than has been known in Whitehall for many years. The incoming Labour Government from March 1974 onwards encouraged them to publish certain reports for public discussion – to the time of writing the reports on *Energy Conservation* (July 1974), *Joint Framework for Social Policies* (June 1975) and *The Future of the British Car Industry* (September 1975) have been laid before Parliament.[1]

The Policy Unit represents a different concept. The appointment of 'policy advisers' to No. 10 and the Cabinet Office, and to a number of departments, is for entirely different purposes. The Fulton Report on the Civil Service[2] recommended a

'. . . practice whereby Ministers make a small number of temporary appointments. We think it important that Ministers should be free to arrange for the holders of such appointments to be closely associated with the work of the many "official" committees (i.e. committees of civil servants without ministerial members) which make essential contributions to policy making: the work of these committees places heavy responsibilities on civil servants to ensure that the choices subsequently presented to Ministers are not unduly proscribed.'

Reference has been made to Edward Heath's political appointments, some of whom were integrated into the official machine as full-time, though temporary, civil servants. The incoming Labour Government in 1974 regularized the position by treating them as a special category of 'political advisers'. Some thirty were authorized, spread round fifteen departments, some senior ministers having one, others two, three or in one case four. At No. 10 a special Policy Unit of around seven was set up, primarily specialists in economic, industrial and social policy –

---

[1] For a fuller account see the evidence placed before the Select Committee on Science and Technology: Science Sub-Committee, and the interim summing-up by Lord Rothschild in the *Israel Sieff Memorial Lecture* (PEP, London, April 1976).

[2] *The Civil Service. Report of the Committee*, Cmnd 3638 (London, June 1968), I, p. 45, para. 129 and p. 94, para. 285.

mainly recruited from the universities, but one from industry and one from social work.

Before the Commonwealth Prime Ministers' Meeting in Jamaica of April–May 1975, I was urged by other national leaders to make a statement on this innovation, and the host chairman put it on the agenda. The statement I made and circulated caused a great deal of interest, and a number of prime ministers on their way home through London visited the Cabinet Office for talks with the secretariat and with members of the Policy Unit. What I think impressed them was the statement that 'most regular senior civil servants', who might have been wary of the idea, 'have openly welcomed the experiment and are co-operating to make it a success'.

The Appendix, Note V, sets out the terms of my statement to the Jamaica Conference.

Reference was made in the previous chapter to ministerial committees of Cabinet, and, in the short sketch of the machinery for the counter-inflation policy, to inter-departmental work by officials.

In modern government this is essential, if ministers are not to be even more seriously over-worked, and if adequate preparation is to be given to all material coming up for final decision. Official committees were created on a considerable scale[1] in World War II, and by successive governments ever since. Increasingly, in peacetime, they came to be exclusively serviced by the Cabinet Office.

In the early sixties, with the impact of the Korean War on the economy, through soaring commodity prices and the resulting effect on the balance of payments, a new and tighter approach to economic policy became necessary. The Treasury took the lead in setting up official inter-departmental committees, some at permanent-secretary level.

Ministers in all governments are sometimes a little worried by this, because they fear that their officials tend to develop inter-departmental loyalties, and even commit their departments (especially if representation is at a high official level) without ministerial authority. It is a serious problem. Inter-departmental committees of this kind cannot make real progress if every department seeks to block agreement, or

---

[1] They tended to be serviced partly by the Cabinet Office, partly by the department principally responsible. For example, when I was in the Cabinet Office secretariat in Richmond Terrace, I was secretary of two official committees (one of which, however, was chaired by a departmental junior minister, both had a joint-secretary coming from the Ministry of Labour). After I moved to head a section in a department, I was the departmental joint-secretary, sharing the work with a representative of the Cabinet Office. After 1943, the non-departmental joint-secretary to such committees tended to be appointed by the newly created Ministry of Production, which was an overlord department with no direct administrative duties. By Clement Attlee's time such duties reverted to the Cabinet Office.

even to enter departmental reservations at every stage: they cannot function on the basis of the lowest common denominator. On the other hand, a collective decision, or line of policy, can be thought to weaken the power of the departments, and particularly the minister, to oppose the recommendations, not merely on departmental grounds, but on general grounds, perhaps broad political grounds. Take, for example, prices and incomes policy which has been a persistent theme of successive governments since the days of Sir Stafford Cripps in the late forties; which led to Selwyn Lloyd's 'guiding light' and the establishment of Neddy; to Labour's statutory policy and the creation of the National Board for Prices and Incomes, Edward Heath's three-stage statutory control, and Labour's 1975 counter-inflation policy. At all stages official committees were required to prepare options for ministers, and in particular to identify specific pay or price problems arising out of the complicated pay arrangements in different industries and crafts, and such thorny price control problems as stock appreciation and provision for new investment. Yet in these committees under successive governments there were undoubtedly civil servants working as a team, some of whose ministers might be standing ready to oppose the whole concept of control.

As a departmental minister, I had the problem in the post-Korean situation more than a quarter of a century ago. My Permanent Secretary in the Board of Trade was one of the heavyweights of Whitehall; indeed, the Treasury were trying to poach him to come as second permanent secretary. His views were needed, and were listened to. Officials had to produce a viable policy, not a hotch-potch of individual views. I raised the problem with him, and we had no difficulty in reaching a solution. He was convinced that the new system had come to stay: he recommended that he should attend in a non-departmental capacity – as a 'wise man' – helping them to reach a conclusion, but on the basis that he would in no way be regarded as committing his president, or even his departmental subordinates. Indeed, he would feed his experience into the committee, and would on the basis of his knowledge of a number of departments (including many years in the Treasury) warn the committee if it was getting into the hands of theorists. We agreed on two propositions: . . . first, he would make it clear, and suggest that others similarly placed should also do so, that he was operating there as an expert and experienced adviser, and was in no way committing his minister or his departmental officials: second, he undertook to keep me fully informed on the way these crucial committees were working and, in particular, to draw to my attention any implications for our own Department, or, more widely, any policy implications or matters where he knew I had strong views going very wide of the preoccupations of our own Department.

The present practice is more sophisticated. Officials represent their departments but are expected to co-operate to the full, e.g. in providing information. They are *not* expected to consult their ministers and get clearance on every question that might come up – or the committees would never get under way. The committees are instructed to get agreement as far as possible on the facts, to prepare material for ministers and to identify options.[1] They do not enjoy any delegated authority, except in those cases where Cabinet, or a ministerial committee, has reached decision in principle, or is near to doing so, and has asked for more detailed work to be done, perhaps the preparation of a parliamentary statement or White Paper, for the consideration of ministers. It is fully understood that they are not in any way speaking for, still less binding, their minister or prejudicing his position in Cabinet or other collective meetings. When something of considerable importance is being studied, particularly if it is the kind of subject that can develop its momentum, they use their discretion in keeping their minister informed, without committing him by doing so.

Committees, ministerial and official, come and go. Some have a specific remit and end when it is fulfilled. For others, it is always a nice point of timing to decide when they can be stood down. Others can remain dormant, to be revived if their special subject again becomes urgent.

What is true of the inter-departmental committee system can be true of the allocation of departmental duties. Departments come and go. Where are the Ministries of Home Security, Aviation, Shipping, Works, Town and Country Planning and the DEA of yesteryear?

Such changes in the machinery of government, in addition to being necessary as priorities change, have a real fascination for some civil servants and ministers, and in the case of prime ministers are almost a temptation.[2]

Different prime ministers are exercised by different priorities: so are

[1] The system of 'identifying' options has become one of the major developments of recent years, and characterizes the work of committees serviced by the Cabinet Office just as much as it does that of the Think Tank. In the immediate postwar years my experience of the system was that *either*, say, three options were identified, the first two clearly unacceptable, pointing the way to the third (usually that of the Treasury); *or* the options were limited by the purposive exclusion of one or more which might have appealed to the Cabinet of the day, but which flouted departmental doctrine.

[2] For a full treatment of this subject, and the rationale of departmental reorganization, see Sir Richard Clarke, 'The Machinery of Government', in W. Thornhill (ed.), *The Modernization of British Government* (London 1975) pp. 63–96. Sir Richard was in fact the permanent secretary of the Ministry of Technology at the time of its absorption of the Ministry of Power.

problems. Administrative fashions change too: there was, in the late sixties and early seventies, a philosophy of big departments, the better to co-ordinate related subjects. It was in my view right, for example, for me to set up in 1964 the Ministry of Overseas Development, in 1969 to merge the then Ministries of Technology (in effect the Industry Ministry), the industrial division of the Board of Trade and the Ministry of Power, and also to announce plans for bringing the housing, local government and planning functions of the Ministry of Housing and Local Government together with the Ministry of Transport.[1]

It was equally right, during the oil crisis, and a threatened crisis in energy supply generally, for Edward Heath to set up the Energy Ministry in 1973 for which indeed we on the Opposition benches were pressing. It is also right for the prime minister to give a junior minister in a large department special responsibilities, virtually to name him as minister for a single subject. In 1964 I created such ministries at minister of state or parliamentary secretary level for the arts, for sport, for industrial training and for higher education, and, in the Foreign Office, for disarmament: again, in 1974, for the disabled, and for particular aspects of devolution.

The same argument applies in the overseas field. When Labour came into office in 1964, there were separate departments and secretaries of state for foreign affairs, commonwealth affairs and the colonies. We had a big programme of granting self-government to dependencies, following a process initiated by Clement Attlee in 1947 with India, Pakistan, Burma and Ceylon, and carried out with determination also by the Conservatives in 1951–64. Tony Greenwood, as secretary of state for the colonies, was given a mandate 'to work himself out of a job' – the Colonial Office was merged with the Commonwealth Office in 1967. For a long time I had it in mind to merge the enlarged Commonwealth Office with the Foreign Office, and as soon as George Brown resigned from the Foreign Office in March 1968 this was announced.

There is a bigger problem in major transfers of functions between departments, and great problems of administrative philosophy underlying it. One thing is certain: whatever is decided will be wrong – it is a choice of evils. If the prime minister, advised by the Civil Service Department, decides that higher education must go with schools, and the whole range of education with science, then either technology has to be separated from industry and brought into the enlarged Department of Education, or technology goes into the Ministry of Industry, whatever its name, and is separated from pure science.[2] Whatever is

[1] See H.Wilson, *The Labour Government, 1964–70*, pp. 708–14.
[2] See H.Wilson, (Patrick) *Blackett Memorial Lecture* (3 December 1975), reprinted and

done will be open to sincere and informed criticism, and no prime minister can be sure he has got it right.

Over-simplifying, I have tried to rationalize the subject by distinguishing between what I call horizontal versus vertical grouping. 'Over-simplifying', because that is to describe the problem two-dimensionally when there are three, possibly four or even an infinity of dimensions.

I developed this thesis in a speech to the annual luncheon of the Parliamentary and Scientific Committee (a mixed body of parliamentarians, scientists and industrialists) on 11 February 1976:

'. . . when I first had to decide these matters, on taking office in 1964, we had a Ministry of Aviation. This logically incorporated the civil aviation function responsibility of commercial aviation authorities – the men who fly planes – and aircraft production. It was logical that they should be in the same Ministry. More than that, it ensured that any argument among those who bought the planes and those who made them, had to be decided by a single minister.

'But the argument on the other hand was that there was a strong case for linking the airlines with shipping, and with tourism.

'There was a no less strong argument for linking the production of highly sophisticated aircraft with avionics generally, the production of missiles and other associated electronic industries.

'There was a similar problem in connection with shipping and shipbuilding.

'There is a strong argument for having the officials sponsoring the companies responsible for *ordering* ships and the companies responsible for building ships in the same Department under the same Minister. But, as I have said, there is an equally strong argument for putting shipping services with aviation services. There is an even stronger argument for putting shipbuilding with other heavy engineering industries, including chemical engineering – the boilermakers' union, once heavily concentrated on the shipyards, now has far more members engaged on chemical plants.'

The same argument justified the transfer of responsibility for the steel industry from Power to Technology, bringing steel production under the same department as the steel-using industry.

Decision on the transfer of functions between departments do not end here: the ministerial dispositions and those of high officials have still to be made, including the decision in a super-department whether, for

published by the Imperial College of Science and Technology (London 1976) on this and associated points.

both administrative and political reasons, there should be dual representation in the Cabinet and a second permanent secretary at official level. The decision here has to take account of any possible aggrievement on the part of industrial organizations who, before the merger, perhaps for very many years, had 'their own department'.[1]

In all these matters a great deal depends on the advice of the head of the Civil Service and the permanent secretaries involved. When I proposed the merger of Technology and Power, they took the plan away for study. They then reported that, while it would create many difficulties, it would have great advantages, and that they 'regarded it as a challenge'. They quickly came up with detailed proposals, and the plan went through. The decision to 'hive-off' what became the new Department of Energy, in 1973, which the Labour Opposition was pressing on the then Government in the autumn of that year, did not represent second thoughts: it was a response to the transformation in the world oil and energy situation caused by the oil crisis following the Yom Kippur war.

In addition to the Technology–Power merger, and the arrangements leading to the creation of the Department of the Environment, I put the Ministries of Health and of Social Services into a new combined department under Richard Crossman, as secretary of state. The officials mainly concerned with the machinery of government told me that, looking back on it, a wiser decision might have been to amalgamate the social services with the Home Office because of the latter's social responsibilities, for example the care of children, delinquency, and the task they had just been given of co-ordinating the urban programme, which I announced in 1968.

This chapter has dealt mainly with the prime minister in his official surroundings. It seems appropriate to add to what others have said about the prime requisites for a prime minister. Reference has been made to keeping in touch with party and people – what it is now fashionable to call two-way communication.

At home and abroad I have repeatedly been asked what are the main essentials of a successful prime minister. Over and above communication and vigilance, there are two factors I have always mentioned. They are sleep, and a sense of history. In a BBC interview with Douglas Stuart on 16 April 1975, and again in a BBC World Service interview

[1] When the Ministry of Power (established 1942 with the semi-autonomous Mines Department of the Board of Trade going back far beyond that) was merged into the Ministry of Technology (now the Department of Industry) I contacted the President of the National Union of Mineworkers, to explain it to him, on the Sunday evening before the announcement.

at Chequers for my sixtieth birthday (less than a week before I announced my impending resignation), I was asked about these things.

Douglas Stuart quoted President Lyndon Johnson's references to the 'pressure of the telephone . . . the battery of telephones by his bed in the White House'. I described a visit there whereby, judiciously sleeping in 'British sleep-time' over the Atlantic (10.30 pm BST–5.30 pm Washington time) followed by sleeping on in Washington to 8.00 am Washington time, I had $11\frac{1}{2}$ hours sleep, and found that the President had had $1\frac{1}{2}$.

> 'I believe the biggest asset a Prime Minister can have is the ability to sleep – a good night's sleep – 8 hours' sleep when I can get it . . . you have got to be able to sleep – a statesman who can't sleep is no good. I remember there was one famous Prime Minister, Lord Rosebery, who spent two years here, couldn't sleep. So he went.'[1]

In the programme in March 1976 at Chequers I answered a question about pressures:

> '. . . the answer to pressure is sleep. My problem is waking up. But I have no problem sleeping. I have never had a sleeping pill in No. 10. I have never needed one. I can sleep and the other evening I was coming out to Chequers and the driver said "You are at Chequers now" – I had slept all the way from Marble Arch in London without intending to.
>
> [*Interviewer:*] Which is about 35 miles?
>
> [*Answer:*] Yes, an hour, an hour's sleep. I can sleep anywhere. I can do it at command if I want to. Winston Churchill could do that.'[2]

On the sense of history Douglas Stuart asked:

> 'But here . . . in this house with its tremendous traditions in it the fact that you have to go to the House of Commons for business and things do you feel yourself hemmed in by the traditions of the past?'[3]

I replied:

> 'I like to think I do. I think that unless you have a sense of history, and of tradition, and of the people who have been here, you can't even apply yourself to the problems of the present. That's why I think some of the greatest statesmen of all parties, in this country and abroad – one thinks of Kennedy in America for example and

[1] BBC World Service broadcast (11 March 1976).
[2] ibid.   [3] Douglas Stuart, 16 April 1975.

Roosevelt, as well as Churchill, Attlee, Harold Macmillan – irrespective of party, they had a great sense of history. Partly to put things in perspective – you know, when you read in the papers, if you have ever been politically dead by lunchtime and even worse by nightfall – well you know, others have been through it before you and you can get a sense of perspective – it doesn't mean you can't take it seriously. But a sense of history – and very often you can get analogies from history – of past wars, of past diplomatic negotiations, of past economic situations.

'*Without a sense of history, a Prime Minister would be blind.*'

V

First Lord of the Treasury

An Hon. Member asked the Prime Minister how he proposes to discharge his duties as First Lord of the Treasury. The Prime Minister (Mr Callaghan): 'Punctiliously.'[1]

The first lordship of the Treasury is not entirely a sinecure. Its holder is the senior of the Lords Commissioners of the Treasury. Until the administration is appointed, including the Lords Commissioners of the Treasury, only he and the chancellor have any being as commissioners, and this meant, on the nights of 18 October 1964 and 4 March 1974, our being presented with most formidable-looking Treasury documents to sign.

There has been some parliamentary interest in the functions of the first lord. On 25 June 1974, in my absence, the then Lord President gave a brief reply.[2] A longer résumé was given by Reginald Maudling (standing in for Edward Heath) on 19 January 1971.[3] The opening answer referred to a statement circulated with the Official Report.

'1. The First Lord of the Treasury is one of the Lords Commissioners of the Treasury and may act as such in the exercise of any of the functions of the Treasury, but does not normally do so. Under Section 2 of the Ministers of the Crown Act, 1964, it is the First Lord of the Treasury who determines the annual salary of the Chief Secretary to the Treasury and all holders of the office of Minister of State.

'2. The First Lord of the Treasury exercises certain powers of patronage. He tenders advice to the Sovereign on appointment to

[1] *Hansard* (13 April 1976), col. 440 (written).
[2] *Hansard* (25 June 1974), col. 407 (written).
[3] *Hansard* (19 January 1971), cols 719–21; the circulated statement is in col. 721.

the Crown livings in the Church of England. The appointments of trustees (and director) of certain museums and galleries are made by the Board of Treasury on the First Lord's recommendation. These are the National Gallery, the National Portrait Gallery, the Tate Gallery, the Wallace Collection, the London Museum, the Imperial War Museum and the National Maritime Museum. Similarly, the First Lord recommends for appointment by the Board of Treasury the chairman and members of the Standing Commission on Museums and Galleries.

'3. In addition, the First Lord is an ex-officio trustee of the Duke of Wellington's Parliamentary Estates, an ex-officio trustee of the Hunterian Collection, an ex-officio member of the Royal Commission for the Exhibition of 1851, an ex-officio Church Commissioner and an ex-officio trustee of the Duke of Grafton's Prisage Fund.'

The principal duties, then, are those of making appointments, and acting as an *ex officio* trustee.

So far as church appointments are concerned, the first lord is responsible only for advice to the sovereign on crown livings. The duty of making recommendations to the Crown on bishoprics, deaneries, canonries and others lies on the prime minister as such. It might, however, be convenient to refer to all ecclesiastical appointments together at this point, as well as the wider question of advice on appointments generally.

The prime minister has the duty of making recommendations to the Queen on church appointments. This was always a matter to which I gave the most careful consideration. But that was not all: I came to look forward, when ploughing through a succession of weekend boxes, to identifying the modest files from the No. 10 appointments secretary. For an hour or more, work on this was an oasis of peace: the appointment might be to a crown living, a deanery or canonry, a bishopric or archbishopric. The papers were always carefully prepared after the fullest consultations in the area concerned. The No. 10 secretary works closely with the archbishop's advisers; if the vacancy to be filled is at episcopal level both of them are fully seized of the views of clergy and laity in the diocese, through the operation of the 'Vacancy in See' committee. Inquiries and consultations in a small rural parish where the living is in the gift of the Crown are no less thorough.

The twenty-five months from March 1974 to April 1976 was a very busy period for top church appointments: it would be interesting to see how far back one had to go in history to find, in so short a period, recommendations from Downing Street to the Queen for the appointment of the two archbishops, Canterbury and York, the deaneries of Westminster – particularly delicate, the Abbey being a 'royal peculiar' – and York, with consequent effects on other appointments, and eleven diocesan bishoprics.[1] On the archbishoprics, the prime minister, in addition to receiving his appointments secretary's advice after painstaking inquiries, naturally consults the archbishops in post, and receives a considerable correspondence from all levels in the Church, from the episcopal bench to the no less sincere advice of parish priests and the laity. All this advice is carefully studied.[2]

On recommendations concerning diocesan bishops, the views of the archbishops are sought and perhaps discussed with them in person. Clergy and laity in the diocese have every facility for making their views known.

The procedure for suffragan bishops is different. By long tradition the submission to the prime minister, and ultimately to the Queen, includes two names, A and B, with the recommendation that the choice falls upon A. I once asked how long this has been the tradition, and was told that it is statutory and goes back to the reign of Henry VIII. When his then Majesty broke with Rome, the appointment of bishops fell absolutely to the Crown. The sovereign appointed the diocesan bishops, but, in accordance with the provisions of a statute of 1534,[3] suffragans were appointed on the basis of a submission to the King with two names, in order, from which he had to make the choice. I was further told that in the 1890s two names came from a particular diocesan bishop to the prime minister, who flouted tradition by choosing to recommend the second. Since the prime minister in the case was Gladstone, it is, perhaps, surprising that Queen Victoria accepted his recommendation.

There has been concern for decades in church circles about the procedure followed in diocesan recommendations, though there are many at all levels in the Church, religion and laity, who would be deeply concerned at suggestions that the process should be institutionalized within the Church itself. Nevertheless, there have been discussions over

[1] The archbishops of Canterbury and York, the bishops of Sodor and Man, Chichester, Lincoln, Winchester, Lichfield, Liverpool, Portsmouth, Bath and Wells, Gloucester, Bristol and Ripon: the formal submission for Coventry also went to the Palace before 5 April 1976.

[2] See also John Wilson's biography of Campbell-Bannerman, *C.B.* (London 1973), chapter 37: 'Bishops and Peerages', pp. 773–86.

[3] 26 Henry 8, c. 14. For Nomination of Suffragans and Confecration of them: '. . . two honeſt and diſcreet Spiritual Perſons, being learned, and of good converſation, and thoſe two Perſons ſo by them to be named, ſhall preſent to the King's Highneſs, by their writing under their Seals, making humble Requeſt to his Majeſty, to give to one ſuch of the ſaid two Perſons as ſhall pleaſe his Majeſty, ſuch Title, Name, Stile and Dignity of Biſhop of ſuch of the Sees above ſpecified, as the King's Highneſs ſhall think moſt convenient for the ſame . . .'

a considerable period between No. 10 and the church authorities, particularly since the creation of a new linking authority within the Church between ecclesiastics and laity, the Synod. In February 1976, at a Downing Street meeting, I communicated formally the official acceptance of a new procedure which would put the initiative more clearly within the Church.[1]

The proposal, due to come before the Synod in July 1976, would continue, and indeed intensify, the existing close relationship between the No. 10 appointments secretary and the archbishop's secretary and others concerned with senior church appointments. Following diocesan consultations, the church authorities will submit two names to the prime minister, with their preference indicated as between the two. It will then be for the prime minister to make a recommendation to the Queen, not necessarily choosing the first of the two. The prime minister would have the right – though this would be regarded as an exceptional procedure – to indicate that the names chosen would place him in a difficulty, in which case he could ask for a third name to be provided. Both No. 10 and church leaders believe that the proposals are workable, and provide adequate assurance to the Church while not unduly restricting the procedure for recommendations to the Crown.

Since these words were written an outline of the proposed new procedure has been made public and led to correspondence in the press, and a great deal of heart-searching in the Church at all levels. Many would consider that there is no proper role for No. 10 in these procedures, and that the Church should control all diocesan appointments. No prime minister could accept this argument, for it ignores the fact that a nomination to the episcopal bench is, directly or indirectly, a nomination to the High Court of Parliament, in that not only the two archbishops, but the bishops of London, Durham and Winchester automatically become members of the House of Lords, and others, up to the total of twenty-one, take their place there on the basis of seniority of their sees.[2]

The first lord's duty of recommending appointments to crown livings is a pleasing one, and again comes after a thorough process on the part of the appointments secretary of considering alternative names, assessing the type of church, and the religious dispositions of the parishioners, as well, of course, as consulting the bishop.

In some parishes the Crown always appoints to a vacancy, in some

[1] Since this was written, the Synod meeting at York, has formally accepted the February proposals.

[2] The Bishop of Sodor and Man is excluded as he is legislatively seated in the House of Keys. Until the dissolution of the monasteries in 1539, lords spiritual exceeded lords temporal, in that abbots and priors were eligible, unless excused by the king.

others the right of appointment alternates between the Crown and a private patron (or between the Crown and the bishop for the diocese). In the latter case, or in those exclusively appointed by the bishop, the Crown appoints when there is a vacancy in a see.

Proposals are sometimes made for an exchange of patronage between the Crown and a private patron. Individual cases can be still more complicated. Recently it was decided to include a parish in the Midlands in a large 'team ministry' to cover a large urban and suburban area. On the existing facts, the right to present the 'team rector' of this team would be exercised in turn by each of the present patrons of the seven parishes – the Crown nominating in one out of every seven turns, say, once every seventy years. The solution, after consultation with the Bishop, lay in the Crown's patronage in this parish being exchanged for an episcopally nominated parish, by the name of Mow Cop. The church wardens of both parishes were consulted and agreed. The Prime Minister, not quite sure whether he was acting in his capacity as first lord, duly gave his authority to seek the royal assent to the exchange.

It is not only church appointments that fall within the recommendation of No. 10: lords lieutenant, and a wide range of appointments to national bodies, art galleries, museums and patriotic funds are subject to the same procedure. Recommendations about the appointments of lords lieutenant are based on intensive inquiries in the area: deputy lieutenants are normally recommended by the lord lieutenant, rather as a diocesan bishop recommends a suffragan, but in a less complicated manner. The prime minister sometimes takes the decision himself, particularly in an area he knows. In the 1960s I faced a difficulty where, in a particular county, I wanted to nominate a lady. There was strong resistance on every conceivable ground, mainly based on resistance to the idea of a female. "There had never been a woman lord lieutenant." I countered this by pointing out that the lord lieutenant of Glasgow is traditionally the lord provost: a woman lord provost had, in fact, exercised both responsibilities. In the event it transpired that my nominee lived a mile or two outside the county in question; but, years later, there was no resistance to the proposal that the Dowager Duchess of Norfolk should succeed her husband, and this proved to be a popular appointment.

Recommendations to the Queen for the two annual Honours Lists, the New Year List and the Queen's Official Birthday Honours, are carefully prepared through an elaborate official machine, with appropriate consultations with outside bodies; for instance, on representatives of the arts through the so-called Mycenas Committee. It would be inappropriate to pursue this highly sensitive subject further, except on two aspects. In 1966, I cut by about half what had been virtually the automatic recognition of civil servants of particular grades. Secondly, in the same year I announced that I would submit no more recommendations 'for political and public services'. Over the years, successive prime ministers have recommended Members of Parliament on their own side, and party officials nationally and regionally, and members of local authorities. I had serious reservations about this practice, both as regards MPs and local councillors (in the latter case, Central Office or Transport House tended to become a fount of honour, which I regarded as undesirable). Within a severely limited list, at Birthday and New Year, this meant a considerable saving: the vacant places, I decided, should be directed mainly to local government service, irrespective of party. The then Ministry of Housing and Local Government (now the Department of the Environment) was entrusted with the duty of making recommendations on purely local government grounds. This worked well: since thirteen years of Conservative rule had ensured recognition for hundreds of worthy Conservative councillors, the recommendations from the Ministry produced a majority (about 2 to 1) in favour of the long-neglected Labour councillors. But what it meant was that, under a Labour prime minister, Conservative councillors were still eligible, in contrast with the previous practice. After 1970, Edward Heath reverted to the older practice: in 1974 I again abolished the 'political services' category. This was no more popular in certain Labour local government circles and perhaps the Labour Party generally than the 1966 decision.

The two annual Honours Lists represent many months of dedicated work by the small but full-time Honours Section. It receives advice for honours at every level from the main departments of state, from Members of Parliament, lords lieutenant, civic heads and the general public. I have noted, week by week, that more of the letters the prime minister receives from MPs of all parties relate to honours than to any other subject: almost all of them are absolutely genuine suggestions, usually coming from their constituencies, of an OBE, MBE or other honour for people who have spent perhaps a lifetime in the service of their fellow citizens, for example as hospital matrons, teachers, social workers, youth service workers and others. Such letters are among the most heart-warming and inspiring a prime minister can receive. He simply replies with thanks, promising a consideration of the name proposed. This is very thoroughly put in hand, including inquiries through the departments and at work level; the problem is that with so many hundreds of thousands of our people engaged in such work, there must inevitably be an element of arbitrariness in preferring that small proportion of them who are finally in the list submitted to the Queen.

The first lord's responsibility for recommendations to the museums and galleries is based, case by case, on different forms of consultation. As a trustee for the other bodies listed previously his duties vary slightly, mainly, and then only on rare occasions, to have to sign and seal a conveyance of some property.

It is as prime minister that recommendations are made to the Crown for the appointment of a royal commission, for assent to the proposed terms of reference and the appointment of a chairman. When this process is completed the home secretary is responsible for setting it up, by the Queen's command. It is usual to announce in Parliament the decision to recommend the appointment of a royal commission, and the prime minister can be pressed in oral questions about its scope and terms of reference. The announcement also usually produces a good deal of oral and written advice on all these matters, from interests likely to be affected and from the general public.[1]

Over some years the late Maurice Edelman questioned successive prime ministers about the number and cost of appointments by No. 10 to offices of profit not made through normal civil service channels. On being told in the House[2] that the total emoluments amounted to £630,830, he asked for a list. Apart from the part-time chairman, vice-chairman and governors of the BBC, the list included the seven most senior judicial officers in London and Edinburgh, selected by the lord chancellor but formally recommended to the Queen by the prime minister. For the rest, the offices included the chairmen of two royal commissions (one paid on a full-time basis, the other £1500), the Crown Estate commissioners, the chairmen of development commissions, the forestry commissioners, the comptroller and auditor-general, the parliamentary commissioner (ombudsman) and the clerks of the two Houses of Parliament.

[1] Between March 1974 and April 1976, the appointment of six royal commissions was announced: on the press; standards of conduct in public life; gambling; the medical profession; the legal profession; and a Standing Royal Commission on the Distribution of Wealth and Income.

[2] 18 March 1975.

VI

Home and Overseas – British Industry and Overseas Relations

'The great duty of a Government, especially in foreign affairs, is to soothe and tranquillise the minds of the people, not to set up false phantoms of glory which are to delude them into calamities, not to flatter their infirmities by leading them to believe that they are better than the rest of the world, and so to encourage the baleful spirit of domination; but to proceed upon a principle that recognises the sisterhood and equality of nations, the absolute equalities of public right among them.' W. E. GLADSTONE[1]

In recent times, the prime minister's first preoccupation has inevitably had to be his responsibility for the nation's economic situation. This is a continuing concern: it dominated the Government's actions and demeanour in 1964–70, as it has ever since. The crisis that followed the actions of the oil-producing states in terms first of the oil famine, second of the effect on the internal cost of living and third of the consequences on Britain's balance of payments has dominated the political situation since the autumn of 1973. Every measure, every Budget or interim financial statement, has been a matter for No. 10 almost as much as for No. 11.

But this crisis, grave and unprecedented though it has been, really represents an external aggravation of a problem that has beset the British economy since the war – indeed, though there were no statistics to measure it at the time, it existed in the years of complacency before 1939.[2] Even before that: Britain's technological lead in the industrial revolution was disappearing in the last quarter of the nineteenth century. By 1900 German steel production had outstripped that of Britain: though few realized it at the time, Britain was no longer 'top nation'. The loss of interest in keeping ahead was symbolized by what I saw as a young president of the Board of Trade in the late 1940s. In

---

[1] W.E.Gladstone, *Midlothian Speeches*, ed. M.D.R.Foot (Leicester 1971), p. 37.

[2] Britain was in balance of payments deficit before the war, despite the high inward flow of interest on capital investments made for the most part in the nineteenth century, plus capital repayments. The balance of visible trade was seriously in deficit.

too many of the cotton mills I visited, the machinery I carefully inspected was inscribed with dates of manufacture before 1900. The problem was not only in textiles. We were falling behind in other manufacturing industries. Although there were no contemporary statistics of the balance of trade and payments, it is clear that our worsening trade position was being financed by interest on our vast capital holdings overseas.

Two world wars ended all that. Our overseas capital had to be run down to meet their cost, and by the end of World War II, thanks to massive borrowings and the accumulation of sterling balances in countries that we had defended, such as Egypt and India, or countries from whom we had bought essential war supplies, we were heavily in debt on capital account – £1100 millions down at old-time prices, of assets and investments that had been built up over more than a century.

That was not all. Under the Lend-Lease arrangements, export markets in Latin America and elsewhere were simply transferred to the United States, to conserve shipping and enable us to concentrate on war production. Those markets were not easy to recapture in a Britain run down by the war; some were never recovered. But more than that, the rights in a generation of unprecedentedly brilliant achievements by British scientists – in jet aircraft, radar and other electronic development, in our break-through in nuclear science and antibiotics – were handed over without charge or obligation, as part of the wartime Lend-Lease arrangements. 'On that surrender alone, I ask, what would our investment income be today, and for 30 years past, from royalties morally due to us on the world's jet fleet, on radar and associated developments, our nuclear know-how and on a generation of anti-biotics?'[1]

Successive governments of both major parties since the war have contended with this inheritance and its implications for Britain's balance of payments, as well as a fact now more widely recognized: that, when Britain emerges from cyclical depression to expansion, each turn of the cycle is shorter, in that growth is held back by physical restraints more quickly; as cycle succeeds cycle; each peak and each trough is marked by higher unemployment than its predecessor.

This is not the place to examine the history or the causes, still less the degree of responsibility of different governments and different policies aimed at putting Britain on a new course. But one devastating fact has become apparent: whereas in the prewar period, and a great part of the time since the war, heavy unemployment and strong inflation did not coincide – we had inflation with low unemployment, or depression

[1] Speech by the present writer on receiving the Freedom of the City of London, Guildhall (12 December 1975).

with no inflation – in Britain, as in other countries, the two have come to co-exist.

Cabinets in recent years, and above all prime ministers and their principal economic ministers, have found their working lives dominated by the balance of payments, inflation and unemployment, particularly since the impact of the world oil and commodity crisis began to be felt at the end of 1973. Cabinet machinery has had to be geared to arrangements for handling crises under successive governments.

The Cabinet, therefore, the prime minister and his immediate colleagues are facing this problem almost perpetually. The action taken by successive governments at times of balance of payments crises – 1947, 1951, 1957, 1961, 1964, 1967 and 1973 – is a matter of history, as is the long succession of occasions when balance of payments crises have cut short cherished dreams of industrial expansion and social advance.

Equally well documented are the attempts made by successive governments to fight inflation, including statutory action to control pay increases, in 1966–7 and 1972–3. The counter-inflation policy based on agreement with the Trades Union Congress in July 1975 has been referred to above. But what is being increasingly realized as of the first importance is the need for structural change, the strengthening of the manufacturing industry and export base, which has been progressively carrying the burden of increased private and social spending, and an approach to investment which can avoid the sudden tightening of industrial constraints as soon as production begins to expand.

The creation of the National Economic Development Council (NEDC, or Neddy) by Selwyn Lloyd during his period at the Treasury was one important advance – but, under successive governments in internationally fair weather and foul, the problem remained unsolved. This is why, quite apart from periods of acute concentration on the balance of payments, the hour-to-hour condition of sterling and the development and refinement of methods of dealing with internal inflation, more and more attention is being given to the basic industrial causes of Britain's malaise.

The prime minister, his immediate colleagues and the relevant Cabinet committees between them devote more of their energies and working time to these questions than to any other subject. This means almost constant consultation with industry, with the Confederation of British Industry, the Trades Union Congress, and with both together, while at departmental level there is constant contact with groups of employers and the relevant trade unions, industry by industry. In addition to innumerable private meetings, many unrecorded in public comment, there are set-piece meetings, on the initiative of either Government or industry, as well as the regular meetings of Neddy and bodies associated with it, such as the 'Little Neddies' (the Industry EDCs), established industry by industry, each with an independent chairman, their work co-ordinated by NEDO (the full-time NEDC secretariat) and their progress and conclusions reported to main meetings of the Council.

The economic ministers, the chancellor, the secretary of state for employment and, as appropriate, those responsible for the specialized departments – Industry, Energy, Trade and Agriculture, with the Transport department of Environment (when transport is discussed) are in the forefront here, operating on policies decided by the Cabinet and its committees. The prime minister, in addition to presiding over key committees, receives regular reports from the leading economic ministers and the industrial departments. Equally, he will be involved in meeting deputations from the central organizations of industry, and also individual industries, in addition to the occasions when he chairs NEDC (roughly quarterly in 1974–6; more often in 1967–70 and less often under the Conservative Government in 1970–4).

A Labour prime minister and his colleagues will also get out into the country, not only visiting industrial centres and work places, but addressing national trades union conferences. From March 1974 to April 1976, I received innumerable trade union deputations, addressed many annual trade union conferences or other gatherings and the TUC, in addition to spending two days in Glasgow with my senior colleagues discussing with the Scottish TUC executive problems of Scottish industry – and a shorter meeting with the Welsh TUC. On the management side, including finance, I had almost as many meetings, lunches and dinners, including formal speeches at annual dinners, e.g. the CBI annual dinner, that of the West Midlands Chamber of Industry and Commerce, the Anglo-French Chamber of Commerce and a number of informal meetings (e.g. the Chamber of Shipping in Liverpool) and discussion lunches and dinners with major firms or groups of experts in the City. On these formal and less formal occasions we were dealing with current industrial issues and emergencies; EEC negotiations; anti-inflation policy; price control or taxation and their effect on profits and investable funds; exports; import penetration and controls; and international economic policy – for example before the Rambouillet Heads of Government Conference on the whole economy, or when important issues were coming up at an EEC summit or a meeting of the Council of Ministers.

A major break-through on the problem that has dogged the British

economy ever since the war was achieved at the Chequers meeting of
NEDC on 5 November 1975. Work had been going on for some time
by ministers, particularly the Chancellor and the Industry Secretary,
the two sides of industry and the NEDO secretariat, working with the
Little Neddies.

The Government's proposal agreed at the meeting was based on a
sectoral approach to industry, in order to classify those that are heading
for successful export penetration and increased and qualitatively relevant investment, those that have the potential for success given assistance
to remedy lack of investment or capacity problems and those key industries that, whether successful or not, are strategically important to
the performance of the rest of industry.

It was, in fact, an attempt, industry by industry, to work on the
constraints that have forced successive governments to slam on the
brakes almost before expansion has got firmly under way – constraints
caused mainly by inadequate capacity, which meant that orders, for
industrial plant and machinery, for example, could not be met in time
to meet the needs of the buyers – or, if they were, would be at the
expense of exports, with the inevitable consequences for the balance of
payments.

It also involved an important counter-cyclical strategy, in harmony
with government policies being announced at that time. Industry tends
to defer the ordering of necessary new plant during a depression, partly
of course because investment funds are low, partly because there is not
enough confidence about the timing or extent of the upswing. When
the economy does begin to pick up, there is a rush to order. The industries producing plant and machinery cannot meet the orders, so
buyers turn to overseas suppliers, or the British investment goods pro-
ducers restrict their exports – in both cases harming the balance of
payments. Government has worked out incentives with industry to
help firms to advance their capital goods orders even when the economy
remains depressed.

The statement made following the Chequers meeting is set out in
Note VI of the Appendix.[1]

How far the prime minister intervenes personally in overseas affairs
has in the past been largely a question of the style and personality of
the incumbent of the day – and to some extent the predominant
challenge of the times. Leaving periods of war out of account, Liverpool
and Peel did not. Palmerston, to a considerable extent Gladstone (quite
apart from his preoccupation with Ireland) and Disraeli were heavily

---

[1] See also answers to questions in Parliament, *Hansard* (6 November 1975),
cols 603–29.

committed; Salisbury was also much involved; Asquith much less. Lloyd George's peacetime administration perished with the Chanak affair; MacDonald was involved in his earlier administration, when he was also foreign secretary; Chamberlain, essentially municipally trained, and as a minister social service-oriented, introduced a system close to personal rule over relations with Germany; Anthony Eden, the most professionally trained in diplomacy of all prime ministers, became most deeply involved, over a period of months, in the Suez question;[1] Clement Attlee left foreign relations mainly to Ernest Bevin but took a close interest in them, and a leading, directing interest in Empire and Commonwealth affairs, particularly the transition from Empire to Commonwealth. After the war, Winston Churchill played a world role in Opposition, relatively little in his remaining years of government; Harold Macmillan took a close and professional interest.

In the early sixties, foreign affairs took the centre of the political stage, two questions being dominant – the European Common Market and defence, particularly the issue of nuclear weapons. Sir Alec Douglas-Home fought the 1964 general election primarily on the nuclear issue, and it dominated parliamentary debates in the first year of the Labour Government almost as much as the economic crisis the incoming Government had inherited. In the sixties I was much involved, personally, in the Rhodesian problem, South Africa, Vietnam, Anglo–American and Anglo–Soviet relations and, later, the Nigerian civil war – as well as in broader issues of Commonwealth affairs. Edward Heath was fully involved in Europe.

In 1974–6, with a foreign and commonwealth secretary greatly experienced in both foreign and Commonwealth affairs – beginning with his period as shadow colonial secretary in the late fifties and early sixties, in the period when so many colonial countries were struggling towards independence – I was more than content to leave the general conduct of overseas affairs to him, and no prime minister was kept more in the picture by his foreign secretary than I was.

But the trend of world affairs in the mid-seventies and its close connection with overriding world economic problems, together with a noticeable trend to meetings between heads of government on overseas affairs, has meant that prime ministers were drawn more and more into the higher reaches of diplomacy. Both bilaterally and in NATO and the EEC, the prime minister was more and more involved.

Between March 1974 and April 1976, the Prime Minister was – had to be – an active participant in heads of government conferences.

[1] Lady Eden was reported as saying that the Suez Canal flowed through her drawing-room.

Altogether, I attended fifteen heads of government meetings, if in that figure are included three socialist leaders' conferences where the majority of participants were prime ministers. This works out at one head of government conference every seven weeks. The prime minister, even had he desired to concentrate almost entirely on domestic and economic affairs, could not have done so.

Another reason for the increased pressure on ministers in Britain and other countries, and even more on their advisers, is the proliferation of international bodies and conferences on interrelated world economic problems, particularly on oil and the world commodity problem, its differential effect on separate groups of developing countries, its implications for world finance, including aid, international credit and the gold problem, and all subjects anyone has suggested may be related thereto.

At Rambouillet in November 1975, more tersely at the Elsinore Socialist Leaders Conference in January 1976, I described this development as the world's leading growth industry, and warned against the rapidly breeding race of 'international beachcombers' moving from conference to conference and spawning new rendezvous as they go. For greater accuracy, I circulated to my colleagues at Rambouillet a schedule of all such organizations and conferences as my advisers had been able to identify, running into seven closely typed foolscap pages – *other than those sponsored by EEC*, whose own contribution to the industry is notable.

On returning to London I published the text in *Hansard* as a written answer to an arranged question. It runs to over 5 columns, $2\frac{1}{2}$ pages, of small type, and includes no fewer than 36 inter-governmental conferences, organizations, boards, groups, councils, committees, working parties, commissions, funds, associations, etc.[1]

There has been a corresponding emphasis on bilateral meetings of heads of government. They are part and parcel of modern diplomacy. In 1964–70 there were nine official meetings between the President of the United States and Britain's Prime Minister, including bilateral contacts at the fringe or, as it is diplomatic to say, 'in the margin' of such multinational gatherings as the two successive NATO heads of government meetings in 1974 and 1975, and the Helsinki Conference. Against the 9 meetings in 68 months in the sixties, there were 6 such meetings in the 25 months of 1974–6. In addition I paid 13 official head of government visits abroad and hosted 59 in Britain. There were 14 official prime ministerial visits overseas, excluding multinational conferences, and 59 official visits to Britain by heads of state or govern-

[1] *Hansard* (24 November 1975), cols 61–8 (written).

ment. A few of these were short courtesy calls, or a working meal: most were full-dress official or state visits, involving two days of discussion, and hosted and reverse entertainment. These 59 visits by heads of government *exclude* formal or informal visits by foreign ministers (including Dr Kissinger, Mr Gromyko and M. Sauvagnargues), deputy prime ministers, finance ministers, trade and other ministers, parliamentary delegations, Commonwealth Parliamentary Association or International Parliamentary Union visits (with one full I P U annual conference), speakers and presiding officers of overseas parliaments, the ambassadors and high commissioners stationed in London, Her Majesty's ambassadors and high commissioners to major countries whenever they are in London (including those accredited to countries to be visited as well as our representative to E E C, and the British members of the Commission, and N A T O), the London-based Secretary-General of the Commonwealth, and the secretaries-general of O E C D and C E N T O, personal emissaries from overseas heads of state or government and leaders of the Opposition in different countries, particularly from the Commonwealth. If these are included the total would be at least three to four hundred – an average of some three or four a week.

Most of these required intensive briefing. For a courtesy call by an incoming or outgoing ambassador or high commissioner, or a restricted visit on a single subject, a written brief in the weekend or overnight box would suffice. For an international conference or major two- to three-day visit, the briefs would be in one, two or even three volumes of background and speaking notes. A major conference would involve one or two, or more, full briefing meetings at No. 10 of the relevant ministers and officials, including usually the Treasury and Trade as well as the Foreign and Commonwealth Office, plus a further meeting on arrival in the conference capital, either the night or the lunchtime before the beginning of the conference, with refresher briefings to review the progress of the conference and decide tactics to meet a changing situation. For all major bilateral visits, either way, Her Majesty's ambassador or high commissioner would normally come back for the briefing.

In the day-to-day work of No. 10 the prime minister's link with the relevant departments is his 'Foreign Office' private secretary, who is responsible to the prime minister for all links with the Foreign and Commonwealth Office, the Defence Department and the Northern Ireland Office (this latter responsibility was added during Edward Heath's Administration). The Foreign and Commonwealth Office usually choose one or two from their own 'flyers' for this appointment, for the prime minister's approval: that they are flyers is proved by their subsequent careers. Chosen from some 330 diplomats of counsellor rank, those who have been in No. 10 in my time have been Oliver Wright (now HM Ambassador in Bonn), Michael Palliser (now permanent under-secretary of state), Edward Youde (now HM Ambassador in Peking), Peter Moon (now HM Minister in Cairo), Lord Bridges (now Commercial Minister at Washington) and Patrick Wright, still at the time of writing in No. 10.

They sift from the hundreds of telegrams and reports from foreign posts those the prime minister should see each night and, at slightly longer range, at the weekend; they produce minutes based on FCO briefing, or those of the other departments they cover, together with any hour-to-hour information on which decisions are needed. This is particularly the case if a senior minister is abroad on important negotiations, especially if the prime minister's clearance is required. It also applies in urgent discussions in the United Nations, whether at Assembly or Security Council level, where the prime minister will have been made aware of an issue reaching the crunch and where the foreign and commonwealth secretary and he have to approve instructions to the head of the British delegation. The time difference, varying from five to six hours, is a help at one part of the day, a problem at another. Overnight telegrams on the state of play allow adequate time for consideration, subject to other preoccupations, because New York is asleep until mid-day, GMT. Late sittings at UN may require attention until well into the small hours.

Reference has been made to the increased number of summit conferences. Three such deserve special mention: the EEC summit, the European Council, and Commonwealth prime ministers' meetings.

The Treaty of Rome in 1957 incorporated the institutions of the Community, with the Council of Ministers – foreign ministers – at the apex of the political decision-making machinery. Each country, in alphabetical order, assumes the presidency of the Council for a period of six months. There were occasional heads of government meetings up to 1974 which took place in the capital city and under the chairmanship of the head of government of the country holding the presidency, e.g. Paris in October 1972, and Copenhagen in December 1973.

It was an inspired idea of President Giscard d'Estaing that created the European Council in 1974. During the French presidency, he called together the heads of government to a short meeting in Paris, in September 1974. Foreign ministers were not invited: officials were not present to take a record. The original purpose of the meeting was to consider the means of advancing European political unity; but Helmut

Schmidt, the German federal chancellor, opened a discussion on the growing unemployment problem and related issues of inflation, oil prices and national balances of payments. It was totally informal – we sat in a group of chairs in one of the Elysée salons, not round a table. All of us spoke, and agreed that the experiment should be repeated. Helmut Schmidt and I deputed to the President that at subsequent meetings foreign ministers should also be present. This was agreed.

In December, France still holding the presidency, we met again, this time prime ministers and foreign ministers, in the Quai d'Orsay. As it happened, the main issue was the 're-negotiation' of the terms of British entry. I had taken the opportunity of a speech at the annual dinner of the London Labour Mayors' Association to refer at length to HM Government's attitude to the re-negotiations, and to reassure our partners about some problems that caused them anxiety. This set the stage for the summit, which in fact was a success. Among its achievements was agreement on the amounts allocated to the European Regional Fund, on which Britain has drawn handsomely.

This meeting was more formal than the September gathering, but the host-President kept the numbers small by excluding all officials – apart from a 'runner' for each delegation outside the door, in case a minister needed to receive from or impart to his official delegation some relevant information. Unfortunately, there was no note-taker, no official sitting behind his prime minister silently and unobtrusively taking a 'note for the record'. This meant that ministerial participants had to keep a record, or leave their delegation without information. Fortunately, the Foreign Secretary, James Callaghan, is an avid note-taker and the 'runner' was kept busy feeding foolscap pages to the waiting and under-employed delegation.

It was at the Paris meeting that we adopted the title 'European Council', and agreed to meet three times a year in future. This was important not only in institutionalizing the heads of government meeting: it meant a major change in the operation of the Community, by inserting into the Treaty of Rome arrangements, a top-level degree of political control, with the prime ministers concerned returning to their capitals and parliaments, reporting back and becoming accountable for the agreed communiqué and the conduct of their own delegations.

Under the Irish presidency, Dublin, in March 1975, was the venue for the first meeting of the new European Council. This was prepared and chaired by the Irish Government with great understanding and restraint, and our hosts refused to use their presidency to press policies on the meeting. The main issue was the conclusion of the 're-negotiation' on the terms of British entry into EEC, which put Her Majesty's

Government in a position to make recommendations to Parliament prior to the national decision in the June referendum.

By the time of the Brussels summit in July 1975, still more in Rome in December of that year and in Luxembourg in April 1976, the European Council was fully established as the ultimate court of political appeal in the Community; though Luxembourg was regarded as a disappointment, in that the decisions hoped for on arrangements for the election of the European Parliament in 1978, on which the Council of Ministers had failed to agree, were referred back to them.

Nevertheless, the European Council had come to stay. In a short and informal meeting on the Tindemans Report[1] there was some discussion on how future sessions of the Council should be conducted. One suggestion was that it should be more informal, in a smaller room instead of the grand state rooms, which hosts liked to offer, with whispering translations in the ears of delegates instead of built-in electronic simultaneous translation. Some of us felt that the admission of a single official note-taker for each delegation would be more to the point. This had been conceded at the Rambouillet economic summit of six leading industrial powers.[2]

The Council, representing the top political direction of each of the nine EEC members, imparts a welcome sense of political reality to a Community that can sometimes become theoretical and bureaucratic. At the same time, preoccupation with national political imperatives can lead to disappointment for many in Europe who look to the Council to take firm decisions on political unity.

Each national leader is inevitably, and rightly, looking over his shoulder at his own parliament. For example, while the smaller nations were resisting a distribution of European parliamentary seats reflecting the population of member countries, and pressing for a minimum figure, regardless of size, Britain, for example, could not welcome proposals such as those approved by the European Assembly under which Denmark, Ireland and Luxembourg, with a total population of 8,390,000, would have 36 seats, while Scotland and Wales, with a combined population of just below 8 million, would have, on the basis of a proportionate share of the United Kingdom's proposed seats, something like 9 or 10.

[1] Prime Minister Tindemans of Belgium had been charged at the Paris Summit, in December 1974, to prepare a report on the future political and institutional development of the Community. This was circulated in January 1976, though the Council of Ministers charged with preparing the European Council agenda for the April meeting had proposed only a short 'second reading' debate prior to detailed consideration by the Council of Ministers and further discussion at a later Summit meeting.

[2] France, Britain, Germany, the United States, Italy as the then president of EEC – and Japan.

When the French President proposed an allocation based on that governing the existing Strasbourg Parliament, not only had Britain to object on the under-representation of Scotland and Wales, but the Italian Prime Minister had to ask for an overnight adjournment to consult the various Italian parties, whether members of the Government coalition or not. (In fact, he received disturbing reports of further fissiparous developments in Rome, on issues bearing no relation to the distribution of seats in the European Parliament, which led to the election the following June. Of such are the political realities of EEC.)

Very different, and developed over a longer period, are the institutions and practices of a Commonwealth Conference, officially 'Prime Ministers' Meeting', it being understood that 'prime ministers' includes those heads of government who are executive presidents.

The Commonwealth Conference goes back to pre-World War I Imperial Conferences, photographs of which hang in the garden-level corridor of No. 10 Downing Street. As a meeting of sovereign independent countries, the series goes back to the days of Clement Attlee.[1] As an attendant minister I was at the one held in Downing Street in 1949. There was adequate room around the Cabinet table: 9 countries, including the partially self-governing Southern Rhodesia,[2] were represented. When I chaired the conference in June 1965 there were 21; the 1966 conference held in London had 22,[3] in January 1969, also in London, there were 28; in Jamaica, 1975, 33.[4] Since then, up to the time of writing, we have celebrated the independence of Papua–New Guinea and the Seychelles, making the present total of Commonwealth countries 36.

The two-day conference in Lagos in January 1966, called on the initiative of Abubakar Tafawa Balewa, prime minister of Nigeria, to discuss the Rhodesian situation following UDI, was the first held outside Britain.[5] At the 1969 London conference I proposed that the next meeting should be held elsewhere, and we agreed that it should

---

[1] 'Looking back over the period of my Prime Ministership one of my most interesting memories is that of my relationship with my fellow Prime Ministers of the Commonwealth.' Clement Attlee, *As It Happened* (London 1954), p. 177.

[2] Under the 1924 constitution Southern Rhodesia had complete internal self-government, but its overseas relations were controlled by Britain.

[3] Tanzania did not attend: two new members, Singapore and Guyana, did.

[4] A further Commonwealth member, Nauru, did not attend.

[5] It began tragically with the news of the death of the Indian Prime Minister Shastri, in Tashkent, where he and President Ayub Khan of Pakistan were ratifying a peace settlement following the hostilities between their two countries. Four days after the Lagos conference we were shocked to hear that our host chairman had been murdered and his body thrown into a ditch, in what proved to be the beginning of a series of tribal struggles for hegemony in his federal country.

take place in Singapore.[1] The British delegation to that conference, and to a subsequent one in Ottawa, was led by Edward Heath. At the meeting held in April–May 1975 in Jamaica, there was unanimous agreement that its successor should be held in London in June 1977, during the Silver Jubilee celebrations of the Queen's accession.

The organization of a Commonwealth Conference has emerged, as the Commonwealth itself has, out of British traditions. Until 1966, it was organized by the British Cabinet secretariat, with the then independent Commonwealth Office making the arrangements. It was invariably held in London. The Conference of 1964, under Sir Alec Douglas-Home's chairmanship, decided in favour of an independent Commonwealth secretariat. Meanwhile Britain organized the 1965 conference, which on 21 June elected Mr Arnold Smith of Canada, the first permanent secretary-general, with a permanent office and secretariat in Marlborough House.

It is an essentially informal gathering: this is as true today with over thirty members as it was with my first conference in 1949. But today it is prepared and serviced by the independent secretariat. The conference at Jamaica, ably chaired by Prime Minister Michael Manley, was the most united I have known, transcending even that held in London in 1969.

The continuing secretariat provides a means of constant consultation; for example, it serviced, in London, the Commonwealth Sanctions Committee to co-ordinate Commonwealth action on Rhodesian sanctions. In 1975–6 it took the lead in co-ordinating action on aid to Mozambique and on other problems consequential on the changed situation on the Rhodesian border.

The foreign and commonwealth secretary is responsible for relations with the Commonwealth. But in a very special sense, the prime minister – through traditions going back in particular to Clement Attlee – is regarded by Commonwealth countries as a link with Commonwealth governments, reflecting on a minor scale the Queen's acclaimed position as head of the Commonwealth. This may be a relic of our imperial past: it is no less a tribute to Clement Attlee's historic role in converting an Empire into the Commonwealth as we know it today.

[1] I had proposed to Lester Pearson in Ottawa in 1968 that our next conference should be held in Canada: he demurred because of his pending retirement and it was felt that his probable successor, Pierre Trudeau, would not be high enough in Commonwealth seniority to chair it. This was why the next conference was, after all, held in London in 1969. See Wilson, *The Labour Government, 1964–70*, pp. 503–4.

VII

The Prime Minister
and Parliament

Get 'em up. (statement attributed to) HAROLD MACMILLAN[1]

The prime minister and his Cabinet are accountable to Parliament. They have no fixed term of office, such as that of an American president, who is secure for four years though perhaps legislatively impotent for part of that time. They survive as a government just as long – not a day longer – as they can count on the support of a majority of Parliament, however small that majority may be.

The crucial test is votes in the House of Commons. An adverse vote in the Lords is not lethal. Even in the Commons the Government can survive after being defeated in a vote on an important division. On 10 March 1976, the Government tabled a motion 'rejecting the demand for massive and immediate cuts in public expenditure which would increase both unemployment and the cost of living, recognizes the need to ensure that manufacturing industry can take full advantage of the upturn in world trade by levelling off total expenditure from April 1977 while keeping under continuous review the priority between programmes'. The motion was defeated as the result of an orchestrated abstention by thirty-nine left-wing Labour members. The following day the Government forced a debate on what was, in effect, and was

---

[1] By a friend. It is recorded that from late June onwards, when parliamentary debates on legislation – often involving late sittings, with votes at any time during the day or night on the Report Stage of Commons Bills or Lords Amendments sent to the other House earlier – Harold Macmillan would view the parliamentary situation, and with the sure touch of an old parliamentarian utter an invocation to the parliamentary deities advocating an early rising of the House and a desire for his parliamentary colleagues to be able to enjoy the peace of beach and moorside.

recognized by every Hon. Member as being, a motion of confidence. It was carried easily.

The Conservatives were voting to cut the forward programme of public expenditure; the Tribune group were voting in protest against restraints on the growth of expenditure in future years. It was an unhappy alliance, to which I drew attention in answer to my regular questions, even before opening the confidence debate.[1]

But votes of confidence are – or should be – extremely rare occurrences. The vote of 11 March 1976 was in effect the only one I had to introduce in nearly eight years as prime minister, despite the fact that in the four administrations the Government overall majority was as follows:

Parliament	*Putative overall majority after election of Mr Speaker – at the beginning of the Parliament*	*Putative overall majority at the end of the Parliament, i.e. immediately before dissolution*
October 1964–February 1966	+ 5	+ 1
March 1966–May 1970	+97	+63
March 1974–September 1974	−34	−36
October 1974–April 1976	+ 4	+ 1

Clement Attlee, when prime minister with a majority of five, went on record as saying that no government could continue with an effective majority of less than ten. Three of the four administrations I headed failed to pass that test, though the Parliamentary Party behind me ensured that we could survive with a smaller majority.[2]

The problem of ensuring parliamentary support is particularly acute

---

[1] 'It is always an arguable question about promiscuity whether one is more open to criticism for going into the bedroom or being the lap-dog outside the door.' *Hansard*, answers to questions (11 March 1976), col. 624.

[2] In the two Parliaments elected in 1974, there was in normal circumstances a sense of safety in numbers, measured not in terms of MPs but of multiplicity of parties. In the Short Parliament of March–September 1974, Labour was the largest party, but 18 short of an overall majority, having a lead of 5 over the largest single Opposition party, the Conservatives. In the Parliament that assembled in October 1974 there was at first a majority of 4 overall, and 43 over the Conservative Opposition. This had been reduced by one by-election defeat, and deaths and a defection, etc., to a small overall minority situation by April 1976; but the total voting strength of the smaller parties was 39, and up to that situation they seldom combined to vote solidly with the official Opposition.

in a House where no party has an absolute majority. We have seen that from Disraeli onwards the prime minister would normally resign after being defeated in a general election, before submitting himself to Parliament for a vote of confidence or reject. This was the course adopted in 1945, 1951, 1964, 1970 and – after a weekend's delay – March 1974. In 1924 the Conservatives, though comfortably the largest single party, faced Parliament on the King's urging, and then were defeated. In 1929, as recorded above, Stanley Baldwin insisted on resigning.

The opening of the first session of a new Parliament is different from that of subsequent sessions. Mr Speaker has to be elected or re-elected. Every member has to take the oath. Ancient privileges have to be sought from and granted by the Crown. Only after that is the session formally opened by the Queen's Speech. On the day it is delivered, a debate begins which usually lasts six days. The last two days are on official Opposition amendments to the 'Address in Reply' thanking the Crown for the Gracious Speech, the amendments usually seeking to express the House's regrets that the said Gracious Speech either included some proposition demanded by the Opposition, or failed to include adequate assurances on points the Opposition regarded, or affected to regard, as essential.

The Queen's Speech, it need hardly be said, is not drafted in Buckingham Palace. It is uniquely the production of the Government. If there has been a change of government there is very little time for the Government to draft and agree on a speech setting out, with full regard for the manifesto on which it was elected, the aspirations in foreign and domestic affairs and the specific items of legislation it is asking Parliament to carry through in the first session.[1]

The draft is first considered by the Cabinet's Queen's Speeches (and future legislation) Committee, and master-minded by the lord president and his secretariat. It then comes formally before Cabinet. In subsequent sessions the pace is more orderly and relaxed: the Legislation Committee will have been at work for months and some of the legislation drafted before the new session.[2]

Any government, especially a reforming government, is faced with two all-powerful limitations on the speed of fulfilment of its objectives: finance and parliamentary time. Once again, it is all a problem of

[1] See p. 44 above.

[2] Until very recently there were two committees: the Legislation Committee, which considers the programme for the session, and acts as a monitor and spur for the current legislative programme, including its duty of approving the introduction of Bills, the need for which would not have been foreseen before the Queen's Speech; and the Future Legislation Committee, preparing in a more leisurely fashion the programme for the coming session. Now there is a single Legislation Committee.

priorities. The chancellor and the leader of the House are responsible to the prime minister and Cabinet, as a result of committee decisions, as well as bilateral meetings: the final decisions are taken by Cabinet.

The Lord President's Committee is responsible also for preparing the Prorogation Speech marking the end of the old session, in these days only a short time before the new session is opened by the Queen's Speech. This time-table is very different from that followed in more spacious Victorian times. Their session was short. The House would assemble for the Speech from the Throne in February: it would usually include one major legislative proposal, for example Disraeli's health reforms (*'sanitas sanitatum, omnia sanitas'*). The rest of the session would involve the debate on the estimates of public expenditure[1] (which in all its forms amounted to £77·1 million in 1876), the Budget, where a shift of £1 million in a major tax would be an important event,[2] followed by adjournment in time for the opening of the grouse-shooting season on 12 August.[3]

Gladstone was able to spend many weeks each autumn at Hawarden, felling trees, broken only by his three or four weeks' compulsory stint as 'Minister in Attendance' at Balmoral, which he hated, and relieved by all-day fifteen mile walks over the hills – if he could get away – and, in the evening, writing miserable letters to his wife.[4]

Once the Queen's Speech has been delivered, the members of the House of Commons who have processed to the Lords to hear it then repair to the Commons, which immediately adjourn until the afternoon, when Mr Speaker informs the House that he has been to the Lords, where the Queen's Speech has been read, 'of which, for greater accuracy' he had secured a copy. Two favoured government back-benchers then formally move and second the 'Address in Reply' thanking Her Majesty

[1] *A Short Fiscal and Financial History of England* (London 1921), pp. 137–8 and 155.

[2] One penny on the income tax would provide roughly £1·5 million. Northcote in the year in question, 1876, raised the tax by one penny.

[3] Taking the session of 100 years ago – 1876 – as an example, the Queen's Speech opening Parliament was on 8 February; the Easter Adjournment 11 to 24 April; the Whitsun Adjournment 1 to 8 June, and the House was prorogued on 15 July, reassembling on 8 February 1877 for the new session.

[4] See Viscount Morley, *Life of Gladstone* (London 1903), Vol II, p. 97 *et seq.* In Queen Victoria's time there was always a Minister in Attendance, the Prime Minister, Foreign Secretary, Lord President or any other. Edward VII spent less time at Balmoral, but when making alterations still provided a suite for the Minister. Records in George V's time refer to such visits, but the practice seems to have ended after the First World War. The reason was the improvement in communications on 26 September 1919; the King was notified by the Prime Minister over the telephone that a general railway strike was to begin at midnight; in 1921 a letter from the Prime Minister was dropped over the grounds from an aircraft. In recent years there has been a weekend visit by the prime minister and his wife, in an entirely informal atmosphere, an event which is one of the highlights of the prime ministerial year.

for her Gracious Speech, and then, by tradition, making a speech mainly related to the experience, achievements and hopes of their respective constituencies, with suitable reference to anything in the Gracious Speech that will be particularly welcome there. They will have been selected by the government whips, and in recent years, under successive governments, I have seemed to sense a disposition on the part of the whips – particularly if a general election is pending – to select Hon. Members defending marginal constituencies.

After the leader of the Opposition has attacked the measures in the Queen's Speech, the prime minister rises, first, to compliment the mover and seconder, with gracious remarks about them and their constituencies; second, to outline the Government's proposals for the use of parliamentary time, with particular reference to the allocation of days for debates initiated by private Members, and the Supply Days, now usually about twenty-nine, when the Opposition has the choice of subject; and third, to make a keynote speech about the programme for the succeeding year, and to deal with the general state of the nation.

The debate then usually runs on to the Tuesday of the following week, each day having its own general subject, agreed between the main parties – though no MP is out of order if he speaks on some other aspect of the Queen's Speech. The last two days are on specific Opposition amendments, usually regretting that the Gracious Speech fails to mention a particular subject, or fails to make adequate provision for some important area of government, and may be – for example on the economic situation – in terms virtually amounting to a censure. The vote is one of the most important of the session. Governments have fallen on such an Opposition amendment, for example after a general election, when the ruling party has lost its majority. The defeat of the Baldwin Government in 1924 was such a case. At one time there seemed a possibility that it might happen in March 1974.

The prime minister will, of course, take part in the principal debates of the session, major economic debates, though not the budget debate, almost invariably on motions of censure, and the very rare motions of confidence, and usually on major constitutional issues – for example, in the sixties the abortive Bill on House of Lords reform, and in the seventies on the referendum and devolution, as well as such dominant issues as the EEC debates following the re-negotiations of the terms of entry.

But his continuing role in the House, the highlight of the daily Question time, is his appearance from 3.15 to 3.30 pm on Tuesdays and Thursdays to answer 'Prime Minister's Questions'. Until Harold Macmillan's time, the prime minister rose to answer the questions put down to him at Question 45 after those put down to the departmental ministers whose turn it was in the rota. Frequently Questions 1 to 44 occupied the whole hour allotted for the question period; every Opposition suspected that, even if ministers were not filibustering to ensure that the Prime Minister's Questions were not reached, government back-benchers were rising in such numbers as to fill in the time. In July 1961[1] the rules were changed, following a report of the Select Committee on Procedure, so that, whatever the rate of progress on the earlier questions, questions to the prime minister would begin promptly at 3.15 pm.

Prime ministers approach the bi-weekly ordeal by questions in different frames of mind, but of two things I am sure: no prime minister looks forward to 'PQs' with anything but apprehension; every prime minister works long into the night on his answers, and on all the notes available to help him anticipate the instant and unpredictable supplementary questions that follow his main prepared answer.

It has been said that Harold Macmillan, a highly successful performer at Question time, used on occasion to be physically sick, or very near to it, before Questions on Tuesdays and Thursdays. In my address to the British Academy I said that, if Britain ever had a prime minister who did not fear Questions, our parliamentary democracy would be in danger.

In seven years eight months as prime minister I answered more than 12,000 parliamentary Questions, oral or written, the figure for 1974–5 reaching over 2000.

The questions are tabled to the prime minister, as to other ministers, well in advance. There used to be a three-week limit on the period ahead for which a question could be tabled; in earlier days, an unlimited period could mean that an MP who wanted to be sure of an oral answer by getting high on the list would table his question many weeks in advance. This led to complaints that questions tabled in a given situation, even a crisis situation, were long out of date when the relevant ministers came to answer them orally. Even the three-week period led to questions that were very *passées*, so a fortnight's limit was laid down. With the speed of events in modern Britain, even this limit fails to prevent time being taken on issues which, while relevant, perhaps sensationalized at the time of their tabling, appear archaic by the time they are answered. A fortnight is a long time in politics.

With Prime Minister's Questions – and some others – there is a rush to table as soon as the Order Paper of the House is open to them. As soon as the prime minister sits down, on a Tuesday or Thursday, after

[1] See *Hansard*, 18 July 1961, col. 1052.

answering the last of the questions on the Order Paper for that day, the Table Office is handling the questions. Some are handed in at that moment; some have been handed in and are awaiting attention preparatory to being placed on the Order Paper; some have been sent in by post. The modern practice is to assemble them all together at 4.0 pm and send them to the printer, without first arranging them in any set order, to establish pride of place on the Order Paper. The actual 'lottery', without fear or favour to any Hon. Member, is done by the printers.

There is a fundamental difference between Prime Minister's Questions and those of departmental ministers. For one thing, most departmental ministers face questions only once every three, four or five weeks, and they can divide the questions for answering between the whole departmental team, no doubt reflecting the devolution of duties within the department. The prime minister has no minister of state or parliamentary under-secretary (except that questions put to him in his capacity as minister for the Civil Service are normally handled on his behalf by the minister of state, Civil Service Department). But the main difference is the extremely wide, indeed totally open-ended, nature of the supplementaries, which can follow the main, usually stylized, question.

Supplementary questions to departmental ministers usually reflect their daily work, and they have a large department ready to brief them on likely supplementaries. Their services are, of course, available to No. 10 – reams of it, attached to the late-night briefing on the eve of Questions.

There are certain standard questions regularly put to the prime minister. One of the most familiar – certainly one of the most open-ended – is when a member asks whether, and when, the prime minister intends to pay a visit to his constituency or some other place at home or abroad. In order to deal with any possible supplementary the prime minister has pages upon pages of briefing for each proposed visit, since the supplementary is virtually unpredictable, unless a friendly MP sends a message through the prime minister's PPS indicating what he is going to ask. This happens more often on the government side, though there are Opposition Members who are more interested in getting a meaningful reply on a matter of constituency interest than in scoring an extremely short-lived political point.

The range of possible supplementaries to a 'visits' question is almost unlimited. First, there are the constituency questions proper. An Hon. Member, whether from the majority or the minority side, on being told that the prime minister *does* plan or 'has no plans' to visit the constituency, may raise some local grievance, such as the delay in placing the promised hospital or school on the relevant department's building programme, the numbers unemployed, prospects for school-leavers, local racial problems, housing, education, the road programme, the long-delayed building of the bridge across the river or the inadequacy of remand accommodation. The list of possible questions approaches the infinite, and almost all of them fall within the responsibility of departmental ministers – but the prime minister has to be briefed and ready, and it is the duty of the No. 10 machine to see that the necessary information is there.

The second group is based on questions designed to open up policy matters, usually on a national or international issue. So when the prime minister has indicated his intentions on the prospects of a visit, the questioner's supplementary presses him to come to hear the views of his constituents on any single subject under the sun, from the imbalance between Soviet and NATO naval forces in the Atlantic to a speech by a trade union leader representing a minority in the TUC on the question of inflation. Again, the range of potential questions is virtually infinite, and covers not only the whole of government responsibility but every conceivable area of national and international life.

The third group is based on invitations pressing the prime minister to visit not the questioner's constituency but that of another Member, very often, if the questioner is on the Opposition benches, a member of the government party. When Clay Cross was in the news over the default of local councillors in relation to the previous Government's rent legislation, Conservative members who might not have heard of Clay Cross three or four years earlier were avid for the prime minister's attendance there – or at least to bring him within range of questions on the said councillors. Another type of area where the prime minister is encouraged to put in an appearance is a town where some conference has been held, or even a speech made, not necessarily by a minister; the supplementary will raise one of the many issues opened up, or touched on, in the speech.

A fourth group, again referring to a journey to a constituency other than that of the questioner, is to give the premier the opportunity of 'hearing the views' of someone there on any subject from agriculture to antimony. Possible supplementaries out of a proposed visit to the City of London, for example, cover a very wide area, from the system of local government there to the level of interest rates or the commodity markets, inflation, the TUC or the latest speech made by the current ministerial target figures – for much of the period in question, Tony Benn.

A fifth group of supplementaries, regardless of whether the questioner is playing at home or away, and more relevantly directed, invites the prime minister to see not only what people are thinking, but what they are suffering – farmers in a particular area allegedly impoverished by government agricultural policy or E E C directives; clothing, textile or footwear workers facing Asian or East European export competition.

On all these questions, the supplementaries will widen further and further from the original, further and further from the place indicated, until they range over the widest possible subjects, for example a speech made three thousand miles away by the leader of the Opposition. The prime minister must stand his ground, produce an answer – usually greeted with cries of 'dodging, dodging', 'answer, answer', or 'resign, resign' – and hold his ground. He must meet carefully prepared supplementaries aromatic with libations of midnight oil with a spontaneous reply which he hopes is at least as good: in any case he has to survive. In the sixties, one prominent Opposition Member, now 'shadow leader of the House', told the press he spent a few peripatetic hours every Sunday evening preparing supplementaries for the Prime Minister's Questions the following Tuesday or Thursday: in fact, over-prepared questions do not always come off.

Then there are questions asking the prime minister to visit likely or unlikely places abroad. Taking the visits questions in the three months from 11 December 1975 to 11 March 1976, 139 questions were tabled for oral answer about intended visits. The great majority of these were not reached, but those that were, and those that might have been, required a great deal of briefing – and estimation of what might lie behind the question.

Some were duplicated questions, with two or more Members pinpointing a place for a visit; some were repeat questions, particularly if on the first tabling the question had not been reached.

Space forbids listing all the places, but some idea of the degree of geographical interest and diversity can be gained from the fact that we had Sweden, Costa Rica, Shoreham and Cyprus on 11 December, the North East, Edmonton, Kirkby, the site of the proposed Scottish Assembly, Bodmin, Leyland and Guyana on 16 December and the Isle of Wight two days later.

Early in the New Year suggestions for a prime ministerial progress included the Isle of Man; on 20 January we had the City of London, Leicester, Tamworth, Perth, Gloucestershire, Merseyside, Bangor (North Wales), Northern Ireland, Moscow, mid-Wales and a tour of the Commonwealth. Late January included Dagenham, Strathavon, Iceland, China, Yugoslavia and Portsmouth. January ended with Dodoma and NATO; 10 February covered ten places, including Helsinki,

Rutland, Hong Kong, the City of London, New York and Devil's Bridge, near Aberystwyth. Late February saw Oslo, Cleator Moor, Skelmersdale, Moscow, Glenrothes and Zambia: on 8 March the list concludes with southern Africa, Staffordshire, the United Nations and SHAPE.

My questioners were ingenious in discovering further ways of opening up supplementaries. If I were not going to place X, would I, with time thus saved, visit place Y? This was countered off-the-cuff, since one has no notice of supplementaries, by the reply that the question was related to visiting X, not inventing new visits out of the time saved. Mr Speaker supported this restriction. Then another one was opened up, on a question from a Scottish Nationalist about visiting Dundee. I had no plans to do so, Sir. One would not normally regard a question about Dundee, whether visited or not, as leading logically to the feats of Queen Boadicea in the first century AD, to a visit by the chancellor of the Exchequer to St Albans, to the ruins of Verulamium or to the qualities of the leader of the Opposition, a lady. But the Hon. Member for St Albans asked:

> 'If the Prime Minister goes to Dundee, will he stop off at St. Albans? Will he make certain that he brings with him his right hon. Friend, the Chancellor of the Exchequer, shows him the ruins of Verulamium – sacked by Queen Boadicea – and points out what the British people will do under a woman leader if they think they are over-taxed?'[1]

My answer, unfortunately of equal length, complained of the irrelevance of the question, dwelt on the sad dénouement of Queen Boadicea's reign and called on the questioner not to advise his Leader to solve the country's problems by unconstitutional methods.

It was all a long way from the very real problems of Dundee.

From then on all similar supplementaries were answered with a general statement of disinclination to go by circuitous routes to places I had already made clear I was not intending to go to anyway.

A few final and not untypical examples to show how far the supplementary, of which the prime minister of course has no notice, can depart from the original venue. I was asked by a Conservative Member to visit Derbyshire. The supplementary question was

> 'Will the Prime Minister answer a question which is being asked in Derbyshire by those dependent on Rolls-Royce as well as in the rest of the country wherever people are concerned about defence and engineering export orders? Who gave the Government the mandate to order the cancellation of commercial contracts between private

[1] *Hansard* (10 February 1976), cols 228–9.

companies and overseas customers? Does streaking into Downing Street with a minority vote empower the Prime Minister to put at risk vast sections of British industry and export orders?'[1]

And so on and so forth. This opened up the whole question of the Government's attitude to supplying naval vessels and other arms to the Chilean dictatorship, on which I had made a statement just two days before and then answered questions covering eight columns of *Hansard*. On this occasion the question was no. 4 on the Order Paper for that day; even so it was allowed to run on for some minutes beyond the normal time of 3.30 pm, and the exchanges covered three and a half columns of *Hansard*.

Another one from the same region wanted me to repudiate a speech by Hugh Scanlon, not made in the region, and not the subject of any government responsibility.

A suggestion that the Prime Minister should visit his own constituency of Huyton, which he did regularly, was designed to express Conservative disapproval of a statement unhelpful to them made during the February general election by the Director-General of CBI, Campbell Adamson, not a constituent of Huyton, or given to speaking there.

A suggestion that I should visit New Zealand elicited a supplementary condemning the Government's cancellation of a good-will visit to Greece, in the days of the Colonels' dictatorship.

The prime minister is not entirely defenceless. When asked to visit a Member's constituency to hear the strength of constituents' views on some particular governmental iniquity, I began to take refuge in a stock reply that I did not regard it as my duty to go round the country visiting constituencies whose residents clearly had no confidence in the ability of their own Member to express their views in the House. This proved something of a deterrent, except to the totally irrepressible.

Another regular ploy is to ask whether a particular speech by a member of the Cabinet or other senior minister – speeches by junior ministers do not qualify for this type of question – represents the policy of Her Majesty's Government. This is a question hallowed by tradition, and must be treated very seriously, since it involves the whole question of collective ministerial responsibility.

Every prime minister at some time, perhaps working through his questions late at night, must harbour the thought that some at least of his colleagues in preparing their speeches entirely fail to give any thought to the dilemma in which they place the prime minister. Some do not

[1] *Hansard* (23 May 1974), cols 595 *et seq.*

have a script; there may be little or no national reportage, and a great deal of effort is often required to trace copies of local, sometimes very local, newspapers.

It is very rare for a prime minister to dissociate himself from a colleague's speech, but sometimes a great deal of ingenuity is required. In the 1960s I once had to dissociate from an interpolation in a ministerial speech caused by noisy interruptions. In 1974–6 I occasionally said that a particular statement was not made as representing government policy but as a political comment, but this was very dubious ground.

What colleagues' speeches do mean is that the prime minister, perhaps well after midnight, has to regale himself by reading seven or eight foolscap pages of a ministerial utterance which, left to himself, he might have preferred to reserve for a more leisured occasion.

Another standard type of question, whenever the prime minister has made a speech, is to ask if he will place the text of that particular speech 'in the Library' of the House of Commons. His office will invariably have done so at the opening of business immediately after the speech. A prime minister who prepares his own speeches will hardly have to sit up late re-reading them. In any case many of the questions are highly tangential, the speech itself usually being used as a coathook on which to hang a regular type of supplementary – on inflation, the Public Sector Borrowing Requirement, the TUC, the CBI, industrial relations, unemployment or import control, or what some minister had said the previous night or that very morning in a radio interview.

What the House – in effect the Opposition – expects at Question time has widened in recent years. Not long ago, the prime minister – certainly Clement Attlee – had no difficulty in dismissing a supplementary by such answers as: 'That is a different question'; 'I would refer the Hon. Gentleman to the statement [or reply] given by the Minister of X, on 31st July' – this is permissible now only by reference to answers in the same session. 'That does not arise out of the original question'; 'If the Hon. Member would put that question on the Order Paper, I will endeavour to see that it is answered.' If and when the question is formally tabled, the prime minister will speedily transfer it to another minister if it relates to the latter's departmental responsibilities. Such a transfer cannot seriously be challenged when a question is tabled, though a prime minister seeking to narrow the field of questions by abusing the conventions governing transfers would probably be quickly called to account. In any case he runs the risk of points of order on his decision to transfer.[1]

[1] In March 1976 I had complaints about the number of questions I transferred, and was questioned about it. After much research had been done in No. 10, I was able to claim

One of the factors inhibiting a prime minister from keeping his Question period tight is the growing, and deplorable, practice of sedentary interruptions. It devalues the democratic process, and it is difficult for a prime minister not to pick up an interruption and seek to fling it back – I myself was far too prone to fall to this temptation.

One safeguard lies in the broadcasting of Parliament, as the radio experiment has shown; television broadcasting would be even more effective. In the radio experiment, ministerial answers came across loud and clear, while the shouting by Opposition MPs sounded to the listener like the yelling of yahoos. (This is not necessarily a criticism of the Conservative Opposition: almost certainly the same would occur if the party roles in the House were reversed, and probably would have been when Labour was in Opposition in 1970–4.)

No. 10 is highly geared for preparing for Question time. The parliamentary section, under the virtually full-time control of one of the five private secretaries, has the most extensive system of records, with what statisticians would call 'instant retrieval'. When I wanted to recall an answer I had given, as president of the Board of Trade, to Michael Foot in the late 1940s about the Rank Organization, the relevant question was turned up in a couple of minutes. If there were complaints about the number of questions answered in any given fifteen-minute period there were up-to-date records to set against those of my predecessors – if I had asked they would have gone back to Palmerston.

But on so many pre-Question nights, I would open the three red boxes needed to house all the questions due for the previous day very late at night. If there was a state entertainment, e.g. for a head of state or head of government visit, or a No. 10 or other public dinner, or if I was returning from one of the places I was always being asked to visit, I would be working on the boxes, containing thirty-five to forty-five questions, until well after midnight, with Cabinet committee briefs and Foreign Office telegrams still waiting. Not all of the questions had to be studied in full. We might – possibly allowing for the grouping of identical questions – hope to reach 'Q5' or 'Q6'. Those further down in the list would be answered in written form, in precisely the same manner as those tabled for 'Written Answer'. With these all that mattered was the substantive answer. Even so, an oral question at, say, No. 23 had to be studied, since Mr Speaker might call the questioner for a supplementary to a question higher on the Order Paper. He might have a substantial

that 'I . . . reply to more questions and transfer proportionately fewer questions, than any prime minister since the war.' The figures were 8·3 per cent in 1974–5 and 7·2 per cent in 1975–6, against figures of 26·7, 16·4, 12·2, 13·4 and 12·2 in the sessions from 1970–1 to 1974 inclusive.

constituency or other point not covered in the main brief – so one had to be prepared for it.

At 2.30 on Tuesdays and Thursdays, the prime minister goes into his room to prepare for Questions, together with the members of the Private Office, the Press Office and the parliamentary private secretary (PPS). He would have been busying himself in readiness: if a government back-bencher had an early question, likely to be reached, the PPS might get an indication from the questioner. Most, though not all, government back-benchers would be unlikely to want to catch the prime minister out; some might have an important constituency question, or one relating to some important national or international preoccupation, and advance information of the supplementary could produce a fuller and more helpful answer.

For the rest, we had to guess from the pages and pages of 'Notes for supplementaries' what might come up. If the departmental minister answering questions from 2.35 to 3.15 was, say, the chancellor of the exchequer or the foreign and commonwealth secretary, then the prime minister would ask the No. 10 Treasury man, or the Foreign Office man, to go to the Officials' box and monitor the questions. Then if one of the prime minister's anticipated supplementary questions was answered by the chancellor or foreign secretary, he would know, and at least hope to get away with, an answer referring to 'the answer given earlier this afternoon by my Rt Hon. Friend'.

Despite all the necessary briefing, I regarded the private meeting before Questions as a time to relax and get into the mood. In a speech after my retirement to the Parliamentary Press Gallery, I described it as

'. . . a toning-up exercise, a kind of kick-about before the match to loosen up muscles, or, as an actor might say, the Green Room.

'As a matter of fact what is one of the greatest ordeals in the democratic world is largely a matter of mental attitude, which I could never get quite right.

'You would expect me to use sporting analogies. Throughout the sixties and for most of the past two years, I got into my head that this was cricket. That the Prime Minister was supposed to be at least a good county-class batsman and he could not afford to have his wicket taken, least of all by an unknown bowler.

'After a recess when the mood of the House can be even more difficult to judge than usual, I used to approach it with all the care of a batsman taking up his stance after the lunch or tea interval, dead bat, limp wrists, etc., though on one or two occasions I was tempted by a fast ball aimed at the eyebrows – when I was tempted to try to hook it over the deep fine leg boundary – usually only to be caught Boycott style. Round about last October, I began to have doubts about this. Why not football – let them score a goal or two. I would try to score more. There was one very stormy period before Christmas, when I decided that that afternoon it was going to be plain Rugby League, the kind I was brought up on.

'From then on the questions got a bit easier.'[1]

The high tribunal of the nation that Question time represents is running into other problems. One is 'syndication', the group organization of questions. This is not a new problem. I noticed the growth of this practice in Labour's Opposition years in the early seventies. Seven or eight back-benchers had small rectangular slips, which I later learned were handed round at a morning meeting by an official of the Conservative Central Office. (Though Members of Parliament are political animals, Parliament is richer in inverse ratio to the intervention of the party machine – of any party – in its functioning.) Most of them had endearing questions directed to the then Leader of the Opposition, mostly challenging him to say where he stood in relation to, and would he condemn, some industrial situation, speech, demonstration. Not only had the Leader of the Opposition no responsibility for these events: the Conservative Prime Minister had no responsibility to Parliament for the Leader of the Opposition. But the questioners made their point, and whatever the Leader of the Opposition refused to answer (an answer that had to be put in question form to the then prime minister) with cries of 'Answer, answer', or did answer, which is what they wanted, he could only lose thereby.

When the Labour Government came to power, syndication continued, but it was of a different order, with a different parliamentary significance. The paper slips were of a different colour, but the syndication was now pre-emptive of parliamentary time, and meant the exclusion from their parliamentary rights of the majority of Members of Parliament.

Let us take, out of forty oral questions to the prime minister, an Order Paper in which a particular question, *ipsissimis verbis* or with minor verbal changes, is listed as Question 1, 2, 5, 7, 9 11 and through the teens and twenties. Parliamentary practice has usually involved grouping to avoid repetitive answers. In other words, the prime minister replies: 'With permission, Mr Speaker, I will answer Questions 1, 2, 5, 7 and 9 together . . .' But he may include eleven, and up to a dozen, questions numbered in the twenties and thirties. If the tablers of each of

[1] 12 May 1976.

these questions are called by Mr Speaker, no other question is called, including those who 'drew' numbers 3, 4 and 6.[1]

To take an example, on 11 June 1974 Questions 1, 2, 7, 8, 14 and 16 asked whether a speech just made by the Chancellor of the Exchequer represented government policy. I grouped them, and the result was that they took the whole of Question time and no other was reached. Questions 3, 4 and 5 never had a chance.

A prime minister, being human, is subject to temptation. There may be a question early in the list which, because of its possible political embarrassment, he may not want to reach. If Questions 1, 2, 5, 7 and 9 are identical, and 11, 13, 15 recurring right up to No. 35 are on the same issue, a simple decision to group them together and admit more supplementaries will preclude everything else from No. 3 upwards. But, equally, if the subject matter of Questions 1, 2, etc. raises difficulties, he is tempted to group 1 and 2 only and expatiate at length, luxuriate even on 3, 4 and 6, with an unbounded desire to impart information to the House.

Prime ministers, have, in the past, yielded to temptation. Edward Heath, I noticed, would one week group up to Question 23, and in the following week follow a more austere grouping pattern. He was not the first: I have recollections of a similar flexibility in the sixties.

In 1974–6 I decided to regularize the practice. I would group identical questions up to 10, irrespective of their helpfulness or otherwise. This I announced to the House, and it was accepted. Even so, it meant a heavily weighted probability in favour of the syndicalists being called as apart from the one-question members. In December 1975 therefore I changed the practice, and answered each single question, even if it meant a degree of repetition on questions after the first.[2] Mr Speaker seemed to be condoning the change, by limiting the number of supplementaries to each repeated question. In default of control over the tabling of syndicated questions, this may be the best answer. Syndicalism, I told the Parliamentary Press Gallery,[3] had increased, is increasing and ought to be diminished, and so far the House has not found a satisfactory means of dealing with it.

The House of Commons Select Committee on Procedure, which in recent years has given useful advice on grouping, might well insist on drafting rules on this matter for the House to endorse or reject. The majority of constituencies are in danger of being disfranchised, if only

[1] Any oral question not reached by 3.30 or soon after is answered in written form, and a copy of the reply immediately sent to the questioner, and also printed in *Hansard*.
[2] *Hansard* (5 December 1975), col. 761 (written).
[3] 12 May 1976.

to a degree, at Question time through the operation of the syndicalists.[1]

The prime minister is not entirely defenceless. Most of them at some time have used the device of 'blocking answers', drafted in such a way as to enable the Table Office to refuse to accept further attempts to raise a particular subject, or to create a peg on which to put supplementaries of varying remoteness. A blocking answer, e.g. to a question on ministerial re-shuffles, or one asking if the prime minister will dismiss this or that minister, would say 'I do not intend to make any government changes until I make a further statement', or 'I do not propose to dismiss any minister unless and until I make a statement to that effect.'

Such an answer can be in response to either oral or written questions. The Table Office then refuses, for a period of three months, to accept any questions on similar lines: the Private Office then has to move quickly to get a question down ready to renew the block.

For some types of question, blocking answers would not be allowed, for example an intention to visit some area at home or abroad, or whether a named minister's speech represents the policy of Her Majesty's Government, or whether the prime minister will place a copy of a particular speech in the Library. Mr Speaker would regard such questions as part of the established methods of opening up prime ministerial Questions.

In 1974 I tried to reduce the time taken on 'visits' questions by grouping all those naming particular places. 'I have at present no plans to visit Rhodesia, Dublin, Christchurch in Dorset, Ormskirk, Bebington, the new local authority district of mid-Sussex or Scotland, Sir.'[2] There were immediate points of order, and it became very clear that the House was not amused. Nor, it seemed to me, was Mr Speaker. The experiment was not repeated.

An important part of the working of the House depends on cooperation between the Government and the principal Opposition party. Contact and consultation between the government chief whip and his opposite number is close and usually friendly, even at times of acute political controversy. The Government in theory has the last word and could dictate a particular parliamentary time-table, through its assumed parliamentary majority, but it would be unwise and contrary to parliamentary convention for it to attempt to do so too frequently.

[1] Labour syndication was encouraged from the autumn of 1975. The difference was that we did not aim for the tabling of large numbers of identical questions designed to dominate the early minutes of Question time. Our people were simply encouraged by the whips, and the prime minister's PPS, to put down questions on any subject, usually a constituency matter, to give an equal chance to Labour Members to bring questions forward to answer.

[2] *Hansard* (20 June 1974), col. 672.

Very occasionally, often towards the end of a tiring and hot late summer session,[1] or following some highly provocative government action (probably on procedure), as seen by the Opposition, all relations are broken off. 'The normal channels', the parliamentary phrase for contact between the whips, 'have ceased to exist', or 'are blocked'. Pairing ceases, marauding parties, thought to have gone home, are concealed in an MP's home near the House, then suddenly descend and vote in a division, defeating the Government if the operation has been well planned.[2]

An example of inter-party co-operation was seen in the first week of August 1975, over a highly controversial Bill, whose introduction had wrecked the parliamentary time-table, and threatened MPs with excessive delay in getting away to the beaches. The Remuneration, Charges and Grants Bill had been introduced following the Government's counter-inflation agreement with the TUC: it had to go through both Houses before the summer adjournment. Business in the Lords was more seriously congested than at any time within living memory, with major, highly controversial Bills on petroleum and submarine pipelines and on the public ownership of land, the setting up of the National Enterprise Board, as well as the Trade Unions and Labour Relations Bill. The Bill providing for the nationalization of aircraft and shipbuilding had been introduced in the Commons almost unpardonably late, owing to delays in preparation and drafting, and was withdrawn in early July, to be re-introduced in the next session. On top of these was thrust the counter-inflation measure. To get the programme through, with the government bills enacted before the normal time for the Queen's Speech opening the new session, would in any case mean the Lords coming back and sitting during the normal holiday period, with the Commons adjourned. Agreement was, in fact, reached, with great good-will, on the entire legislative programme (subject to postponing the Shipbuilding and Aircraft Bill to the 1975–6 session) at the price of extending the old session well into November – the Queen's

[1] It is particularly at this season that any prime minister, leader of the House and chief whip whose love of parliamentary democracy is not tempered by a high degree of masochism, echoes the words attributed to Harold Macmillan at the head of this chapter, 'Get 'em up'. After these words were written, a similar crisis occurred in May 1976, following parliamentary arguments and accusations about voting procedures, over the Shipbuilding and Aircraft Bill.

[2] For decades, Lord North Street, SW1, has been regarded as the centre for such operations: see *The Labour Government, 1964–70*, pp. 120–1, for an account of two such successful forays carrying amendments to the Finance Bill (the Budget legislation) on the night of 6–7 July 1976. This was in fact out of the blue; 'the normal channels' were functioning as usual. The Conservatives were following the practice of Geoffrey Byng and George Wigg, who organized similar forays in the early fifties from Richard Crossman's house in Vincent Square.

Speech was in the event on the twentieth, some three weeks later than normal. But as the price of this co-operation the Opposition exacted a not unreasonable promise that in the new session no seriously 'controversial' legislation would be introduced after Easter. Consequently there was something of a rush to get certain controversial Bills laid before Easter 1976, for Second Reading and subsequent stages thereafter. Only very rarely are the prime minister and the leader of the Opposition directly concerned with parliamentary business, though during that period each of us was fully and repeatedly consulted by our respective chief whips and business managers. But there are many occasions when the two leaders meet on privy councillor terms, for example on security matters. On cases which have been reported to the House, for example, I was asked to call on Harold Macmillan on the defection of Philby,[1] on the Dr Stephen Ward case (mentioned in the Profumo affair)[2] and on the Denning Report. The present leader of the Opposition came to see me on my proposed Committee of Privy Councillors on mercenaries, following the Angolan atrocities. Consultation has been close and continuous between the respective leaders, together with the minister or shadow minister concerned, on successive constitutional matters relating to Northern Ireland, such as the imposition of direct rule in March 1972 and again after the breakdown of power-sharing in 1974, and also on security there. Edward Heath called me in when a court case in Belfast threw some doubt on an aspect of the legal position of soldiers, and asked my agreement to co-operate in rushing a short Bill through all its parliamentary stages in one day to clear up the confusion.

Edward Heath, and later Mrs Thatcher, saw me a number of times for a general review of the Northern Ireland position in 1974–6, and following the Armagh shootings in January 1976 we set up two formalized Downing Street meetings, with a number of representatives of the Government and the Opposition, together with the Liberal and Ulster

---

[1] Subsequently Harold Macmillan refused in the national interest to give any information in reply to Questions. I intervened as follows:

'Is the right Hon. Gentleman aware that I can confirm what he has just said? In the two meetings which we have had, he has given my right Hon. Friend and me a very full and frank account of this case, which raises a number of issues which, frankly, cannot be discussed across the floor of the House. While we still have some grave anxieties about the way in which it has been handled, which I think it best we should pursue in further confidential discussions with the right Hon. Gentleman, we feel that in the public interest this is a matter which should now be left where it is and not made the subject of further public discussion or public inquiry.'

Harold Macmillan expressed his thanks, but some of my back-benchers were severely displeased. *Hansard* (16 July 1963), cols. 335–6.

[2] See Macmillan, op. cit., pp. 436–53 and the quotation heading Chapter IX below.

Unionist Leaders and the SDLP, with the intention that this should continue if the situation so required.

It is customary, when White Papers or other documents preparatory to legislation are on constitutional matters, for the leader of the Opposition to be handed an advance copy on embargoed terms, as in the case of Command Paper 6348 on Devolution, which I took to Mrs Thatcher's room.

Defence is a question that can be divisive politically, but which nevertheless should be a matter for intimate discussion between the prime minister and the leader of the Opposition. In 1963, when I became leader of the Labour Party, defence, particularly the nuclear issue, was a subject more divisive between sections of the Labour Party than between the two main parties. After 1963 I had little trouble with it, and even less when we took office and announced the Government's defence policy. As leader of the Opposition in those days, I formally asked for defence briefing on privy counsellor terms. This was refused, no doubt because Sir Alec Douglas-Home had been told that he must use the subject as a political weapon in the forthcoming election. After the Labour Government was formed, it was still a major issue in parliamentary debates, particularly as our defence policy was unfolded. After Edward Heath's election as leader of his party in July 1965, I pressed it again, but he was singularly resistant. On being pressed further, it was finally agreed that he would go to the Ministry of Defence headquarters for a full briefing, visual 'presentations', the lot. The date was fixed for 11 November, the day on which Mr Ian Smith in the event proclaimed Rhodesia's 'unilateral' – but illegal – declaration of independence. Edward Heath's defence briefing was cancelled: instead he was visiting me at No. 10 to discuss the Rhodesian situation. Following that, no interest was shown. As outgoing prime minister in 1970, briefing for me was not an issue, except for special situations in Northern Ireland – for example Edward Heath asked me over to Chequers to put me in the picture on Operation Motorman, the highly successful operation in Londonderry, due to take effect early the following morning. After the 1974 change of government, Edward Heath, too, was up to date with his briefing, so no special arrangements were necessary, and after his replacement by Mrs Thatcher the question did not arise again – apart from my arranging full security briefing for her and, as already mentioned, the all-party consultations on security and the military situation in Ulster.

Reference has been made to the prior issue, under embargo, of appropriate draft White Papers to the Opposition. It has also been the practice, for many years, that a copy of any government statement on a major issue to be announced in the House of Commons at 3.30 pm should be made available to the leader of the Opposition and relevant colleagues some fifteen minutes or more beforehand. This is done on embargo and privy counsellor terms. Clearly, there are occasions where advance disclosures would not be justified, and might be positively harmful. For example, the Budget speech is not handed to the leader of the Opposition in advance: copies begin to be handed over just as the chancellor, after two to two and a half hours of careful exposition, embarks on the final heart-warming, but by that time uninformative, passages of the peroration to the Budget speech.

Relating to the prior issue of White Papers is the question of what is issued to the press. Clearly, the advance issue of documents bearing on financial plans can be undesirable: although these 'Confidential Final Revises' (CFRs) are embargoed, MPs do not have entire confidence that the embargo will be fully honoured. The furore that followed the publication of the Public Expenditure White Paper (Cmnd 6393) in February 1976 was directed not only to the advance issued to the leader of the Opposition and used by the shadow chancellor; the issue to the press was strongly attacked and the point made that capital gains could have been made by any recipient, or any individual in whom a recipient confided, before the hour of publication. There was no evidence in fact that anything improper occurred.

At the Parliamentary Labour Party meeting on the evening following publication, there were strong demands that the practice of issuing CFRs should be ended, as being derogatory to the rights of Members themselves. It is a difficult problem. Members have been infuriated on the publication of a White Paper to hear, within a minute of the release, on radio or television, another Member answering questions in a way that showed a detailed knowledge of the subject matter which could not have been assimilated within so short a time. This occurred over the Devolution White Paper: some MPs received press copies and were asked for comments before the White Paper was available to MPs generally.

The CFR system is undoubtedly valuable to the Government of the day in publishing its statistics, expanding its policies and announcing forward programmes of public spending or other politically sensitive issues. Undoubtedly it is of value to the press, but not only to them: the public throughout the country benefit from the summary, analysis and commentary which would be less informative, and perhaps even downright wrong, if the writer had been unduly rushed: editions, whether of evening papers or broadcast programmes, will not wait.

There is a strong case for retaining the system, but better arrangements are needed to ensure equal treatment of MPs. Perhaps the answer lies in ending the custom of 'approach embargoes'. Up to the time of writing, there are two kinds of embargo – the absolute kind which bans approaching M Ps or others and the more relaxed variety, which allows such approaches. It is much to be doubted whether back-bench Members on both sides of the House will be satisfied until 'approach embargoes' are universally applied.

A significant development since the mid-sixties has been in the appointment of select committees of back-bench Members covering an ever-widening area of government operations. For very many years the only such committee was the Public Accounts Committee (PAC), founded by Gladstone in 1861 as part of his reform of our financial institutions. At a time when there was little confidence in the integrity of the system of controlling expenditure, he was particularly concerned to strengthen the safeguards against 'alienation', that is, diverting to another purpose, perhaps even a corrupt one, moneys that had been specifically voted by Parliament for a particular use. In the 1880s the then PAC made parliamentary history by deciding to define alienation as wasteful expenditure even if channelled to the original voting purpose. The precedent was set in relation to the purchase by the War Office of medal ribbon. A contract had been signed with Messrs Thorp and Sons for 14 shillings. This was later cancelled and another contract signed with Messrs Davies at 20 shillings. The War Office rejected the C and AG's demand for an explanation on the ground that the governing act gave the C and AG no power to query administration. The PAC stood their ground and asserted their right to query wasteful expenditure. The Treasury supported the PAC and the battle was won.[1]

From then on if the House had voted, say, £400,000 for some military construction project, and the final expenditure rose to £700,000, there was 'alienation', namely waste. From that time the PAC became a major, prestigious parliamentary institution, and the scourge of the bureaucracy. It summons no witnesses, except the civil service head of the department under examination, and the comptroller and auditor-general (C and AG) nominally as a witness, in reality the committee's servant, the high and independent officer who guides and inspires their investigations. Take, for example, the examination in the early sixties of the expenditure record of the Ministry of Defence on the missile programme, including the ill-fated Blue Streak. The Permanent Secretary attended in his capacity of accounting officer, which every department has to appoint under the Exchequer and Audit Acts – he

---

[1] See the Treasury's 'Epitome' supporting the Committee, with their reasons. *Second Report*, Public Accounts Committee 1888, pp. 207–8.

is invariably the head of the department, and he can be summoned to account not only for his department's stewardship, but also in respect of departmental grants-in-aid to outside bodies. In addition, the Treasury is represented by the 'Treasury Officer of Accounts', a senior official on the public expenditure side. Neither he nor the C and AG can intervene, unless called on by a Member: but in fact most of the questions put by chairman or members begin life as the work of the C and AG.

Even the toughest, most experienced permanent secretaries have expressed feelings amounting almost to terror when they face examination. They are briefed for days, by their departmental finance officers and under-secretaries responsible for the issues under examination. They will have read the comptroller and auditor-general's notes, comments and criticisms on the particular spending programmes of their department for the previous financial year, and will arrive with masses of files, supported by their financial advisers. I recall my permanent secretary in the 1940s, a war hero of World War I, tough, experienced in departmental and inter-departmental battle, who had served a wide range of senior ministers in war and in peace, telling me that he had survived a Cripps and a Wilson, and many others, month in, month out, without any anxieties, but that the night before he appeared before the PAC each year he never slept a wink. Other accounting officers have told me the same.

Membership of the PAC has traditionally carried great prestige with it; senior Members of the House, ex-ministers and usually some of the most promising younger Members, with bright prospects of promotion, are selected by their whips for an apprenticeship there. Many brilliant ministerial careers began as a result of PAC service.[1]

The chairman of the committee is always a Member of the Opposition, usually an ex-minister. For many years the tradition was to appoint the former financial secretary to the Treasury, or other high Treasury minister.[2] In an age when hardly any MP, back-bench or front-bench,

[1] When I made my proposals for a fully empowered PAC for the European Parliament, in a public speech on 26 September 1975, and again when I submitted a formal scheme to the European Council (Heads of Government Summit) in December of that year, aimed at bringing the flabby financial arrangements of the Community under control, I mentioned that, as with the Westminster PAC, young European parliamentarians could make their reputations there, and this would give the strength to the Parliament, in its early years, that supporters of EEC would welcome. In the early 1970s Edmund Dell added to his already high reputation, earned as a minister, by his handling and exposé of the North Sea oil situation, as acting chairman of the PAC.

[2] Though I had no direct Treasury experience, as a former president of the Board of Trade I was chairman from 1959 to 1963, and was thus able to preside over the centenary celebration. On the day of the centenary the Committee was examining Sir Henry Hardman, the permanent secretary to the Ministry of Agriculture, who had had pretty

had a room, the PAC chairman had. He had regular detailed briefing from the C and AG and his staff. I calculated that it meant two full days' work a week (plus home-work) 'in the hunting season'. (Accounting officers are 'hunted', according to the Committee's priorities, from December to July–August.)

Although the Committee consists of active party politicians, it tends to act as a single all-party, even non-party, body of high detachment and integrity. I learnt a lesson as chairman when we were due to devote four committee sessions to examining the egregious record of expenditure on various missile projects, where the funds authorized at the outset were exceeded, in some cases many times over. I approached Sir John Arbuthnot, then, as the Americans would have put it, 'ranking' Conservative Member on the Committee. I pointed out that, as shadow chancellor, I had in a number of debates, and at Question time, made some strong comments on some of the projects, particularly 'Blue Streak'. Would it not be better if I stood down from these meetings? He was horrified. What is said in political debate in the Chamber, he said, has nothing to do with what happens in Committee Room 15. If it had been thought that I could not tread the stairs from the Chamber level to the Committee corridor, I should not have been chairman.

During the years I was chairman, there was a great demand in the House that Parliament should exert a much greater control over expenditure. This was urged in particular by a ginger group on the Government side, headed by the then Lord Hinchingbrooke. They organized well, by intervening at the beginning of each Supply Day. The twenty-nine Supply Days, when the subject for debate is chosen by the Opposition, have for many years been directed to any subject on which the Government's policies can be lambasted. While nominally directed to examining and querying individual expenditure programmes, far more Supply Days involve calls to spend more than those devoted to calls for retrenchment. To set the debate in motion, the estimate of the department to be criticized would be tabled for discussion and usually carried formally, so that the main debate could begin early, either on a formal motion, or as a general airing of the announced subject. Lord Hinchingbrooke and his colleagues made clear that they would initiate a detailed debate on the estimate before the House, to the embarrassment of the Government of the day and the fury of the main Opposition speaker.

In the event, as shadow chancellor, I proposed that their point should be met by the House setting aside three days for debate on public

rough handling in previous sessions. He asked leave, at the beginning of the meeting, 'as the toad beneath the harrow', to congratulate the Committee on its centenary.

expenditure, two to be provided out of Government time, and the third by the Opposition allocating one of 'their' Supply Days. One of the three would debate the most recent report of PAC, a second the report or reports of the Select Committee on Expenditure, and the third a more general debate on controlling expenditure. It has not been a successful experiment. Attendance is usually poor: there is no vote; the debate has tended to dwell on particular items in the PAC or other committee report.

Junior to the PAC, but of long standing and prestige under different names, is the Select Committee on Expenditure. It was originally established in 1912 as the Estimates Committee. In 1914 its activities were suspended because of war secrecy, but in 1917 it was reconstituted as the Select Committee on National Expenditure, reverting to its former title in 1920. In the war of 1939–45 it again became the Select Committee on National Expenditure,[1] and Estimates again in 1945. In 1970 it was again named as the Select Committee on Expenditure, with terms of reference 'to consider how, if at all, the policies implied in the figures of expenditure and in the estimates may be carried out more economically, and to examine the form of the papers and of the estimates presented to this House'. The Committee consists of forty-nine members with a quorum of nine.

Another committee that has earned great respect is the Select Committee on Nationalized Industries, first set up in 1951. In 1958 its terms of reference were widened, and now are: 'to examine the Reports and Accounts of the Nationalized Industries established by statute whose controlling Boards are appointed by Ministers of the Crown and whose annual receipts are not wholly or mainly by Parliament as advanced from the Exchequer'.

Again, a still younger committee, that on Science and Technology, has earned wide respect both in Parliament and in the wider scientific world.[2]

Up to 1964 there were only the three select committees dealing with government operations (as opposed to regulating the affairs of the House, such as Privileges, Procedure and Services), namely, Public Accounts, Estimates and Nationalized Industries.

---

[1] Its terms of reference were 'to examine the current expenditure defrayed out of moneys provided by Parliament for the Defence Services, for Civil Defence, and for other services directly connected with the war, and to report what, if any, economies consistent with the execution of the policy decided by the Government may be effected therein'.

[2] See an article in *The Times* (27 May 1976), 'Ten Years of the Select Committee on Science and Technology', by Arthur Palmer, MP, its chairman. (He pays credit to Richard Crossman for the part he played in its creation as one of the first experiments in widening the select committee system.)

In August 1966 Richard Crossman became leader of the House, and immediately began on a programme of reform, which many Members, especially the new entrants of March 1966, most of them impatient of ancient procedures, felt to be long overdue. He moved to set up each select committee for a single session only, with no undertaking that it would be reconstituted in the succeeding session.

His reforms have been built on by successive leaders of the House. At the beginning of the 1975–6 session there were twelve main Select Committees – Armed Forces; Cyprus; European Secondary Legislation (with three sub-committees); Expenditure (with six sub-committees); Nationalized Industries (with three sub-committees); Overseas Development; Public Accounts; Race Relations and Immigration; Science and Technology (with three sub-committees); a joint select committee with the Lords on Statutory Instruments, and a separate Commons select committee on the same subject; and Violence in the Family.

There is no doubt that the select committees have steadily gained in experience and prestige, their reports going very far to open up the work of ministers and departments to the press and the public – and they undoubtedly are creating a remarkable standing in Whitehall.[1] One danger that can be foreseen is the assertion of one or two chairmen and other members of committees or sub-committees, that they are seeking to assimilate their work into that of the Committees of the two Houses of the United States Congress, where, as argued above, and in chapter X, the system is entirely different, in that the US president and his departmental secretaries are not accountable on the floor of either House, as are members of the British government. Another problem which could come to a head would arise if and when a committee seeks to put questions, or raise issues, which would be ruled out of order by Mr Speaker if raised on the floor of the House, and similarly by the chairman or deputy chairman if raised in a standing committee of the White House.

Just before the change of government in April 1976, I was in trouble over select committees. The (usually feverish) pre-Christmas week had been attended by high drama over the Chrysler affair. This is not the place to argue the rights and wrongs of it, but the Trade and Industry Sub-Committee of the Select Committee on Expenditure, which in August had issued a report on the automobile industry critical of government policy over Leyland, quite appropriately decided to apply

[1] Select committee activity is now prodigious, and some of them take their evidence in public. For example, in the week ending 21 May 1976 there were 23 meetings, 7 of them in public; the following week 20 of which 9 were in public. Certain national newspapers published daily lists of committees meeting in public each day, so that anyone interested can attend.

themselves to the Chrysler affair. This had been most unfortunately and almost unprecedently attended by a grotesque series of leaks, involving ministers. The sub-committee, having naturally read reports, about a suggested Rasputin-like role undertaken by Harold Lever, chancellor of the Duchy of Lancaster – reports which, by whomsoever inspired, did not in my view accurately reflect what actually happened – called on him to give evidence before the Committee. Rightly or wrongly, I felt it to be contrary to the principle of collective responsibility for a number of ministers to be called in an endeavour to establish the attitude each had taken up in Cabinet and the individual advice each had given to his colleagues. I ruled that the only ministers to go should be those who bore in Parliament the responsibility for the issues under investigation: on the floor of the House questions are directed to the responsible minister, regardless of the presumed opinions of other Cabinet members. In any event I could not lend my support to the selection of ministerial witnesses on the basis of press leaks, still less on press speculation.

Questions followed in Parliament. I made it clear that I was not saying that *only* the responsible minister, as recognized in questioning on the floor of the House, should go: for example, while the minister of agriculture and the foreign and commonwealth secretary could properly be invited to give evidence on negotiations they had conducted in the E E C, it would be perfectly appropriate for the relevant committee to invite, say, the secretary of state for prices and consumer protection to answer questions on the effects of any agreement on the cost of living. The whole question was still unresolved when I submitted my resignation as prime minister.

This work is not the place to discuss reform of parliamentary procedure, on which the Leader of the House has announced the appointment of a select committee. I have always been among the minority who consider that the House should sit in the mornings, though most ministers in all administrations oppose this because they need the mornings for consultations in their departments, and it is certainly the case that an early start, say 11.0 am, would not guarantee a 7.0 pm finish: parliamentary business would tend to expand to fill all the waking hours and some beyond.

I would, however, mention one possible area of reform, which since, I proposed it in July 1964, before Labour returned to office, did lead to a not insignificant innovation, and for which there is a case for taking it further.

On 4 July 1964, speaking at Stowmarket, I made three proposals. The first, a commitment, was the appointment of an ombudsman: I had referred this to Shadow Cabinet and National Executive Committees; after six months nothing had happened, so I announced it as policy. The second was for a different method of initiating Bills on issues where there was little inter-party controversy, but where MPs and members of the public could have very different views on the best course to pursue. Recalling my Gladstonian studies at the university, I pointed out that important decisions on parliamentary control of the developing railway system, presenting totally new problems for the House, were referred to a select committee chaired by the responsible minister, Gladstone, at that time vice-president of the Board of Trade. After taking evidence and holding a number of deliberative sessions, the Committee, despite its all-party membership, produced an agreed report, *to which was attached the draft of a Bill* for introduction into the House. As amended by the House, this became the Railways Regulation Act of 1844.[1] (A similar practice is followed by the Law Commission, the law review body set up by the Labour Government of 1964: its authoritative reports frequently append a draft of suitable legislation for Parliament to consider.)

In the event, the reforms of 1964–70 did not go so far: instead the 'Second Reading Committee' proposal for uncontroversial legislation, particularly on matters of some complexity, was adopted, relieving the House of some of its legislative work. The over-burdening of Parliament, under any government, has now become so acute that the saving of time on the floor of the House, without weakening parliamentary control, must be one of the urgent preoccupations of the special Procedure Select Committee. Unfortunately, what I hoped for, and still in principle support, is made more difficult by the fact that there are now so many committees, select and other, that the available members are chronically over-worked, to the detriment of attendance in debates on the floor of the House.

The third Stowmarket proposal involved a reform of the White Paper system. Government policy on major issues, especially those arousing controversy (including manifesto commitments made before and during an election), should appropriately be White Paper material where the Government states its view, and fights to ensure that the view prevails. There are, however, many issues not of this kind, but on which honest differences of opinion can be held by men and women of good-will, and no less of experience – I instanced such questions as legislation on the care of children, where it was not to be assumed that all wisdom resided in a government department. The result was the invention of the 'Green

[1] 7 & 8 Vict. c. 85.

Paper'. This sets out the Government's provisional views, but on the basis that there will be no loss of face if free public discussion provides better solutions. The first Green Paper, in 1967, was issued by Michael Stewart as secretary of state for economic affairs, and consulted public opinion on the concept of the Regional Employment Premium and other proposals to help reduce the economic disparities between regions.[1] After public discussion, its principal ideas went forward to legislation. In another case, reform of the organization of the National Health Service, the Green Paper of the then minister, Kenneth Robinson, failed to impress, and a second attempt was made by Richard Crossman a year or two later, gaining greater acceptance.

To use a phrase that has become more popular since, these proposals were designed to advance 'open government', and indeed did so. It is a tribute to that very limited start that, since then, new ideas have proliferated almost daily to get a fuller popular participation in the processes of government.

[1] *The Development Areas: A Proposal for a Regional Employment Premium* (April 1967).

VIII

The Prime Minister and his Party

'Party is organised opinion. . . . I had to prepare the mind of the country, and . . . to educate our party. . . . I believe that without party Parliamentary government is impossible.' BENJAMIN DISRAELI[1]

The prime minister is leader of his party, not only in Parliament but in the country. Without the support of his party he is nothing. If he loses the support of the majority of his parliamentary party he is out. If he loses the support of his party in the country he is in danger. In saying this I do not necessarily identify the party in the country with the party machine. He may have clear support in his party in the country – and here it is sometimes necessary to draw a distinction between party activists and the broader mass of party supporters. If he loses the support of the party machine he is in trouble. If he loses the support of his party in the country, and cannot get it back, he should contemplate cultivating roses.

In saying this, I rule out coalitions as normally defined. I always have, save in extreme circumstances, such as war. Cabinet government is about decisions. Peacetime coalitions almost invariably produce fudged decisions, where words matter more than actions, and the achievement of the lowest common denominator is regarded as the highest act of coalition statesmanship. Moreover, except in cases of an election providing a 1923 or a 1929 situation, an inter-party coalition inevitably produces – it is sometimes designed to produce – a paralysis of opposition. And when an important and self-conscious section of the country is denied effective parliamentary representation, frustration leads to extra-parliamentary action.

[1] The first two sentences are taken from a speech at a meeting of the Society for Increasing Endowments of Small Livings in the Diocese of Oxford, 25 November 1864; the third from his speech at Manchester, 3 April 1872.

In any case, every party leader who forms a party-based government is the head of a coalition. Every major party is itself a coalition: I have described the Labour Party as a broad church. So are the Conservatives. A party claiming, as is so often done, the support of half the country will almost certainly embrace within its parliamentary representation a range of views covering more than half the views held in the country.

This chapter inevitably will describe relations between the prime minister, the party leader, the Cabinet and the party (party machine and party in the country), in terms of the Labour Party, which I know. I cannot write with authority about the Conservative Party, even though over the years I have devoted some academic study to the subject. Suffice it therefore to record some basic differences which it would appear exist between the two major parties, on the relationship between the leader (be he prime minister or Opposition leader) and his party.

First, the Conservative leader governs Central Office. He appoints the chairman and principal directors.[1] He is not totally unfettered: Edward Heath ran into resistance from regional chairmen when he sought to remove Edward du Cann. He bided his time, chose a suitable moment, and replaced him by Anthony Barber. Lord Thorneycroft was Mrs Thatcher's appointment after her election: she exercised her powers, with some criticism but no interference, to dismiss Edward Heath's recent personal appointment, Michael Wolff, as director-general of the Conservative Party Organization. Other dismissals followed. This means that the Conservative leader is fairly well proofed against trouble with the machinery; it is his fief, an appointive bureaucracy. On the other hand, this method does not ensure the active support of the party in the country.

In contrast, the appointment of the Labour Party machine owes nothing to the leader. He himself sits on the thirty-strong National Executive Committee *ex officio* as leader – though the three leaders chosen since the war were elected in their own right before becoming leader. The NEC is elected by the Annual Conference in sections representing constituency parties, trade unions, women members, affiliated socialist societies and the Young Socialists. The remaining members are the leader, deputy leader and treasurer; the general secretary, elected by the Executive itself, is also a member, but without a vote. It is therefore much more responsive to Conference, and much more closely related to the power groups – constituency, trade unions and the others – that elect the various sections.

Second, the Conservative leader naturally nominates the Cabinet

[1] I use the word 'he' throughout as I am commenting on a system, not any particular individual.

when the party is in office, but he also nominates the members of the so-called Shadow Cabinet and allocates the shadow 'portfolios', and also appoints junior spokesmen. This means that in the parliamentary party those who would regard themselves as the best fitted for appointment (usually not less than eighty per cent of any parliamentary party, of whatever colour) tend to harbour disappointment. Their basic loyalty to the leader tends at times when morale is low to cause them to criticize not the leader, but the inadequate qualities and performance of those he appoints.

I have commented in chapter II above on the great advantage a Labour leader in Opposition has in having his Shadow Cabinet elected for him by the whole parliamentary party, and the help this gives to the leader on forming a government. This reduces, though it does not eliminate, criticism of his appointments.

Third, the Conservative Party programme between elections, and the manifesto issued at the beginning of the campaign, is virtually dictated by the leader, together with his closest associates, assisted of course by party officials. In contrast, the Labour Party programme and policy statements issued between elections are the responsibility of the NEC – major ones usually being thrashed out at joint meetings between NEC and Cabinet (or Shadow Cabinet). The procedure followed for the manifesto is laid down in Clause V of the Party Constitution.

While the 'party programme' is made up of decisions taken by party conference, and requires a majority of not less than two-thirds of the votes recorded on a card vote,

> 'The National Executive Committee and the Parliamentary Committee of the Parliamentary Labour Party shall decide which items from the Party Programme shall be included in the Manifesto which shall be issued by the National Executive Committee prior to every General Election. The joint meeting of the two Committees shall also define the attitude of the Party to the principal issues raised by the Election which are not covered by the Manifesto.'

When the Constitution was drawn up by Sidney Webb in 1918, the Party hardly envisaged the possibility of a Labour government. In modern times the clause has been interpreted as meaning that, while in Opposition, it is the Parliamentary Committee (including the elected leadership) that conducts the discussions with the NEC; in Government it is the Cabinet. Despite the Constitution, the Parliamentary Committee would be inappropriate when Labour is in office, because it is elected from the ranks of the back-bench Labour MPs, ministers being excluded and having no vote. Nevertheless, the Constitution is flexible enough to allow the joint meeting both to agree on a policy for issues that may only have emerged since Conference, and to select 'programme' issues for inclusion in the manifesto.[1] In recent years, with the makeup of the NEC on the one hand and of the Shadow Cabinet (or Cabinet) on the other, the meetings have tended to be the occasion for the more left-wing NEC members to press particular areas of conference policy for inclusion (e.g. sweeping defence cuts, nationalization commitments and heavy social spending), while the Parliamentary Committee, still more the Cabinet, tends to be more cautious. A Cabinet has access to full cost estimates of party programmes, and can usually insist on keeping them within the bounds set by the Government. Most party programmes emphasize that the party looks forward to a period ten or fifteen years ahead, beyond what can be done within a single four- or five-year Parliament, because of the limitations of expenditure and of parliamentary time.[2]

It is clear, therefore, that the Conservative leader has, in theory at least, far more authority than the Labour leader, in respect of control over the party machine, appointments to the Shadow Cabinet and therefore consequently to an incoming government, and also in determining the policy on which the Party fights a general election. How far this power is exercised in practice, in both Government and Opposition, depends on the style of the individual leader and how he can secure his objectives without standing too much on his authority. A great deal of analysis, not least by Conservative writers, of the respective styles of Harold Macmillan and Edward Heath tends to bear this out. In the last resort the leader's effectiveness depends on the considerations set out in the quotation from Lord Rosebery at the head of chapter III. Whatever constitution or convention may say, party management is essentially man-management, as in every other walk of life.

For the reasons given, the analysis of the rest of this chapter relates to relations between the prime minister in the Labour Party setting.

[1] For example, take the February 1974 manifesto. The two bodies met in January and February 1974. The issue of 'confrontation', the then Government versus the miners and TUC, had not emerged in any serious form at the time of the Labour Party Conference in the previous October, when the then Government were still talking with the TUC, but it played a dominant part in the manifesto and in the election. A further complication was that NEC members naturally wished to include in the manifesto policy proposals included in 'Labour's Programme', 1973, which had been debated throughout the week at Conference, *but not specifically put to Conference* or endorsed by it: it therefore did not have the status of the two-thirds majority enjoyed by the Constitution for inclusion in the 'programme', something I had been watching very carefully before and during Conference.

[2] The manifesto of February 1974, for example, after setting out the Party's general aims and policies, lays down, 'Of course . . . these aims, like the particular items in the programme, cannot all be fulfilled at once.'

The leader of the Labour Party is Labour's man; he must be capable of being described by the press in a kind moment – perhaps after his retirement – as the 'people's premier', or he is nothing. This means preferably that he must have spent a political lifetime with the Party at local level, organizationally, on propagation of party philosophy and policies, and that, as leader, he has to be constantly accessible to every area of the country.

As the political, as well as administrative, head of the Government, a Labour prime minister has to operate in a number of intersecting party political circles.

The first is PLP meetings. There is a routine meeting every Thursday at 6.0 pm, after the parliamentary business for the next week has been announced. This is first and foremost to discuss the business, and receive a report from the chief whip on the vital votes where he must ask for a full attendance. But almost anything can be raised under 'Any other business', and sometimes the parliamentary back-bench leadership tables on the agenda a specific item for discussion. Special meetings are held every week or two, usually on items shortly to come before the House, as, recently, the defence White Paper, public expenditure, import controls, Europe or a more general discussion on broad economic policy, counter-inflation policy or longer-term problems such as parliamentary reform. The responsible ministers are in attendance and either open or wind up the debate. A vote can be called for on an issue of which notice has been given, and motions or amendments tabled.

Within the Parliamentary Party there is a network of 'subject groups', some of which beget sub-committees. At the beginning of the 1975–6 parliamentary session, there were thirty-four main groups, some with sub-groups.[1] In addition there are, besides the Scottish and Welsh groups, seven main regional groups, with further regular meetings of MPs concerned with a particular area such as Merseyside. Ministers, senior and junior, are regular attenders at their meetings.

The prime minister is frequently asked to receive deputations from 'subject groups', regional groups or informal groupings formed for some immediate purpose. In the sixties my door was always open. In 1974–6, I tended rather to insist that they should see the minister concerned with the subject they had in mind. The prime minister should be wary of being asked to receive a deputation desirous of asking him to direct a minister to take a particular line on some decision (e.g. the siting of a factory) – there may be in the wings another shadow group wanting precisely the opposite decision to be taken. The right forum is the floor of the House, or the appropriate group of the PLP, or, better, a direct

1 Two more were set up in May 1976.

approach to the minister, who, from other deputations he may have received as well, can assess the arguments which should govern his decision.

Having led three governments with minuscule – or minus – majorities, there is one type of deputation to which I have always been particularly resistant. This is the one which, as a reason for seeking a meeting, or when the meeting is held, is anxious to make clear that it exceeds in number the Government's titular majority, and that therefore the prime minister must be prepared to accept its urgings. If this information is tendered in advance, the deputation is curtly informed that the meeting will not take place. If it is deferred until the meeting begins, the ending is speedy.

In 1964, with a titular majority of four, with, at times of a three-line whip, sick members being accommodated in something approaching a hospital ward administered by Britain's first woman whip (until a more compassionate pairing arrangement was worked out between the two parties), I was asked to receive a deputation. They began with the warning that their numbers exceeded the majority. I told them we could not meet on such a basis, for every formal or informal group in the Party exceeded the majority. Indeed, there could well be an even larger group taking a diametrically opposed view, and if this principle were accepted other deputations concerned with entirely different subjects could endeavour to operate a similar blackmail. In past times, not recently, they were told, the number of committed Henry Georgeites, or Douglas Social Creditors, might have put forward similar claims: not very long before 1964 – some would say since – a deputation from the Flat Earthers might have sought to exercise a similar degree of pressure. The Government would govern as long as it commanded the support of a majority, however narrow, in the House. If individuals or caucuses destroyed that majority for sectional motives, those responsible would have to face the electoral consequences. The Government had announced that it would act as though it had a majority not of four, but of forty: we would continue the implementation of the policy on which we had fought the election, not be forced to pick our way through factional puddles on the road. They left.

Politicians and journalists have sometimes raised in discussion the question, is a parliamentary situation with a single-figure majority easier or harder to operate than one based on a landslide? It is very arguable. Clement Attlee explained to the 1950 Labour Party Conference the problems of living with a majority of five – not disloyalty, he said but 'a question of health'.[1]

[1] Labour Party, *Conference Report* (London 1950), p. 98.

There is no such anxiety with a majority such as Labour had in 1945 – 246 – or 1966 – 97. The problem in those conditions is the tendency of pressure groups within the Parliamentary Party to indulge their differences with the Government, and increase their popularity with their constituents or factions within the party, and to organize spectacular collective abstentions, or even votes against the Government. This is highly inconvenient, and much is made of it by the Opposition and the press.

My impression is that there is a scientific 'law of majorities'. Let x be the Government's overall majority. Then x is greater than y, where y is the organized abstention; it is also greater than $2z$ where z is the number of government back-benchers collectively voting against the Government: x minus y, and x minus $2z$, is thus almost always a finite number but usually fairly small, perhaps single figures.

Apart from formal parliamentary meetings, groups and deputations, more regular means of co-operation have been developed by the appointment of a Liaison Committee between the Cabinet and the PLP; the prime minister nominates the leader of the House, the chief whips in both Houses, and three other ministers, the PLP being represented by its back-bench chairman, vice-chairman and five other elected members of the Parliamentary Committee, together with a back-bencher in the House of Lords.[1]

The second intersecting circle is the National Executive Committee. The prime minister, as party leader, is a member, and usually attends important meetings, especially, of course, joint meetings with the Cabinet. He would rarely attend a meeting of a sub-committee of the NEC. Hugh Gaitskell, as leader of the Opposition, frequently did, in a period of somewhat divided counsels, but not of course as prime minister.

One thing must be made clear. The prime minister and his Cabinet cannot be instructed by the National Executive Committee or by Conference.

In what is the *locus classicus* of this constitutional doctrine, Clement Attlee, in the interview quoted in previous chapters, said this:

> '[*Williams:*] *There's a great deal more formal machinery of party decision in the Labour Party than in the Conservative Party. Did this reduce your freedom of action?*
>
> '[*Attlee:*] No. Naturally as the leader of a party any Prime Minister has been sent in to carry out a party programme. That is what electors have voted for. He wouldn't be leader if he didn't believe in

---

[1] For organization, membership and terms of reference of the (back-bench) Parliamentary Committee with Labour in government, March 1974, see the *Annual Report* of the National Executive Committee (1974), p. 74.

it. But he must always remember that he is more than a party leader. His government is responsible primarily to Parliament and through Parliament to the nation. If you begin to consider yourself solely responsible to a political party you're halfway to a dictatorship. You must always have in mind what is in the best interests of the country as a whole at a particular time.

'In the Labour Party the Annual Conference passes resolutions which are party policies. It is for the National Executive to interpret these in a national sphere. But as far as work in the House goes they must always be interpreted and dealt with in the light of circumstances by the Parliamentary Party. They are a guidance to the Parliamentary Party, not an absolute mandate. They couldn't be. You can't have a non-parliamentary body arranging things, saying, "You mustn't do this. You mustn't do the other." What you do must depend on the circumstances. The National Executive is useful in giving a consensus of opinion, keeping you in touch with feeling but there can never be any question of orders being issued by the National Executive to a Labour government. That would be quite out of the question. You must always remember you are the government of all the country and act accordingly . . .'[1]

In 1970 the disappointment that followed Labour's election defeat, together with memories of the gap that had opened up in 1968–70 between the Government and the Party, led to strongly backed assertions that a future Labour Government should be under tighter direction from Conference. A resolution was moved at the Conference in October, of which the operative opening paragraph sought to lay down that: 'The Parliamentary Labour Party leaders, whether in government or opposition, should reflect the views and aspirations of the Labour and Trade Union movement, by framing their policies on Annual Conference decision . . .' The resolution then went on to 'deplore the Parliamentary Labour Party's refusal to act on Conference decisions . . .'

This would in fact have been difficult in the 1960s, when Conference took diametrically opposite decisions in succeeding years on, for example, EEC and other questions. In my reply to the debate, I repeated the Attlee doctrine:

'. . . even when the Movement tore itself apart in 1960 there was no one then who suggested that, in the day to day work of the Labour Government, Conference decisions should be binding. We recall the 1945 correspondence, now I suppose almost written into our national

[1] Francis Williams, *A Prime Minister Remembers* (London 1961); reprinted in *The British Prime Minister*, ed. Anthony King (London 1969), pp. 78–9.

Constitution, between Clem Attlee and Winston Churchill, when the Conservatives sought to create a constitutional bogey in the person of Harold Laski.

'We recall the precise terms in which Nye Bevan, defeated at Annual Conference on the question of tied cottages, explained the position of a Labour Government in relation to Conference decisions. . . .

'. . . A Prime Minister is responsible to the House of Commons and acts on the basis of the Cabinet judgment of what is necessary in the public interest in so far as and as long as he commands the confidence of the House of Commons, and he cannot be from day to day instructed by any authority other than Parliament . . .'

I went on to assert, as Clement Attlee had said, that any Labour Government would seek to act in accordance with the general policy, and indeed wishes of the movement:

'But timing and priorities must be a matter for a Labour Government, because an interventionist government, a Socialist Government, has to decide priorities every day of its life.

'In particular, I do not think anyone would suggest that a government operating within the broad strategy, laid down by the Party programme, itself stemming from Conference, which Conference has asked should be included in the manifesto, should be required automatically to carry out each and every decision of each and every annual Conference.'[1]

On the subsequent card vote, the resolution was carried by 3,085,000 to 2,801,000. I made it clear that no future Labour Government would be bound by it. Nor has it been.[2]

The prime minister, in keeping in touch with the National Executive Committee, is not limited to attendance at formal NEC meetings and joint Cabinet–NEC discussions. After Labour's return to office in 1974, the Liaison and Campaign Committees that had existed in Opposition were merged, and the new Liaison Committee, with Cabinet ministers nominated by the prime minister and Executive members elected by the NEC, have met regularly.

More informally, a high-level liaison committee consisting of the leading parliamentary ministers and the NEC have met at No. 10 at 9.30 every Tuesday morning when government and international com-

[1] Labour Party, *Conference Report 1970*, pp. 183–4.
[2] See Richard Crossman, *Bagehot Revisited* (op. cit.), pp. 114–15, referring to relations with the NEC and Cabinet; 'I think there is nothing more enjoyable than watching the skill of a good Labour leader riding those two horses and not coming unstuck.'

mitments made this possible: the Government was represented by the prime minister, lord president, foreign and commonwealth secretary (also treasurer of the Party), chief whip; the NEC by the chairman, vice-chairman and general secretary of the Party, to consider any question affecting relations between the two, including arrangements for joint meetings.

But even more important, in my experience, has been the prime minister's travels, away from Parliament and the NEC, to meet party members all over the country.

In my statement to the Cabinet on 16 March, announcing my impending resignation, I gave a piece of gratuitous advice to my, as then, unchosen successor.[1] I said:

'You must find time to stand back and think about the problems of the Administration, its purpose, its co-ordination and its long-term strategy. Equally, you have to watch for that cloud no bigger than a man's hand which may threaten not to-morrow's crisis, but next month's or next year's. In all this you have got to think and feel politically as well as in constitutional and administrative terms.

'It is not only the job here in Westminster, Whitehall and Parliament. It is the job in the country. The leader of the Party, and no less the Prime Minister, has a duty to meet the people, to address political and other meetings. For 13 years I have averaged well over 100 a year, covering nearly every constituency, some of them many times.'

What I was stressing in that figure did not relate to public meetings, where the speaker is cut off from the audience, whom in days of television glare he might not be able to see, but the practice I began in February 1967, of attending receptions of some 300–500 active members of, say, six or seven constituency parties, in a city, conurbation or county, meeting everyone, listening to comments, advice, criticism and sometimes praise, signing hundreds of autographs – saying a few words of greeting from the platform at the beginning and end.[2] These speeches were usually informal, though if any great developments dominated

---

[1] See the Preface, above.

[2] Compare W. Bagehot, *Collected Works*, ed. Norman St John-Stevas (London 1974), VII, p. 67. 'The Prime Minister is at the head of our business and like every head of a business he ought to have mind in reserve. He must be able to take a fresh view of new contingencies and keep an animated curiosity to coming events. If he suffers himself to be involved in minutiae, some great change in the world, some Franco-German war may break out, like a thief in the night, and if he has no elastic thought, and no spare energy he may make the worst error. A great Premier must add the vivacity of a lazy man to the assiduity of a very laborious one.'

the political scene, I could use the occasion for a major, on-the-record statement of five to ten minutes, with press and broadcasting services present. For example, two of my most widely reported statements on Northern Ireland in 1971–2 were at such gatherings.

Finally, the prime minister's own constituency. Successive holders of the post, ever since the war, have maintained a good record of frequent visits to their constituencies. Clearly, this is easier for a prime minister with a London constituency than for one who has to travel long distances. It does not do any harm for him to have a provincial seat, however; prime ministers are too much subject to London influences.

Most of us have found considerable understanding from our constituencies, particularly our constituency parties. They recognize that their MP cannot be there as much as others, and that he can hardly be moved by them to record his dissent from government policy by speech or vote. But it is right that he should attend meetings of his constituency supporters whenever he can, and listen to the views of those he has known and worked with for many years: they are, in any case, as entitled as any other party workers to hear directly about the problems their Government is facing, and the reason for particular government actions. It is right, too, that he should take a close interest in his constituency correspondence, replying personally to letters asking for help or advice, and that, when possible, he should be in his constituency office to meet individuals and deputations.

On this particular question, it soon became clear to me that care was needed. There was no problem about meeting the constituents with pension or education or housing problems, or a deputation from a factory in or near the constituency faced with redundancies or even total closure. But in the sixties I noticed that local representatives of national organizations were coming to depute on behalf of those organizations. In one case a local bookmaker came with a representative from his national organization to complain about some aspect of the betting tax, thus using his constituency membership as a means of making a formal approach to the chancellor. Constituents should not be prejudiced because their MP is prime minister: equally, they should not expect undue and discriminatory advantages – still less that any of them should become contacts for national organizations.

On the other hand, a prime minister has everything to gain, and so have his constituents, by his maintaining the closest contact with his local authority leaders, committee chairmen and officials, especially during these recent years when local authorities and elected representatives have been trying to settle down after the much-criticized 1973 re-organization of local government.

IX

The Prime Minister and National Security

'It is dangerous and bad for our general national interest to discuss these matters. It has been a very long tradition of the House to trust the relations between the two parties to discussions between the Leader of the Opposition and the Prime Minister of the day. I ask the House now to revert to the older tradition which I think is in our real interests. Otherwise we would risk destroying services which are of the utmost value to us.' HAROLD MAC-MILLAN[1]

The prime minister has the ultimate responsibility for the national security authorities at home and abroad, though the home and overseas organizations concerned come departmentally under the Home Office[2] and the Foreign and Commonwealth Office responsibility.

The No. 10 responsibility is exercised through the secretary of the Cabinet, who is the prime minister's link with the authorities concerned. The Cabinet Office account for the Secret Service vote which is published under the heading 'OTHER EXTERNAL RELATIONS: SECRET SERVICE being the ESTIMATE of the amount required in the year ending . . .'[3]

In 1975–6 it amounted to £22 millions. No other details of estimates or expenditure are made available to Parliament either in the estimates or the accounts. By agreement with the Public Accounts Committee,

[1] op. cit., Vol. VI, p. 434. See reference to the Philby case, p. 145 above.
[2] Until 1952 the Prime Minister was directly responsible for the security service. Following a report by Sir Norman Brook, responsibility was transferred to the Home Office, and a directive was accordingly sent to the Director-General of the Service, by the Home Secretary, Sir David Maxwell-Fyfe. 'In your appointment as Director-General of the Security Service you will be responsible to the Home Secretary personally. The Security Service is not, however, a part of the Home Office. On appropriate occasion you will have right of direct access to the Prime Minister.'
This was first publicly quoted in The Denning Report on the Profumo Affair, Cmnd. 2152, of September 1963. It came as a complete surprise to Members of Parliament and the Press, and apparently just as much of a surprise to No. 10.
[3] See, for example, *Supply Estimates, 1975–76* (year ending 31 March 1976) HMSO No. 210, printed 11 February 1975, pp. 11–30.

the account is supported by the personal certificate of the Comptroller and Auditor General in a unique form: 'I certify that the amount shown in this account to have been expended is supported by certificates from the responsible Ministries of the Crown.'

The prime minister is occasionally questioned on matters arising out of his responsibility. His answers may be regarded as uniformly un-informative.

There is no further information that can usefully or properly be added before bringing this Chapter to an end.

X

Transatlantic Comparisons

'*Noes, seven, ayes one, the ayes have it.*' ABRAHAM LINCOLN

On overseas visits and lecture tours, I have found that the British system of government can be most easily explained by comparison with that of other democracies. Clearly, in this work it is not possible to range over the whole world: that would require a volume, or series of volumes, in itself. I am therefore confining the task to comparisons with the United States, whose constitution some historians have ascribed to a desire to follow a French writer's inaccurate rationalization of what he conceived to be British constitutional practice in the eighteenth century.

When I sat for my final honours school at Oxford in 1937, the first question on the paper on comparative political institutions went something like this: 'Would you prefer to be Prime Minister of the United Kingdom or President of the United States? *State your reasons.*' My reply was unequivocally for the Westminster post, and the reasons I gave represent my attitude today. Put simply, the president, elected directly and separately, is virtually secure from all possible removal. Nevertheless, part or even the whole of his tenure may be frustrated by inability to get his legislation, including vital tax and other financial legislation, through a hostile Congress. He is not all that sure of success in a Congress reflecting a majority from his own party.

The prime minister, however, lives far more dangerously in that he can be ousted from office at very short notice if he loses control of Parliament. Nevertheless, since he exists only because of the confidence of Parliament, he has a much greater assurance that while the confidence persists he can get his legislation, or most of it, carried through to the Statute Book.

This distinction is not always fully understood in the United States, even at top level. In 1965 I was visiting President Johnson, and went into the Oval Office to meet him at 5.0 pm (10.0 pm GMT). As a practised politician he told me – as his Embassy had – that he took a close professional political interest in the struggle of our Government to survive; at that time our majority was down to 1, in a House of 615, with a by-election pending. I looked at my watch and said that at that very moment the House of Commons was dividing (on the Territorial and Reserve Forces Bill); that one (possibly more) of our Members had announced the intention of abstaining, and that we might be facing a defeat which, if not reversed by a motion of confidence, would mean either resigning or seeking a fresh mandate through a general election. We won by a single vote. At lunch the next day, he told my colleagues that I was a pessimist. 'How often, when I was Senate Majority Leader, would I have thrown my hat in the air over a majority of one?' The point, as I explained to him, was that a defeat in either House in Washington would not carry with it any risk of the removal vans entering the White House drive.

Broadly speaking, a British government, even with the smallest of majorities, gets the greater part of its legislation through. It is more constantly at risk, but the confidence that sustains it in being is at the same time a virtual guarantee that most of its legislation will be passed by the Commons.

It is, of course, a fact that the president, being directly elected by the people, not by the legislature, enjoys a unique prestige, quite apart from that adhering to his office.[1] But in terms of power, he suffers from the doctrine of separation of powers which underlines the United States Constitution. Resiling, particularly as this is written during the bicentennial year, from all the constitutional arguments about how the Constitution came to be so devised, I will simply assert the British view that the founding fathers leaned too heavily on the concept of *la séparation des pouvoirs*, which Montesquieu in the early eighteenth century claimed to identify in the British Constitution. There was, in fact, no such separation between the three constituents, legislative, executive and judiciary, which Montesquieu thought he discerned – even today we have a Cabinet member, the lord chancellor, who is independent

---

[1] Against this, British general elections have been increasingly related to personalities. It has been noted above that this was true of Palmerston's election and the Disraeli–Gladstone rivalry; with television this has grown still further. Even before television, Sir Denis Brogan, in *The American Political System* (London 1933), p. 118, claims that 'an English General Election has as decidedly a plebiscitary character as an American presidential election'.

head of the judiciary, speaker of the Upper House of the legislature and a member of the executive.

Constitutions based on theory, particularly when the theory is wrongly conceived, tend to produce different solutions from those based on seven hundred years of mainly pragmatic experience.

The result, put simply and – as many would argue – crudely, is that the United States has a constitution, nominally based on theory, which has had to become one based on compromise, and give and take. The fact that it had to be tested in a bloody civil war no more detracts from that assertion than does the traumatic experience of that war, which was fought not on *séparation des pouvoirs* but on states' rights and the issue of slavery and secession.

Whether this is an over-simplification matters less than the practical working of the system. Even in almost equally divided Parliaments, basically the Government party of legislators aims loyally to sustain the executive, the Opposition to dislodge it. The confrontation, roughest at those times when the going is tough for the Government, is between parties, not between legislature and executive. And when, through the attrition of by-elections or the defection of one or two government supporters, a situation is created where the Government no longer commands an effective majority in the House, a general election can be forced, with incalculable results, or the Government can be pushed into resignation. This happened far more between 1832 and 1867[1] than in the period of more than a century since the second Reform Act.

But the significant fact of Westminster politics is that, as long as the Government can win its battles in the division lobby, even by single-figure majorities in a House of over six hundred members, it can in general get its business through. Nowhere is this more clear than in financial legislation, expenditure and taxation.

In Westminster, the Government has complete control over expenditure. No private Member, no Opposition party except in the exuberance of debate, can put forward proposals to increase government expenditure; a motion or amendment involving the increased expenditure of a single pound requires Treasury certification. Every Bill involving expenditure requires a Financial Resolution to authorize the expenditure involved, which is usually put to the House immediately the Bill has had its Second Reading, and usually takes an hour or less to be voted through. Any Private Member's Bill, such as those which under Standing Orders can be introduced for a limited period of the year under a

---

[1] See p. 18 above. This is so, even though three of my four administrations had overall majorities (in one case an overall *minority* of 34) which most commentators would have regarded as unviable.

procedure of balloting for priority, must if a penny of public expenditure is involved carry with it the cachet of 'Queen's recommendation signified'. This has to be moved from the Treasury bench, and is in effect a signal of Treasury approval. Without that approval, the Bill is nullified. Sometimes with Private Members' Bills that the Government has, by collective decision, supported – in many cases sponsored and drafted on behalf of a private Member who has drawn a place in the ballot – 'QRS' is vouchsafed.

Thus, in Britain, 'pork barrel' expenditure is ruled out. No Member, be he on the Government or Opposition side, can seek to increase expenditure on an object near to his heart or his constituency; still less can he do a deal with another Member, or group of Members, that he will support their spending objectives if they will support his. There may be arguments about the effectiveness or otherwise of Treasury control – such arguments are usually doctrinal battles about policy – but not a penny gets through which the Treasury has not authorized.

The same is true of taxation. No back-bench Member on either side can propose an increased tax burden of a single penny, even if it affects only a single taxpayer. Ingenious amendments to the Government's Finance Bill (the legislation that embodies the annual Budget proposals), many of them designed to reduce taxation, fall, on the fiat of the authorities of the House, if in their ingenuity they involve even a modicum of increased taxation for one taxpaying citizen. In a wider sense it follows, therefore, that, once the Budget has been 'opened' and the Finance Bill introduced, any amendment from any part of the House, designed to relieve taxation here by increasing it there, is out of order.

The undoubted fiscal impotence of any part of the House other than the Treasury bench has another consequence. As long as the Government commands the confidence of the House – give or take one or two fiscal sops most chancellors like to give towards the end of the tax legislation season – the Government's proposals go through with exemplary speed.

The contrast between the two systems is clear. Most studies of the Civil War period, when the Union was fighting for its existence, point to the delays in getting financial decisions through. Lyndon Johnson, in his autobiography, records the protracted legislative delay that supervened over his clear perception, on economic management grounds, that increased taxation was essential.[1]

In December 1965, Gardner Ackley, chairman of the Council of Economic Advisers, submitted a 'memo' calling for a tax increase.[2] In

[1] Lyndon Baines Johnson, *The Vantage Point: Perspectives of the Presidency, 1963–69.* (London 1971), pp. 440 *et seq.*
[2] ibid., p. 440.

January 1966, the President's State of the Union message called for tax 'adjustments' of $6 billions, to which he had some response. Two months later he took a further initiative. Throughout 1966 he discussed it *ad nauseam* with individual Congressmen who told him that they were with him 'in spirit' but that it would be political suicide to vote for it. The Ways and Means Committee were against it. There was no support for his tax bill. In the State of the Union message of January 1967, he pressed again. Lyndon Johnson sets out the variegated nature of congressional, business and union opposition.[1] On 3 August 1967 he made a further proposal for increased taxes. Hearings began on 14 August, but the proposals were not carried until June 1968, after the President had announced that he would not accept nomination for a further presidential term.

At a time of economic emergency, not to mention full mobilization for the fighting in Asia, two and a half years were needed between the Gardner Ackley memorandum and the President's acceptance of the need for increased taxation, and its enactment in Congress; and it is arguable that it would not have gone through then had he not taken his presidency out of the field of controversy by his announcement at the beginning of 1968.[2]

With these delays we may contrast British practice. The Budget Speech is delivered usually on a Tuesday afternoon at 3.30 and its contents are kept totally secret until the chancellor of the exchequer reveals them in Parliament. Tax changes are embodied in a list of resolutions for approval by the House, and these form the financial authority for the Finance Bill, which gives legislative form for the tax and other financial changes. But while the Bill proceeds through Parliament at a reasonable legislative pace, usually taking up to the four months allowed, the resolutions embodying the tax changes are passed by the House immediately after the chancellor ends his speech, *and have legal effects at once* under the Provisional Collection of Taxes Act, 1913.[3] Thus, whereas an American government convinced of the need to raise taxes can be forced to wait for two or even three years, a British government resolved

[1] ibid., pp. 446–7.
[2] Richard Neustadt, 'White House and Whitehall', in *The British Prime Minister*, ed. Anthony King (London 1969), p. 144, mentions that a tax cut which President Kennedy felt to be necessary had to be delayed to the point where he was aiming for it only for the beginning of his fourth year.
[3] Until recently the House could express its immediate reaction to the Budget or any of the tax changes by a parliamentary vote on each resolution as put to the House on Budget Day, without debate. The Standing Orders were changed in October 1967 to provide that certain tax changes designated by the Government to take immediate effect should be put to the House for decision at the end of the Budget speech. At the end of the Budget debate (usually six days later). The House could vote for or against any or all of the resolutions.

on the need to change tax rates gets them into legal effect within a few minutes, the only relevant stipulation of the 1913 Act being that the authority given by the passing of the resolutions ceases if they are not given legislative form within four calendar months. The course of debate on the Finance Bill can, of course, lead to changes in some of the chancellor's proposals, as given immediate force by the passing of the resolutions: some changes in tax law run into heavy criticism; some may be argued to be unworkable, or to inflict unforeseen hardship on a particular section of the community. As long as the chancellor has a parliamentary majority he can, of course, stick to his guns and reject all amendments, but most chancellors keep a little up their sleeve for the purpose of offering, usually minor, concessions at the later stages of the Bill. Where the Bill, either on the chancellor's initiative or as a result of conceding points to his critics, leads to a change in the content of the original resolution, it is the final shape of the Finance Bill, not the Budget Day resolutions, that is overriding.

Even in wartime an American president has been inhibited in securing congressional assent to policies he felt to be essential for the conduct of that war. Bagehot, in his Introduction to the second (1872) edition of *The English Constitution*, refers to the delay in imposing necessary wartime taxation and the consequent increase in the Government's borrowing requirement, and to the 'capital error made by the United States Government, . . . the "Legal Tender Act" as it is called, by which it made inconvertible paper notes issued by the Treasury the sole circulating medium of the country.'[1] His point here is not so much congressional delay in meeting a demand for tax increases demanded by the president as a failure of Congress, first to see the need for increased taxes when war began; second, in relation to the debauchment of the currency, and third, in over-reaction by Congress in terms of excessive and almost arbitrary taxation when they reacted from their earlier over-relaxed fiscal attitudes and in their panic introduced ill-considered tax burdens which, by their very nature, were so unfair and counter-productive that they failed to produce anything like the yield they were seeking.[2] The charge here was not, as in the Lyndon Johnson case, an inadequate and delayed response to the presidential tax proposals: it was a lack of initiative on the part of Congress.

In discussing the relations between the chief executive and the legislative authority in the two countries, the differences are in no sense limited to financial legislation. It is a question of fundamental differences in the

[1] See also Henry Jones Ford in *The Presidency*, ed. Aaron Wildavsky (Boston 1969), p. 436.

[2] Walter Bagehot, *The English Constitution*, 2nd ed. (London 1963), pp. 304–9.

relation between the head of government (and opposition elements) and the parliamentary institutions: it is the difference between a constitution based on a strict separation of powers, constitutionally defined – and therefore a matter for legalistic argument and judicial review by the third element in the separation – and (in the United States) changing presidential attitudes to Congress.

Richard Crossman, in his Godkin Lectures, emphasizes the *parliamentary* conflict between the prime minister and 'his rival', the leader of the Opposition, both of them senior elected representatives, one of whom is chief executive, the other aspiring to be: the whole parliamentary struggle is a series of skirmishes directed to one final battle for political control, a general election. Referring to the twice-weekly Prime Minister's Questions:

> 'This regular conflict between the Prime Minister and his rival, in the ambience of Parliament, represents the essence of our Prime Ministerial system – the fact that the conflict takes place in the parliamentary milieu. The whole of British politics is centred there . . .
>
> The man that's running the Executive has to be there at the dispatch-box, has to present himself to fight the contender for power, and the whole press and television will report that evening on what happened to him. He's being tested, and the House of Commons feels itself to be participating in the test.'[1]

In a later comparison of the two systems, Crossman stresses two of his constant themes; first that in the United States, as distinct from Britain, there is no national party, while the national party in Britain operates first and foremost through parliamentary combat; second, that for more than three years out of four there is in the United States no leader of the Opposition, no alternate (or shadow) chief executive. In Britain the challenge is identified and publicized; he or she receives virtually equal (and free) television time, but above all enjoys full parliamentary equality with the head of government, and equal reporting by the media.

Presidential elections are generally reckoned to begin about Labour Day, fourteen months before the voters go to the polls, though in fact the Opposition candidate is not selected, and may not be predicted with any confidence, until some four months before the electoral decision. In Britain, the next general election campaign begins, but at considerably less total expense, the day that Parliament meets after the preceding election. Most British governments are extremely wary about taking

[1] R. Crossman, op. cit. pp. 34–5.

action in the year before a presidential election which might influence voters' attitudes.[1]

In this context, Richard Crossman might well have made the further point: that, unlike the situation in America, the prime minister and his principal contender are, unequivocally, leaders of their parties – indeed, since the Conservative Party in 1965 adopted the Labour system of election by a secret ballot of their parliamentary party members, both are unchallenged democratically elected leaders.

This raises another interesting contrast of some importance: the relative cost in the two countries, first of becoming a national party candidate, and second the cost of the general election (presidential) contest.

In the United States the cost of being selected as the presidential candidate has always been inordinate, and inflation, increased by the cost of buying television time and of public relations generally, has raised it to the point where, despite legislation – which in 1976 was hamstrung by a Supreme Court decision – valid candidates were dropping out of the primary campaign through lack of funds.[2] In describing this, as most British political observers would agree, as barbarous and undemocratic, I have to justify such adjectives by wearying the reader with a personal story.

In January 1963, I was on a lecture tour in the United States – most years in the late fifties I used to lecture in Chicago, and a number of other distinguished institutions. I left Chicago early in the morning of 20 January, for two speeches in St Louis, Missouri. When I arrived there, H M Consul-General met me with the news that Hugh Gaitskell, leader of my party, whom I had seen on his sick-bed a number of times before leaving for the United States, had taken a serious turn for the worse; indeed, there were growing anxieties about him.

From St Louis, I flew east to New York, where I was due to address the Council of Foreign Relations. In the course of the pre-speech dinner I was called out no less than eight times to take telephone calls from London, pressing me to return. At the end of my speech and questions, I returned to my hotel with an American friend of long-standing.

He realized I would have to go back, and though I refused, at such a

---

[1] This rule was grotesquely infringed by the then British Government which invaded Egypt only hours before President Eisenhower's 1956 election. On coming into office for the first time in 1964, I laid down a new rule: don't rock the transatlantic boat within six months of a mid-term election. When I told him of this, President Lyndon Johnson warmly approved.

[2] To a British student, the most pathetic story in US pre-election history is that of Hubert Humphrey retiring, defeated and exhausted, in his buggy from West Virginia, in contrast to the expensive caravanserai of the Kennedy machine.

time, to discuss the question of the election of Hugh's successor, if Hugh were to die, he would not be put off.

'As I understand it,' he said, 'this is the British equivalent of a convention for the choice of the presidential candidate!' I agreed. 'In that case,' he said, 'I'd like to present a cheque of 10,000 dollars towards your expenses.' I replied that I could not take a penny from him, or any other American friend; moreover, the campaign, as he would put it, would not cost $10,000 in all. He was amazed, and when he asked me how much I estimated, I said, 'Two bob, at most'; i.e. two old shillings, ten new pence – at the then current exchange rate, twenty-eight cents. He was frankly unbelieving, recalling comparable US primary and convention expenses. I explained that all the candidates would be Labour Members of Parliament, and that the 'convention' electorate would consist exclusively of elected Labour MPs. All likely candidates would have been MPs for nearly eighteen years, and known to their electorate. Canvassing would be counter-productive, and if I stood there would be none by me or my supporters. It was for all the world as though the selection of the presidential candidate had to be made, by each party, from members of the Senate of that party, and voted on by secret ballot by all Senators accredited to that party. To quell his disbelief, I undertook to send him an audited account of my 'primary and convention' expenses. After being elected I did so: it amounted to eight (old) pence, a little over nine cents, and was accounted for by telephone calls to two over-enthusiastic supporters of mine who were defying my ban on canvassing. It is my impression, subject to verification from the published figures when available, that candidates' primary and convention expenses in the US 1976 contests will exceed that figure, perhaps substantially.

A similar contrast exists between the two countries in respect of legally permitted expenditures in the election itself – the general election in Britain and the presidential election in the United States, which coincides with the election of the House of Representatives and one-third of the Senate.

In Britain the permitted cost per candidate, because of inflation, is now at an all-time high by British standards. The present limits, including election literature, the cost of hiring halls for meetings, the travelling and overnight expenses of visiting speakers, use of cars (which had to be certified by my political agent) *and all the candidate's personal expenses*, including hotel accommodation, are as follows: in 'county' constituencies, £1075 *plus* 1p per elector; in borough constituencies, £1075 *plus* ¾p per elector. The candidate is allowed £100 for hotel and other bills. If he spends more his agent has to account for it, and bear the excess over £100.

Thus, with an average constituency of about 60,000 electors, the maximum permitted expenditure for a county seat is £1675 and £1525 for a borough seat. The total legal expenditure permitted to a national party fighting every seat in Britain would thus be just over £1,000,000. These limits are rigidly enforced. All returns are certified on oath, and elected members can be, and have been, unseated for expenditure which exceeded them.

Moreover, national parties are allowed free television time, simultaneous on both channels during the campaign: the two major parties are each allowed five programmes of ten minutes at peak viewing time, the Liberals three, and minor provision is made in other cases, in addition to a large number of equally free programmes on the main election issues on regional programmes.

I have referred above to differences between our two systems in the sphere of finance. But these cover an important, but in numerical terms only a small proportion of, relations between chief minister and Parliament and Congress on respective jurisdictions, particularly the initiative in, and influences over, the passing of legislation.

If it is true that the United States Constitution has remained somewhat ossified – the preserve of the Supreme Court and the legal profession[1] – relations between the president and Congress, the president and the people, have depended very much on the character and style of individual presidents, and have, almost extra-constitutionally, evinced powers of evolution and even presidential idiosyncrasy.

The doctrine of the separation of powers in the Constitution gave the president no specific authority greater than that enjoyed by other citizens – indeed, it has been argued, less.[2] 'Of legal authority for presidential leadership of Congress . . . the Constitution was nearly as bare as Mother Hubbard's cupboard.'[3] Many writers on constitutional history have referred to the charges in the 'Jeffersonian era', stressing the absence of counter-presidential pressure groups and the congressional experience of presidents of that time. Attributing the main responsibility

---

[1] See Brogan, op. cit., the opening paragraph of his book, p. 15. Having stated that the Constitution in a year and a half had acquired all the sanctity of the Twelve Tables in ancient Rome, he describes it as having 'acquired a patina of age that discouraged the irreverent hands of the renovator. Almost from the start, it was put into the care of a priesthood, the lawyers, who from time to time, have opened the Sibylline Book, and told the multitude what was the judgment of the ancestors on situations which it is highly improbable that the ancestors had ever foreseen.' The United Kingdom has no system of judicial review: see p. 145 above, where a High Court decision in Northern Ireland threw doubt on the position of the troops. The legal issue was settled in a little less than twenty-four hours, by a Bill that went through both Houses and regularized the position of the Army.

[2] James Sterling Young in Wildavsky, op. cit., p. 411.

[3] ibid., p. 412.

to Jefferson, they refer to Jefferson's enlistment of legislators to act as his agents in Congress, the designation of particular members of the Cabinet to undertake liaison with Congress, social invitations to legislators to come to the White House and the use of the press. Jefferson, too, made articulate the use of patronage through elected members of both Houses, in return for which he expected political support in Congress. Madison instructed departmental heads to give to Congress advice about intended legislation; Monroe, while resisting the right of Congress to direct communications to heads of departments, was active in encouraging traffic in the opposite direction.

> 'It has always been considered as a practical rule that the Committee of Foreign Relations should be the confidential medium of communications between the Administration and Congress. . . . The Chairman . . . has always been considered as a member in the confidence of the Executive . . . the President has . . . directed me to communicate freely to him.[1]

The use of patronage goes back to the same era. American historians have stated 'the institution of bartering patronage for legislation did not exist'; before Jackson, 'no President . . . undertook to buy leadership with patronage . . . the practice of using patronage to get votes in either House was rare and would have been thought corrupt.'[2]

Jefferson was opposed to creating vacancies in order to give patronage its head; Jackson initiated the practice. Jackson equally used his personal popularity to circumvent congressional opposition: Senator Webster observed, 'Was it not for the fear of outdoor popularity of General Jackson, the Senate would have negatived more than half his nominations.'[3]

The next qualitative change in presidential power has been attributed to Abraham Lincoln's wartime leadership. Lincoln, one of the greatest statesmen, *qua* statesman, in the history of democracy, attained his objectives by the most assiduous use of his unrivalled powers as a politician. His objectives were clear: to save the Union, to end the secession. At no point was he concerned to end the ownership of slaves until, in his mind, that became essential to save the Union and end the bloodshed.

Against these categorical objectives, two things stand out from his record as president. One was that his relations with Congress were dominated by his assertion, not of a new presidential role *vis-à-vis* Congress, but of the war powers of the chief executive. The second was his political

---

[1] Secretary of State Adams – see Young, op. cit.
[2] ibid.
[3] ibid.

strategy; while the war must be won by a bloody confrontation, congressional acquiescence in all he had to do must be won by stealth, even deviousness.

In the assertion of his war powers he was helped by the long recesses, even in wartime, and by the long period in which a lame-duck congress sat in the New Year after its successor had been elected.

A recent judgement on Lincoln as war president draws on and synthesizes some of the historic pronouncements over more than a century:

> 'In his relations with Congress, Lincoln was no Woodrow Wilson or Franklin Roosevelt or Lyndon Johnson. He did not attempt to exercise strong, positive leadership over the legislative body; he presented to it no legislative programme; he accepted from it, with apparent meekness, various unwelcome acts and decisions; he vetoed only one important bill in four years. He showed remarkable deference to Congress but he showed equally remarkable independence of it. He allowed Congress to go its way in the optimistic hope that Congress would allow him to go his. . . .
>
> 'Lincoln firmly believed in the doctrine of the separation of powers; but he took a very comprehensive view of the war powers of the president, and was determined to keep the crucial matters – conduct of the war, slavery and reconstruction – under presidential control. He was a strong president in those fields which he believed to be essentially his concern, but a modest one elsewhere, notably respectful of Congressional rights in the field of legislation as being each supreme in its own field; his major battles with Congress were fought over the boundary between them.'[1]

Had he not been murdered a week after Appomattox, it might have been possible to assess how far his assertion of war powers was in his view required by war needs only, or whether in the reconstruction period, perhaps longer, he would have felt that he had to fight for powers not exercised by his peacetime predecessors. Certainly the total breakdown between his successor, Johnson, and Congress, culminating in the humiliating impeachment proceedings, would not have occurred had Lincoln lived.

What is of intense interest is his success in managing Congress. Admittedly this was in the midst of the most dangerous crisis his country had faced, but his problems were compounded not only by the fact that there were no precedents for the actions he felt it right to take, but also by the disappointment and disillusion of a protracted war, a succession of defeats and heavy casualties.

[1] Peter J. Parish, *The American Civil War* (London 1975), pp. 203 and 204.

In terms of presidential–congressional relations, his handling of the Proclamation of Emancipation is instructive. He repeatedly resisted pressure from anti-slavery organizations for such action. He was fighting to save the Union. It was only when he felt that this was a necessary step to ending the bloodshed and keeping the Union together that he slowly began to move. He drafted his Proclamation and quietly took it through Cabinet, but did not announce it because of the military situation. He was determined that it would be justified on intrinsic grounds as a means to securing peace and the maintenance of the Union; therefore it was important not to announce it in the absence of military victories, as it would have been denounced as an action of desperation. When the military situation improved he announced it, but still in a pragmatic, low-profile way; and even after he had cleared it with Cabinet, and with the Proclamation in his pocket, he met a passionate anti-slavery demonstration and discounted their arguments for that very Proclamation.

In common with many statesmen, before and after him, who are more concerned to secure objectives than to react to day-to-day clamour, he was concerned with timing.

'Many of my strongest supporters urged Emancipation before I thought it indispensable, and, I may say, before I thought the country ready for it. It is my conviction that, had the proclamation been issued even six months earlier than it was, the public sentiment would not have sustained it. . . . A man watches his pear-tree day after day, impatient for the ripening of the fruit. Let him attempt to *force* the process, and he may spoil both fruit and tree. But let him patiently *wait*, and the ripe pear falls into his lap! We have seen this great revolution in public sentiment slowly but surely progressing, so that, when final action comes, the opposition was not strong enough to defeat the purpose.'[1]

An American historian described Abraham Lincoln's Proclamation as having had 'all the moral grandeur of a bill of lading'.[2] This was deliberate.

'His sensitivity to all shades of Northern opinion made him as much concerned with the style, the justification and above all, the timing of emancipation as with the deed itself. Even Horace Greely admitted that Lincoln was well ahead of the bulk of Northern opinion, and that there was probably a majority in the North against emancipation

[1] From a letter to George Thompson, a British anti-slavery leader, quoted by Frank B. Carpenter, *Six Months at the White House with Abraham Lincoln* (London 1866), p. 77.
[2] Richard Hofstaater, quoted in Peter J. Parish, op. cit., p. 246.

until mid-1863. In fact, he was the arch-exponent of the indirect approach to the slavery issue, the strategy of the "soft sell". In deference to the fears and prejudices of many, perhaps most, Northerners, he played down moral principle and high ideals, and denied himself grand gestures as outbursts of righteous indignation.

'He took the low road to emancipate rather than the high. It was slower and more circuitous, but it was safer and it led to the same place. . . . Lincoln knew where he was going, although his intentions were more frequently obscured by the fog of war or a smokescreen of his own making. He was the Great Emancipator, but the road to emancipation was paved with equivocation.'[1]

These comments are fully justified, and I have included this long digression on Lincoln partly to show that the apparently unworkable relations between president and Congress could be made to work. Because of his death, we shall never know whether these methods would have been equally effective without the compulsion of war. Even though these questions remain unanswered, this episode is instructive, for his methods stand as a model for democratic statesmanship in the easier Westminster relationships; whenever it is results that are needed, some apparently unattainable objective to be reached, rather than the excitement and plaudits that inevitably accompany a failed confrontation.

Lincoln secured not only his Proclamation: he carried public opinion.

What is relevant in our transatlantic comparison is the question; how successful, in Washington and Westminster respectively, is the government in securing the passage of the legislation it considers necessary to fulfil its programme? Here again, institutional differences make comparisons difficult.

In Westminster the great majority of Bills that reach the Statute Book as Acts of Parliament are government-initiated, government-drafted and carried through from the Government Front Bench, 'with the Whips on', i.e. pressed as policies on which the Government has the right to expect, even demand, the support of its back-benchers. In the last three full parliamentary sessions up to the time of writing,[2] the following is the number of Bills carried into law, showing in brackets those introduced on the initiative of back-benchers, usually though not exclusively those who have drawn a place in the ballot for Private Members' Bills early in the session.

[1] Parish op. cit., pp. 237–8.
[2] I have excluded the sessions of 1973–4, and that of the 'short Parliament' between the two general elections of 1974, because in both cases the legislative programmes foreshadowed in the relevant Queen's Speeches could not be carried through to completion. Of the three sessions, the first two were in Parliaments with a Conservative majority (elected in 1970); the third with a Labour majority (elected October 1974).

Session	Government Bills	Private Members' Bills	Private Peers' Bills	Total Public Bills Enacted
1971–2	59	12	5	76
1972–3	57	13	2	72
1974–5	73	10	Nil	83

Even these figures may somewhat exaggerate the proportion of genuinely inspired back-bench Members' Bills. Quite often back-bench MPs successful in the ballot to introduce Private Members' Bills approach the Government for suggestions, and are encouraged to sponsor what is in effect a Government Bill. This may be because of pressure on the Government's legislative time-table, or because it is felt that the nature of the Bill suggests that back-bench introduction is appropriate.

These figures should be compared with studies that have been made of experience on Capitol Hill. Because of the division of functions between the executive and the legislature, Bills normally stem from the legislative arm; though it is sometimes difficult to establish the operative paternity. For example, there are cases of strong public and presidential pressure for particular legislation and a Bill is spontaneously introduced in Congress. Alternatively, there will be cases where there is good reason to suspect that the Bill was drafted in the executive and quietly fathered on a friendly senator or congressman.

The president's constitutional right to 'recommend' to the consideration of Congress 'such measures as he shall judge necessary and expedient' was in fact a deliberate attempt to follow and codify the practice of the Westminster prime minister. Gouverneur Morris, who did the actual drafting of the Constitution, explained this in these terms: 'Our President will be the British minister.'[1] In fact, though the proportion of legislation directly or indirectly initiated by the executive has grown over two centuries, as it has in Westminster, at no point has it been as high as in Britain.

White House initiation, in fact, has been in the main 'a twentieth century phenomenon'. When Woodrow Wilson wrote his classic treatise, *Congressional Government*, in 1885 he detected little tendency on the part of the president to take an active hand in shaping legislation.[2]

Although Dr Chamberlain refers to the success of Washington,

[1] Quoted from Madison's Journal of 24 July 1787 by Ford in Wildavsky, op. cit., p. 432.

[2] Lawrence H. Chamberlain, 'The President, Congress and Legislation' in Wildavsky, op. cit., p. 440.

through Alexander Hamilton, his personal congressional representative, and also of Jefferson, Jackson, Lincoln and Cleveland with Congress, he concludes: 'It was only when Theodore Roosevelt came into office that the philosophy of the executive dominant in legislation received conscious application. During his seven years in the White House, Roosevelt invested the presidency with a dramatic and aggressive personal spirit.' Woodrow Wilson's contribution he sets as a more deliberate and a more effective party leadership – while '. . . the multi-dimensional leadership of Franklin Roosevelt did much to create the impression that the congressional role in legislation had become definitely secondary'.[1] He cites Theodore Roosevelt's record in railway and conservation legislation, Wilson's on tariff, banking and business regulations, and Franklin Roosevelt's more widespread legislative record.

The results of a survey[2] by Chamberlain of the origins of 90 major legislations over a period of some 65 years are set out in tabular form. Those listed as 'Presidential Influence Preponderant' were 19; 'Congressional Influence Preponderant', 35; 'Joint Presidential–Congressional Influence', 29; and 'Pressure Group Influence Preponderant', 7. Of the 23 passed after 1932, the President is credited with 8, Congress with 2 and the President and Congress jointly with 13.

In the international field the United States Congress has, in practice, a far greater power over international treaties, through withholding ratification, than the Westminster Parliament.

The whole course of world history between the two wars was driven into tragedy by the refusal of Congress to ratify Woodrow Wilson's actions in the leading part he played in creating the League of Nations. Less spectacular, and as it has turned out less tragic, was the failure of Congress in 1947–8 to ratify the Havana Charter setting out new rules for international trade, which again owed much to American leadership in the person of Will Clayton, under-secretary at the State Department. The Geneva sixty-four-nation conference that had negotiated the Charter had, however, drawn up an interim set of trade rules, the General Agreement on Tariffs and Trade (GATT), to run until the Charter was adopted by national governments and parliaments. This intendedly temporary measure has thus governed world trade for nearly thirty

[1] Lawrence H. Chamberlain, 'The President, Congress and Legislation' in Wildavsky, op. cit., pp. 440-1.

[2] Covering ten categories: agriculture, banking and currency, business, government credit, immigration, labour, national defence, natural resources, railways and tariffs. The classification is weakened by the number of measures in the list marked by an asterisk, indicating that one or more Bills on the same subject had been introduced without administration support and had received substantial consideration in Congress before administration backing led to the enactment of the measure as listed: 74 of the 90 were so asterisked in this sense.

years, lending support to the French thesis that only the provisional endures.

In Westminster, Parliament, on whose authority alone can governments survive, has all the power needed to reverse any international action taken by HM Government. In fact, no international treaty has been nullified by parliamentary process. Under the so-called Ponsonby rules specific parliamentary ratification is not required. The Government assumes authority in respect of any treaty or agreement it has negotiated if Parliament has not reacted within twenty-one days.

The practice, based largely on previous conventions, was laid down in a Commons statement on 1 April 1924 by Arthur Ponsonby, undersecretary of state for foreign affairs. He made clear that there was no constitutional obligation to compel the government of the day to submit treaties for parliamentary ratification, except where a Bill or Financial Resolution had to be sought from Parliament to make the necessary legal or financial provision to underwrite it.

He asked for – and received – the endorsement of the House for a more clearly defined procedure to enable Parliament, if it wishes, to examine, consider and if need be discuss any treaty that had been negotiated before the Government finally ratified. Pointing out that this could be achieved either by legislation or by instituting the procedure of 'an address to the Crown, which, constitutionally speaking, is the Treaty-making power', he went on to propose a new procedure:

> 'It is the intention of His Majesty's Government to lay on the Table of both Houses of Parliament every Treaty, when signed, for a period of 21 days, after which the Treaty will be ratified and published and circulated in the Treaty Series. In the case of important Treaties, the Government will, of course, take an opportunity of submitting them to the House for discussion within this period. But, as the Government cannot take upon itself to decide what may be considered important or unimportant, if there is a formal demand for discussion forwarded through the usual channels[1] from the Opposition or any other party, time will be found for the discussion of the Treaty in question . . .'

He went on to remind the House that there are many other agreements, some purely technical, which are not subject to ratification:

> 'His Majesty's Government desire that Parliament should also exercise supervision over agreements, commitments and understandings by which the nation may be bound in certain circumstances and which may involve international obligations of a serious character

[1] The Government and Opposition whips.

although no signed and sealed document may exist. . . . We shall inform the House of all agreements, commitments, and understandings which may in any way bind this nation to specific action in certain circumstances . . .'

The essential point was that the Crown, advised by the Government, is the treaty-making power, and that while Parliament can always set aside any treaty, as it can any other action of Government, including proposals for legislation, the Government can negotiate, and in default of parliamentary rejection ratify – and in any important question the Government could make a treaty, as it can make any domestic action, a matter of confidence and call on its supporting parliamentary majority to ensure its endorsement.[1]

In the respective parliamentary settings there is a further difference between the two capitals. The president appears in Congress only on set-piece occasions for a message or statement. The prime minister faces Parliament every Tuesday and Thursday when the House is sitting – something like sixty times a year – to answer questions of which notice is given and also the supplementaries which follow each oral question.[2] He speaks in a number of major debates, particularly the debate on the Address in reply to the Queen's Speech opening each Parliament, substantial constitutional debates and critical economic or foreign affairs debates. He himself makes a considerable number of government announcements in Parliament and is subject to oral questioning on them; he reports to the House, usually orally, on most important international conferences, visits he has made abroad or his discussions with visiting statesmen.

But this is not all. The president's ability to influence the voting of an individual member of either House is limited and indirect. As Sir Denis Brogan has said,

'He has no such resource as parliamentary government gives a party leader, he cannot challenge votes of confidence or rather cannot do so with any real results; a failure to support the executive has no immediate terrors for legislators, even of the President's party, and there is no very effective means of transmuting a promise of support into action with the certainty of disciplined voting that the party in power can rely on in the House of Commons.'[3]

Traditionally there has been the power of party whips to visit on a

---

[1] See Geoffrey Wilson, *Cases and Materials on Constitutional and Administrative Law* (Cambridge 1966), pp. 453–4.
[2] See pp. 131–43 above.
[3] Brogan, op. cit., p. 131.

recalcitrant member all the horrors of a withdrawal of the party whip, which involves his expulsion, temporary or lasting, from the Parliamentary Party and the loss of his right to attend party meetings and committees. It can lead, and has led, to his failing to get his party's support as a candidate in a forthcoming election, though this is not automatic, for in the Labour Party, membership of the Party nationally, and hence the Party's *imprimatur* as an official candidate, is a matter for the National Executive Committee, subject to an appeal to annual Conference. Aneurin Bevan, for example, lost the party whip at a PLP meeting just before the 1955 general election, but at the NEC was saved by one vote, after an adjourned meeting.[1]

An American president has no such power, even in theory. If he has, therefore, much less influence over the legislative process than a British prime minister has, given a majority in Parliament, there is nevertheless one area where his power is transcendent: relations with his Cabinet.

Previous chapters have set out the limits within which a prime minister operates in relation to his colleagues. The president's position is absolute. In fact, in the sense in which the term has come to be understood in Britain, the president's Cabinet is not a Cabinet. Again, to quote Sir Denis Brogan,

> 'The American Cabinet is composed of ten heads of departments under whose control, some, but by no means all, the administrative machinery is placed. These are officers bound to give the President advice should he ask for it, but have no authority to tender it. They meet regularly, and are known as the President's Cabinet, but they are not merely liable to dismissal individually, or in bulk. They have no corporate rights which are uniformly recognised by custom.'[2]

Even in appointing its members, the president is constrained by the need to balance his selection in geographical terms and in party terms. In many cases he selects a technician, e.g. in finance or social services, rather than a political leader.

The power of the Cabinet is illustrated by the famous story of Abraham Lincoln. At the end of the Cabinet discussion he collected the voices, and found himself in a minority of one – 'Noes, seven, ayes one, the ayes have it'. The decision is that of the president and his alone. The Cabinet's role is consultative, and after consultations are complete the president decides. Those who sit round the table are in effect heads

---

[1] No Labour MPs lost the whip in my thirteen years as party leader: in fact I insisted on the restoration of it to five MPs, including Michael Foot, as soon as I was elected leader in February 1963.

[2] Brogan, op. cit., p. 125.

of departments, and could in practice be a group of British permanent secretaries – except for their lack of permanence.

In the 800 pages of *The Presidency*, to which frequent reference has been made, it is significant that the Cabinet is hardly mentioned, even in the contributions dealing with presidential power and relations with Congress. In the section on 'The President's Cabinet' it is clearly stated at the outset that:

> 'In the first place, the structure of the American Executive fixes a lower limit to Cabinet activity. The President's power to use or not to use it is complete and final. The Cabinet is his to use when and if he wishes, and he cannot be forced into either alternative. He has the power of life or death over it at this point.'[1]

Citing Lincoln's statement, he goes on to quote Jonathan Daniels, 'No institution is more a body of one man's man than the American President's Cabinet.'[2] While certain presidents, such as Harding, Truman and Eisenhower, made some use of their Cabinets, his analysis supported the view that 'The political help which the President receives comes not from the group but from individual Cabinet members, who can and do augment the President's effectiveness in his leadership roles.'[3]

As individuals, the Cabinet members interact with many outside bodies, political, legislative, interest and party groups, but the final conclusion is that 'It frequently makes more sense to describe the Cabinet member as part of a "feudal" pattern of fiefs, baronies and dukedoms than an orderly and symmetrical pyramid of authority.'[4]

There is an important further difference between the two Cabinets. In Britain, Cabinet experience is an essential qualification for the top position, that of being head of government. In modern times no prime minister has been elected who has not had Cabinet experience. Indeed, in every case of a new prime minister this century, and for the great majority of nineteenth-century premiers, every incoming prime minister has sat in his predecessor's Cabinet, if he succeeds a premier of the same party, and every incoming prime minister being appointed after an interval because his party had been in Opposition had been a member of the last Cabinet formed by his own party.[5] The only exception was Ramsay MacDonald: there had been no previous Labour Cabinet of which he could have been a member.

[1] Richard F. Ferno Jr. in Wildavsky, op. cit., pp 491–512.
[2] ibid., pp. 491–2.
[3] ibid., p. 511.
[4] ibid., p. 512.
[5] When Labour won the 1964 general election we had been in opposition for thirteen years, but the tenuous link was preserved from my membership of Clement Attlee's Cabinet.

The Cabinet is therefore the training ground for selection for No. 10. There is no other, and it is virtually inconceivable that there could be.

In the United States the odds are much more against the emergence of a Cabinet member, save for the vice-president. Hoover's reputation was built up by his eight-year service as commerce secretary, it is true, and Roosevelt had been secretary of the navy, though in his case it was his reputation as governor that created his national reputation. Since 1928, five of the eight presidents (Truman, Kennedy, Johnson, Nixon and Ford) established themselves through Congress; one, Eisenhower, was a general; the only two with Cabinet experience were Hoover and Roosevelt.

Richard Neustadt's comparative studies are designed to show that, despite very different constitutional forms and conventions, there is more similarity of working in the two capitals than many academics have conceded.[1]

'First, we have counterparts for their [UK's] top civil servants – but not in our own civil service.

'Second, we have counterparts for their Cabinet ministers – but not exclusively or even mainly in our Cabinet.'[2]

Having referred to 'Treasury flyers' in Whitehall, he identifies their opposite numbers as

'non-careerists holding jobs infused with Presidential interest or concern – "in-and-outers" from the law firms, banking, business, academia, foundations, or occasionally journalism, or the entourages of successful Governors and Senators – along with up-and-outers (sometimes up-and-downers) who relinquish, or at least risk, civil service status in the process. Here is the elite-of-the-elite, the upper-crust of our "Administrative class".'[3]

[1] Richard Neustadt has a close and intimate knowledge of both the White House and the principal power-centres in Whitehall. His Westminster studies began as an academic, but President John F. Kennedy used him for important contacts with Downing Street. After the deep misunderstandings between the two heads of government leading to the cancellation of Skybolt, which was at the time at the centre of Harold Macmillan's defence planning, the President charged Dr Neustadt with preparing a full report on what had gone wrong. His document, which he told me was 170,000 words long, reached the President the weekend before his assassination in Dallas. President Johnson sent him to see me in 1964 on the eve of my first prime ministerial visit to Washington – where the proposed 'mixed-manned fleet', the so-called MLF, was 'torpedoed' – to ensure that there were no prior misunderstandings on defence matters: see Wilson, *The Labour Government, 1964–70* (London 1971), especially pp. 45–6, and Anthony King (ed.), *The British Prime Minister* (London 1969), pp. 131–47. Neustadt's '10 Downing Street', an interview with Henry Brandon, ibid., pp. 119–30, is also a perceptive study.

[2] Neustadt, op. cit., pp. 113, 133.

[3] ibid., p. 137.

Comparing Cabinet with Cabinet, he judges:

'British government may not be Presidential but our government is more Prime Ministerial than we incline to think. Unhappily for thought, we too have something called a Cabinet. But that pallid institution is in no sense the equivalent of theirs. Our equivalent is rather an informal, shifting aggregation of key individuals, the influentials at both ends of Pennsylvania Avenue. Some of them may sit in what we call the Cabinet as Department heads: others sit in back rows there, as senior White House aides; still others have no place there. Collectively these men share no responsibility nor any meeting ground. Individually, however, each is linked to all the others through the person of the President. . . .

'The functional equivalence between a British Cabinet and our set of influentials – whether Secretaries, Senators, White House staffers, Congressmen or others – is rendered plain by noting that for most intents and purposes their Cabinet members do the work of our congressional committees, our floor leaderships, and our front office downtown, all combined.'[1]

For, he concludes,

'a President like a Prime Minister lives daily under the constraint that he must bring along *his* "colleagues" and get action from *their* liegemen at both ends of the Avenue. A sensible Prime Minister is always counting noses in Cabinet. A sensible President is always checking off his list of "influentials". The P.M. is not yet a President. The President, however, is a sort of super Prime Minister.'[2]

Let that judgement provide a fitting end to a chapter-long record of differences – and to any other differences that may arise between our two countries.

[1] Neustadt, op. cit., pp. 144–5.
[2] ibid., p. 147.

APPENDIX

I *Collective Responsibility* (see Chapter III)

(a) Following is the text of a statement on the collective responsibility of ministers in all circumstances, with special reference to the National Executive Committee of the Labour Party, read to Cabinet on 3 April 1969, and authorized by Cabinet to be released to the press.

The Prime Minister said that there had for some time been a growing tendency for some Ministers to act in ways which called in question the collective responsibility of the Cabinet, in so far as they had apparently felt free, in their personal dealings both with members of the PLP and with the Press, to dissociate themselves from certain of the Government's policies and to allow this to be known to outside bodies, particularly the Trade Unions, with whom their colleagues were often conducting difficult and delicate negotiations in the name of the Government as a whole. Before a decision was reached on any item of Government policy a Minister was entitled to defend his own point of view within the Cabinet as strongly and persuasively as he wished. But once a decision had been taken the principle of collective responsibility required every member of an Administration to endorse it and to defend it to any outside body on any occasion, whether private or public. This remained true even if the Minister was himself a member of the outside body concerned. There was no objection in principle to Ministers retaining affiliations of this kind provided that no conflict of interest or allegiance resulted. But this proviso was especially important in the case of Ministers who were members of the National Executive Committee of the Labour Party

(NEC), where any clash of loyalties was liable to be particularly embarrassing. It had to be recognised that the NEC's concept of its relationship to the Parliamentary Party had changed since the Labour Party became the Government Party. During the Labour Government of 1945–51 the Executive would never have sought to enforce a decision of the annual conference of the Party on the Government. And even in 1960, when the Labour Party were in Opposition, the Executive had refused to try to impose the decisions of the conference on the PLP. Now, however, it was seeking to assert a right to withhold support from the Government on issues on which the annual conference had not yet expressed a view.

It would be unfortunate if circumstances developed, perhaps later in the year, in which it proved impossible to deal with this situation except by means of a ruling that no member of the Cabinet might offer himself for election to the NEC. He himself would greatly regret it if he were forced to give such a ruling, since the result would be not only to weaken the links between the Government and the NEC but also to reduce the latter to a body which was competent merely to discuss and to protest but not to exercise influence or to accept responsibility. Nevertheless, this situation could be avoided only if Ministers themselves recognised and accepted that, where any conflict of loyalties arose, the principle of the collective responsibility of the Government was absolute and overriding in all circumstances and that, if any Minister felt unable to subscribe to this principle without reservation, it was his duty to resign his office forthwith.

14 May 1974

(b) In 1974 the issue arose again in relation to Chile and other matters. I wrote the following letter, which was published at the time, to three ministers who were members of the NEC. After some little difficulty, satisfactory assurances were received.

In my minute of 14 May 1974 I reminded Ministers of the principle of collective responsibility, as it applies to Ministers in their dealings with the Labour Party and in particular to Ministers who are members of the National Executive Committee. I attach a copy of that minute herewith.

That minute restated the rule that, where any conflict of loyalties arises, the principle of the collective responsibility of the Government is absolute and overriding in all circumstances and that, if any Minister feels unable to subscribe to this principle without reservation, it is his duty to resign his office forthwith.

I reminded all members of the administration at the Eve of Session Reception at 10 Downing Street as recently as Monday of this week of their duty to comply with the requirements of collective responsibility. I made it clear that it is inconsistent with the principle of collective responsibility for a Minister who is a member of the National Executive Committee to speak or vote in favour of a resolution of that body which is critical of Government policies or actions, or which seeks to impose on the Government views or decisions which are manifestly inconsistent with Government policy.

Your vote in support of the Simonstown resolution at yesterday's meeting of the National Executive Committee was clearly inconsistent with the principle of collective responsibility. You will be well aware of the embarrassment which this has created for your colleagues.

I must ask you to send me in reply to this minute an unqualified assurance that you accept the principle of collective responsibility and that you will from now on comply with its requirements and the rules that flow from it, in the National Executive Committee and in all other circumstances. I must warn you that I should have to regard your failure to give me such an assurance, or any subsequent breach of it, as a decision on your part that you did not wish to continue as a member of this administration. I should of course much regret such a decision; but I should accept it.

31 October 1974

II *Chequers and its Ambience* (see Chapter III)

When Lord Lee of Fareham gave Chequers to 'England for the rest and recreation of her Prime Ministers for ever' he included in the Trust Deed a statement of his reasons:[1]

It is not possible to foresee or foretell from what classes or conditions of life the future wielders of power in this country will be drawn. Some may be as in the past men of wealth and famous descent; some may belong to the world of trade and business; others may spring from the ranks of manual toilers. To none of these in the midst of their strenuous and responsible labours could the spirit and anodyne of Chequers do anything but good. In the city-bred man especially, the periodic contact with the most typical rural life would create and preserve a just sense of proportion between the claims of town and country. To the revolutionary statesman the antiquity and calm tenacity of Chequers and its annals might suggest some saving virtues in the continuity of English history and exercise a check upon too hasty upheavals, whilst even the most reactionary could scarcely be insensible to the spirit of human freedom which permeates the countryside of Hampden, Burke and Milton.

Apart from these more subtle influences, the better the health of our rulers the more sanely will they rule, and the inducement to spend two days a week in the high and pure air of the Chiltern hills and woods will, it is hoped, benefit the nation as well as its chosen leaders. The main features of this scheme are therefore designed not merely to make Chequers available as the official country residence of the Prime Minister of the day, but to tempt him

[1] Part of this statement is included as the Schedule to the Chequers Estate Act, 1917.

to visit it regularly and to make it possible for him to live there, even though his income should be limited to his salary.

The concluding words are a reference to the Trust provision, directing the trustees to pay to the prime minister, in respect of any week in which he spent one period of thirty-six hours at Chequers, £15 (in 1922 money) to pay his expenses. The requirements of thirty-six hours was ingeniously calculated; it covered, roughly, two days and a night, or two nights and a day. Thus, if a prime minister with a distant constituency visited it on Friday and returned on the overnight rail sleeper, motoring from the London main-line station and reaching Chequers at, say, 8.15 am on the Saturday, he would qualify for the grant if he left Chequers for London not earlier than 8.15 pm on the Sunday. Alternatively, if he cannot leave London until Saturday evening, he qualifies if he stays till Monday morning. Clement Attlee, like Neville Chamberlain a devotee of Chequers, tried whenever possible to leave London early on Friday afternoon and return to Downing Street on Sunday evening or Monday morning.

III *The 'Agreement to Differ'*

(a) Statement in Parliament on the 'agreement to differ' on the Referendum, 23 January 1975.[1]

It is the declared policy of the Government that, once the outcome of our renegotiation of the terms of membership is known, the British people should have the right to decide, through the ballot box, by means either of a General Election or of a referendum, whether Britain should continue in membership of the European Community or should withdraw.

The Government have decided that this should be done by means of a referendum.

Prolonged uncertainty and delay on the decision of the British people are in the interests neither of Britain nor of other members of the Community. After 15 years of discussion and negotiation, it is an issue which all of us in this House and in the country want to see settled; and uncertainty about the future of British membership is inhibiting the work of the Community. The Government are committed to putting the issue to the people before 10th October this year. Provided that the outcome of renegotiation is known in time, we intend to hold the referendum before the summer holidays, which means in practice not later than the end of June. We shall, therefore, propose to the House arrangements which would make it possible to hold the referendum on that time-table, tight though it will be.

[1] *Hansard*, Vol. 884, No. 52, cols. 1745–7.

When the outcome of renegotiation is known, the Government will decide upon their own recommendation to the country, whether for continued membership of the Community on the basis of the renegotiated terms, or for withdrawal, and will announce their decision to the House in due course. That announcement will provide an opportunity for the House to debate the question of substance. That does not, of course, preclude debates at any earlier time, subject to the convenience of the House.

The circumstances of this referendum are unique, and the issue to be decided is one on which strong views have long been held which cross party lines. The Cabinet has, therefore, decided that, if when the time comes there are members of the Government including members of the Cabinet, who do not feel able to accept and support the Government's recommendation, whatever it may be, they will, once the recommendation has been announced, be free to support and speak in favour of a different conclusion in the referendum campaign. . . .

As to the arrangements for the referendum, I told the House on Tuesday that the rules for the test of public opinion must be made by this House. The Government propose within a very few weeks to publish a White Paper on the rules and arrangements for conducting the referendum. The White Paper will set out the various possible courses on each issue and the Government's proposals on such matters as, for example, the information policy of the Government during the referendum campaign, broadcasting arrangements during the campaign, the question of expenditure by campaigning groups, the form in which the question is to be put to the British people, and arrangements for conducting the poll, the counting of the votes and the announcement of the result.

The Government will provide time for a debate on the White Paper on referendum procedure in this House before the Easter recess. That debate will, of course, be separate from, and will precede the parliamentary debate which will be necessary on the outcome of the negotiations. The debate on the referendum White Paper will enable the Government to take full account of the views expressed by right hon. and hon. Members of this House, and by public opinion generally, in drafting the necessary legislation for the referendum.

The Government propose to introduce the legislation around Easter-time. We shall, of course, propose that all stages should be taken on the Floor of the House. If we are able to hold the referendum before the summer holiday, the Bill will need to complete its passage through both Houses and to receive Royal Assent by the end of May.

(b) The 'Guidelines for the Agreement to Differ', approved by Cabinet in March 1975, and reported to Parliament.

In accordance with my statement in the House on 23rd January last, those Ministers who do not agree with the Government's recommendation in favour of continued membership of the European Community are, in the unique circumstances of the referendum, now free to advocate a different view during the referendum campaign in the country.

This freedom does not extend to parliamentary proceedings and official business. Government business in Parliament will continue to be handled by all Ministers in accordance with Government policy. Ministers responsible for European aspects of Government business who themselves differ from the Government's recommendation on membership of the European Community will state the Government's position and will not be drawn into making points against the Government recommendation. Wherever necessary Questions will be transferred to other Ministers. At meetings of the Council of Ministers of the European Community and at other Community meetings, the United Kingdom position in all fields will continue to reflect Government policy.

I have asked all Ministers to make their contributions to the public campaign in terms of issues, to avoid personalising or trivialising the argument, and not to allow themselves to appear in direct confrontation, on the same platform of programme, with another Minister who takes a different view on the Government recommendation.[1]

(c) The 1932 'Precedent'

The 1932 precedent alluded to in Parliament, when my statement was questioned, was not an exact precedent, though there was wide acceptance of the view I claimed, that it was a 'sound' one.

The main difference lay in the circumstances of the formula of the respective governments.

The Government in 1975 was a single-party administration, with an overall majority. The decision to hold a referendum had been put to the electorate in two successive general elections.

The 'agreement to differ' in 1932 was in the context of a National (coalition) Government, formed during the crisis of 1931. In the landslide general election in 1931 the issue of tariff protection was carefully laid on one side: the Prime Minister (Ramsay MacDonald) asked simply for a 'doctor's mandate'. It has been recorded that, when the Cabinet was formed, MacDonald was advised by King George V to make certain that the Cabinet would not subsequently be broken up by either Sir Herbert Samuel or Philip Snowden over the protection issue. MacDonald replied that he would prefer to 'let sleeping dogs lie'.

Within months of the election, the tariff issue came to the fore. There was a most difficult meeting of Cabinet, leading to a statement issued from Downing Street, on 22 January 1932, that the Cabinet had

[1] *Hansard* (7 April 1975), Written Answer 351.

'. . . determined that some modification of usual Ministerial practice is required, and has decided that Ministers who find themselves unable to support the conclusions arrived at by the majority of their colleagues on the subject of import duties and cognate matters are to be at liberty to express their views by speech and vote.'[1]

When the relevant clauses of the Finance Bill came before the House, the minority exercised their right to speak and to vote, though the divisions were whipped by the Government. This did not happen again in that particular coalition: the same members were unable to accept the decision of the Ottawa Conference, imposing more generalized tariffs and preferences, and after the Cabinet meeting called to endorse Ottawa on 28 September 1932, they resigned.

The events of January–April 1975 were not, as I conceded at the time, an exact precedent. MacDonald's Government was a coalition. But feelings on the question of membership of the Common Market ran deep. The referendum had been agreed in Labour's days of Opposition; indeed, it was the basis on which some of us at a most difficult Conference in 1973 had been able to persuade a narrow majority of the NEC and Conference not to bind itself in favour of withdrawal from the EEC on the formation of a new Labour government.

Procedurally, too, there were differences between 1932 and 1975. In 1932 the dissident minority of the Government was allowed not only to speak freely in the country but to vote *and speak* against the Cabinet's recommendation to the House. In 1975, under the 'Agreement to Differ' guideline, there was freedom of speech in the campaign in the country, freedom of voting in the House, but no right to express in the House views different from the majority Cabinet and PLP point of view. One minister of state was dismissed from the Government for insisting on speaking.

IV *The Supply Estimates* (see p. 68 above)

Following are two typical pages taken from the Supply Estimates, 1975–6 (HMSO, 11 February 1975) followed by two from Public Expenditure to 1979–80 (HMSO Cmnd. 6393).

[1] Ivor Jennings, *Cabinet Government*, 3rd ed. (Cambridge 1935), p. 280; A.J.P.Taylor, *English History 1914–1945* (Oxford 1965), p. 324; Harold Nicolson, *King George V* (London 1952), p. 495; Viscount Snowden, *An Autobiography* (London 1934), II, p. 1012.

1974–75	SUBHEAD DETAIL	1975–76
£		£

PROGRAMME 7.1
SUBSIDIES

SECTION A: SUBSIDIES

—	**A1 Subsidies under the Housing Rents and Subsidies Act 1975**	618,205,000
	(1) Grants to Local Authorities:	583,205,000
—	(a) Basic element £450,000,000	
—	(b) New capital costs element £90,000,000	
—	(c) Supplementary financing element £13,000,000	
—	(d) Special element £30,000,000	
—	(e) Expanding towns subsidy▼ £105,000	
—	(f) Transitional town development subsidy▼ £100,000	
	(2) Grants to Development Corporations and the Commission for the New Towns	35,000,000
—	(a) Basic element £19,000,000	
—	(b) New capital costs element £14,000,000	
—	(c) Special element ·£2,000,000	
	A2 Grants to Housing Associations under the Housing Act 1974	209,500,000
—	(1) Housing association grant	194,000,000
—	(2) Revenue deficit grant	14,000,000
—	(3) Management grant	500,000
—	(4) Hostel deficit grant	1,000,000
548,457,200	**A3 Arrears of subsidy entitlement under previous legislation**	21,350,000
5,956,000	(1) Annual grants under Housing Acts prior to the Housing Finance Act 1972	1,000,000
	(2) Subsidies under the Housing Finance Act 1972	20,350,000
523,201,100	(a) Grants to Local Authorities £20,000,000	
19,300,100	(b) Grants to Development Corporations and the Commission for New Towns £350,000	
7,000,000	**A4 Grants to Development Corporations and the Commission for the New Towns under Section 42(2) and 42(3A) of the New Towns Act 1965**	9,000,000
16,904,800	**A5 Miscellaneous grants to local authorities and other bodies**	249,970,000
79,500	(1) Provision of Hostels by housing associations under Section 15 of the Housing (Financial Provisions) Act 1958	70,000
1,000	(2) Temporary and emergency housing	1,000
12,500	(3) National Federation of Housing Societies	13,800
115,000	(4) To meet increased cost of constructing or equipping houses by approved experimental methods	1,000
10,000,000	(5) Slum clearance subsidy under the Housing Finance Act 1972▼	20,000,000
6,220,800	(6) Subsidies to housing associations under the Housing Finance Act 1972	4,808,000
50,000	(7) Private enterprise housing under the Housing (Financial Provisions) Act 1958 and earlier legislation	75,000
426,000	(8) Other grants	1,200

▼*See* Notes at beginning of Volume.

1974–75	SUBHEAD: DETAIL	1975–76
£		£

SECTION A: POLICE

GRANTS TO POLICE AUTHORITIES

272,182,000	**A1 Grants for Police Expenditure▼¹** (50 % of net approved expenditure) Grants to county and combined police authorities and to the Metropolitan Police Fund	310,724,000
1,035,955	**A2 Special Grants for Metropolitan Police▼**	1,538,421
	(1) Salaries, &c, under the Metropolitan Police Act 1899. Commis-	
26,396	sioner (£16,350), Receiver (£10,428)	27,284
9,559	(2) Superannuation of Commissioners	11,137
	(3) Contributions under the Police Act 1909 for imperial and	
1,000,000	national services	1,500,000

CENTRAL SUPPORT SERVICES

4,402,000	**A3 Training and Education: Current Expenditure**	4,271,000
3,492,000	(1) Police District Training Centres	3,324,000
	(a) Salaries, &c, of 634 civil servants and 301 staff	
	on loan £2,183,000	
	(b) General expenses £1,141,000	
690,000	(2) Police College	709,000
	(a) Salaries, &c, of 119 (139 at 1 April 1974) civil servants and	
	26 staff on loan £442,000	
	(b) General expenses £267,000	
188,000	(3) Police Promotion Examinations Board	204,000
32,000	(4) Crime Prevention Training Courses	34,000
984,000	**A4 Training and Education: Capital Expenditure**	2,273,000
610,000	(1) Police District Training Centres	1,638,000
374,000	(2) Police College	635,000
8,627,000	**A5 Scientific and Technical Support: Current Expenditure**	9,597,000
1,726,000	(1) Forensic Science Laboratories	1,915,000
	(a) Salaries, &c, of 409 (352 at 1 April 1974) civil servants and	
	19 staff on loan £1,350,000	
	(b) General expenses £565,000	
3,589,000	(2) Police Wireless Services	3,914,000
	(a) Salaries, &c, of 857 staff £2,467,000	
	(b) General expenses £1,447,000	
2,836,000	(3) Police National Computer Centre	3,245,000
	(a) Salaries, &c, of 190 civil servants and 192 staff	
	on loan £1,264,000	
	(b) Professional fees £488,000	
	(c) General expenses £1,493,000	
476,000	(4) Part cost of Metropolitan Police Laboratory	523,000
6,038,000	**A6 Scientific and Technical Support: Capital Expenditure**	8,384,000
537,000	(1) Forensic Science Laboratories	964,000
4,091,000	(2) Police Wireless Services	5,272,000
1,410,000	(3) Police National Computer Centre	2,148,000

▼ *See* Notes at beginning of Volume.
¹ *See* Notes at end of Vote.

TABLE 2.10

10. EDUCATION AND LIBRARIES,

				1970–71	1971–72	1972–73
Schools						
Under fives	...	capital[1]...		—	—	—
		current[2]		—	—	—
Primary, secondary and other	...	capital	...	492·0	569·3	687·8
Primary	...	current	...	997·6	1,069·9	1,122·4
Secondary	...	current	...	1,087·2	1,178·8	1,250·3
Other	...	current	...	215·9	242·9	259·5
Meals	...	...	...	202·2	201·7	222·7
Milk	...	...	...	16·1	10·5	8·2
Higher and further education[3]						
Universities	...	capital	...	110·5	110·6	110·1
		current	...	450·8	463·8	474·3
Further education	...	capital	...	129·2	123·5	105·6
		current	...	539·0	572·7	613·5
Teacher training	...	capital	...	19·5	23·3	18·7
		current	...	199·6	206·7	214·1
Libraries						
Purchase grants	...	...	...	1·3	1·3	1·5
Other	...	...	...	115·0	124·1	137·6
Miscellaneous educational services, research and administration						
Youth services, etc.	...	capital	...	14·6	15·2	18·5
		current	...	41·1	42·9	49·0
Research and other services ...	...	...	...	6·2	6·1	7·4
Administration	...	...	...	170·8	176·8	192·6
VAT paid by local authorities	...	...	...	36·9	39·5	41·4
Total education and libraries...	...	capital	...	788·7	867·7	975·5
		current	...	4,056·8	4,311·9	4,559·7
Total	...	...	4,845·5	5,179·6	5,535·2
Research Councils, etc. ...	...	...	...	177·4	194·9	201·1
Arts						
National museums and galleries						
Capital expenditure ...	...	...	...	1·9	3·7	1·2
Annual purchase grants ...	...	...	...	2·3	2·1	3·0
Other current expenditure	...	...	...	12·8	14·2	14·5
Local museums and galleries	...	capital	...	1·6	3·4	3·3
		current	...	10·0	10·7	11·9
Arts Council and other arts ...	...	capital	...	3·5	3·7	5·5
		current	...	18·5	21·5	22·8
Total arts	...	capital	...	7·0	10·8	10·0
		current	...	43·6	48·5	52·2
Total	...	...	50·6	59·3	62·2
Total education and libraries, science and arts	...	capital	...	822·5	908·4	1,015·7
		current	...	4,251·0	4,525·4	4,782·8
Total	...	...	5,073·5	5,433·8	5 798·5
Changes from Cmnd 5879 revalued ...	...	...				
Cmnd 5879 revalued	...	...				

[1] New nursery programme only.
[2] Separate expenditure figures not available before 1973–74.
[3] Decisions have still to be made on the apportionment of the totals for Higher and further education from 1976–77 onwards.

SCIENCE AND ARTS

1973–74	1974–75	1975–76	1976–77	1977–78	1978–79	1979–80
—	18·0	31·9	22·5	10·6	6	6
96·5	104·5	131·3	145·1	150·7	152	155
662·3	469·7	386·4	378·2	298·0	238	217
1,087·2	1,146·3	1,243·5	1,232·9	1,215·5	1,189	1,158
1,354·4	1,451·3	1,404·5	1,447·8	1,485·9	1,511	1,532
271·9	279·8	290·8	301·0	304·5	308	311
259·5	309·1	314·9	300·3	277·6	248	207
8·3	8·3	10·8	11·8	11·5	12	11
122·6	82·8	104·5 ⎫				
527·0	548·9	571·1 ⎪				
104·6	83·8	53·7 ⎬ 150·1	151·6	122	121	
624·6	649·7	677·9 ⎪ 1,499·4	1,498·6	1,514	1,551	
16·7	11·4	4·9 ⎪				
219·8	210·2	208·9 ⎭				
2·4	3·0	3·2	3·5	3·7	4	4
147·6	149·5	151·7	156·3	147·9	145	149
19·9	14·1	19·3	17·8	18·0	17	17
52·8	50·3	53·3	54·6	53·0	53	53
7·4	7·9	11·1	12·2	13·3	13	13
199·8	197·1	198·1	202·2	201·7	202	203
40·1	42·5	38·7	40·5	39·5	39	39
963·3	708·4	623·4	595·8	495·3	396	374
4,862·1	5,129·8	5,287·1	5,380·4	5,386·3	5,377	5,373
5,825·4	5,838·2	5,910·5	5,976·2	5,881·6	5,773	5,747
185·1	185·5	172·3	175·8	175·7	172	171
3·9	4·2	5·3	5·1	3·9	3	2
2·4	2·0	3·6	3·8	3·8	4	4
15·6	16·7	18·1	19·0	19·7	19	19
5·3	5·2	2·5	2·6	3·7	3	1
12·7	16·7	17·9	17·8	17·8	18	18
4·8	7·8	4·9	2·4	1·7	1	1
25·7	27·4	29·2	30·9	33·2	31	32
14·0	17·2	12·7	10·1	9·3	7	4
56·4	62·8	68·8	71·5	74·5	72	73
70·4	80·0	81·5	81·6	83·8	79	77
1,003·9	751·7	664·9	634·7	533·3	431	406
5,077·0	5,352·0	5,499·4	5,598·9	5,607·8	5,593	5,589
6,080·9	6,103·7	6,164·3	6,233·6	6,141·1	6,024	5,995
	+ 130·8	+ 27·6	− 84·2	− 331·1	− 618	
	5,972·9	6,136·7	6,317·8	6,472·2	6,642	

V *The 'Political Advisers' Experiment*

Following is the statement I made to the Commonwealth Heads of Government Conference, Jamaica, May 1975.

The general doctrine is of course that Ministers take political decisions and civil servants carry them out. Why then do we want political advisers? What can they do that Ministers cannot?

There are two reasons which have caused us to experiment in this way.

The first is the pressure of work on Ministers. In less hectic days Ministers were their own political advisers. To a large extent this is still true. A politician with decades of experience and accountable to his electors can only survive if he can scent the changes of mood in the country and in his Party. But the burdens of modern government as developed in our country, the immense volume of papers, the exhausting succession of departmental committees, of Party gatherings and meetings with outside interests make it almost impossible for him to carry out his departmental and political responsibilities and at the same time sustain a detailed analysis of all the various political nuances of policy. If he can keep on top of his own department's work he is doing very well, but he finds it increasingly difficult to play a constructive part in the collective business of the Government as a whole.

The second is the nature of our Civil Service. The British Civil Service takes a pride in its political impartiality. As a result – unlike for example the United States – political change does not mean drastic changes in the Civil Service. This gives our system a degree of continuity and stability which is often admired. The ability of senior civil servants to change and often reverse policies is achieved both by a genuine wish to serve the Government of the day to the best of their ability and also by a certain amount of contingency planning in a pre-electoral period based on a careful on-going study of the proposals of potential Governments.

This system has not been without its critics however. There are those who say that the social and educational background of senior Civil Servants remains too narrow and that the 'Whitehall mandarin', coming as he does from such a background and guaranteed stability and continuity in his office, can become isolated from changes of mood and structure in our society.

We have tried to meet these problems in two ways.

First we have established a Central Policy Review Staff – or think-tank as it is often called – to assist the Government in the identification and evaluation of priorities. It works mainly on issues submitted to it by the Cabinet, but has sufficient spare capacity to work on issues which it chooses for itself. It is involved in regular presentations to the Cabinet of synoptic views of Government strategy and detailed analysis of selected particular issues. The CPRS tries to divide its work between both short-term and long-term issues but has to struggle with Gresham's Law that consideration of today's problems drives out consideration of tomorrow's.

The CPRS is a small unit (15–20). It was set up by our predecessors but we have found it very valuable and have continued it.

Members of the CPRS are *not* political appointments. Half are civil servants secured for a short term of duty and half are outside appointments, again for a short number of years, recruited on a non-political basis and subject to strict civil service rules and disciplines. They are a young staff, drawn from the widest possible range of civil service departments and outside disciplines and experiences. They work with departments rather than separately but their papers and their conclusions are independently arrived at. Uniquely, they put their papers directly to Cabinet Committee meetings without going through the Minister, and are invited to speak to their papers.

The CPRS is located in the Cabinet Office and serves all Ministers collectively. Thus it helps greatly over the problem of busy departmental Ministers who have little time to think about their colleagues' policies. It projects an independent, objective analysis – and often an alternative view. But it is in no sense a 'party' organisation.

Accordingly when we came into office in March 1974 I authorised the appointment by Cabinet Ministers of Political Advisers. This is not of course a wholly new concept – previous administrations had brought in advisers from outside, normally chosen from political sympathisers – and even now we have only 30 such advisers spread around 15 departments. The increase is however of considerable significance and Political Advisers now play a definite role in our affairs.

Since a Political Adviser is the personal appointment of his Minister his specific role within any particular department will vary to some degree or another. His role will also depend on his particular background and experience.

Examples however are:

1. *As a 'sieve'* examining papers as they go to Ministers, drawing attention to problems and difficulties, especially ones having Party political implications or electoral considerations, and looking for 'landmines' – especially in politically sensitive areas.

2. *As a 'deviller'* chasing up Ministerial wishes, checking facts and research findings outside Whitehall, spotting obstacles and ensuring that particularly sensitive political points are dealt with in an appropriately sensitive way.

3. *Medium- and long-term planning.* Since the Adviser is not under the same pressure of political, Parliamentary or constituency work he has the time to prepare 'think pieces' for his Minister which can generate long-term policy thinking within the Department.

4. *Contributions to policy planning within the Departments.* Most Departments have planning groups looking at medium- and long-term problems. A Political Adviser is eminently suitable to contribute ideas at this early planning stage, particularly ones which are new, or at least outside the mainstream, originating from outside the Government machine, and

perhaps running contrary to long-established departmental views. The Adviser can thus extend the range of options available to a Minister.

5. *Liaison with the Party*. This is an important function if Party and Government are not to 'grow away' from each other. Such liaison will involve close co-operation with the Party's own research departments.
6. *Outside interest groups*. The Adviser can ease the Minister's burden in contact with outside interest groups.
7. *Speech writing and research.*

It is for the Minister to decide what papers the Political Adviser sees and what work he does. Much depends on the Political Advisers' background. Some are 'ideas men' or academics: others are former Party officials with specialist knowledge of their areas: and others are recent graduates and young Party activists. They do not however normally see papers ot a high security classification and their contributions are made within their departments. They do not attend interdepartmental official committees.

I have set up a special Policy Unit in my own office. This team, which I have deliberately kept small (now 7), is made up of people with expert knowledge of the fields of economic, industrial and social policy. They advise me directly on the immediate decisions to be made, whether in Cabinet or elsewhere, and on longer term issues and developments. They work closely with my Private Office staff as well as with the network of Special Advisers serving other Ministers and with the CPRS and Cabinet Secretariat, and keep in touch with thinking outside Government through contacts in universities, industry, trade unions and pressure groups.

The purpose of this Policy Unit is not only to bring in experts to extend the range of policy options from which the Government – and particularly the Prime Minister as head of the Government – has to choose. The Policy Unit was set up, and its members were selected, to provide a team with strong political commitment to advise on, propose and pursue policies to further the Government's political goals. For policies without politics are of no more use than politics without policies.

To sum up. The Political Adviser is an extra pair of hands, ears and eyes and a mind more politically committed and more politically aware than would be available to a Minister from the political neutrals in the established Civil Service. This is particularly true for a radical reforming party in government, since 'neutralism' may easily slip into conservatism with a small 'c'.

Problems have arisen, but much less than some predicted. They are usually problems:

(i) of *relationships* – with civil servants and, surprisingly perhaps more delicate, with other ministers – and
(ii) of *confidentiality* since not all Special Advisers are accustomed to Civil Service reticence with the media.

We are still in the early stages of this experiment and, in a typically

British way, prefer to work out the problems as we go along. But we can say at this stage that these developments are worth-while. Three dozen Political Advisers are not going to overturn our powerful government machine – nor should we want them to. They can however make a distinctive contribution. The reason why they are successfully doing that is that the nature and value of that contribution – and its limitations – has been recognised by all concerned. Indeed, most regular senior Civil Servants have openly welcomed the experiment and are co-operating to make it a success.

10 Downing Street, SW1

May 1975

VI *Statement on Industrial Strategy* (see Chapter VI)

This is the Prime Minister's statement following meeting of NEDC, 5 November 1975.

At the National Economic Development Council today at Chequers, Cabinet Ministers, including the Chancellor of the Exchequer and the Secretaries of State for Industry and Employment, had a long and constructive discussion, under my chairmanship, on the Government's new approach to industrial strategy.

The whole future strength of Britain's economy was bound up in our discussion. For our prosperity is ultimately dependent upon the prosperity of our manufacturing industry. Of course, many sectors are already highly efficient and very competitive by international standards. Agriculture, retail distribution and financial services are good examples. But the backbone of our economy is manufacturing industry, which now accounts for about thirty per cent of our output and employment and over 80 per cent of our visible exports.

The fact must be faced – the performance of British industry since the war has been steadily deteriorating under successive Governments in comparison with our competitors. There are many explanations for this decline. Some people blame managements; some the unions; while others put all the blame on Governments. But the important thing today at Chequers was that no-one was blaming anybody. Everyone present, Government, unions and management, recognised the decline and that we all had to work together, taking account of each other's legitimate interests, to reverse it.

The objective – accepted by all of us today – is to transform a declining economy into a high-output, high-earnings economy based, as it must be, on full employment.

That is the task we face; it is not something we can achieve overnight. But we must start the process now.

It is for this reason that the Government have put forward their proposals for a new approach to tackle our industrial problems. At this stage it is only an approach – not an immediate solution – and there are a great many details to work out. But it is now a *common approach* shared by Government and the representatives of the unions and management on the NEDC.

The Government believes that a successful approach to industrial strategy must satisfy two conditions. First, it must be realistic and flexible. The proposals we discussed and are publishing today involve a careful analysis of the performance and prospects of key industries which will be continuously adjusted as experience grows and circumstances change. This analysis does not itself constitute a strategy, but it provides a flexible framework within which strategic decisions can be made. Second, we must get away from policies of confrontation. Instead we must engage the co-operation and drive of both management and labour in both the private and public sectors.

Our industrial strategy will rest on these two principles. In particular:

– We must ensure the better co-ordination of policies affecting the efficiency of industry. The Government intends to give greater weight, more consistently than hitherto, to the need to increase the national rate of growth through regenerating our industrial structure and improving efficiency.

– We must ensure the more effective use of the instruments of industrial policy and the deployment of financial assistance to industry.

– We must ensure that industry, both public and private, is able to earn sufficient profits on its investment to spur management to expand and innovate.

– We must ensure a more effective manpower policy, including measures to provide a better supply of skilled manpower for growth industries and to cope with the human problems of people transferring from contracting to expanding industries. There was general agreement that much higher priority should be given to training and re-training.

– We must ensure improvements in planning, both in industry and by Government, which will flow from the regular discussion of the prospects of key industries.

As a first step the Government will provide a framework for assessing the prospects of the more important sectors of industry over a period of five or more years ahead. It will also indicate the role of these industries in meeting our overall economic objectives. This framework will take full account of likely developments in world trade and the competitive position of British industry. It will be discussed extensively with both sides of industry and it will be reviewed at regular intervals.

The framework for five years ahead will be based on a rolling programme, taking stock together each year of changes needed for later years. While meeting the essential criterion of industrial flexibility, this is designed to give industry a greater measure of continuity than it has enjoyed over the last twenty years under successive Governments.

The framework is expected to classify these industries under three main heads:

– Industries which are intrinsically likely to be successful;

– Industries which have the potential for success if appropriate action is taken;

– Industries whose performance is most important to the rest of industry.

For each of these categories there will be a detailed study drawing attention to the prospects, strengths and weaknesses of the industries concerned.

We intend that Government, Management and Unions, working together, will ensure that the programme is master-minded by the National Economic Development Council. Both planning agreements and the National Enterprise Board will be important in this work.

Regularly each year, both sides of industry, together with the Government, will identify the areas for improvement and action by each of the three parties, Government, Management and Unions. This will be done at national level – for example in the NEDC – at industrial level – for example in the EDCs – and at company level, primarily though not exclusively in the context of planning agreements. This process will provide the background for discussions by Government, Unions and Management.

The national approach, through Neddy, is of fundamental importance on strategy and policy. Still more important is the sectoral approach, where EDCs (little Neddies) acting more as action Committees, will need to be extended to cover the areas highlighted as essential to the strategy. But most important of all is the company approach. For it is at company and plant level that the real decisions are taken.

Much of the discussion at Chequers today dealt with the question of method and procedure. But this was essential if our future industrial strategy is to be soundly based. What was significant about today's discussion was that for the first time Government, Management and Unions have agreed on a common approach. This is the essential first step.

INDEX